# THUCYDIDES MYTHISTORICUS

# THUCYDIDES
# MYTHISTORICUS

## FRANCIS MACDONALD CORNFORD, 1874-1943.

Ἴσως τὸ μὴ μυθῶδες αὐτῶν ἀτερπέστερον φανεῖται

University of Pennsylvania Press
Philadelphia

First published 1907 by Edward Arnold, Ltd. Reprinted here by arrangement with the publishers.

First *Pennsylvania Paperback* edition, 1971

ISBN: 0-8122-1021-2

Printed in the United States of America

TO
JANE ELLEN HARRISON

ὄναρ ἀντ᾽ ὀνειράτων
πολλῶν τε καὶ καλῶν

# PREFACE

THE title of this book needs a word of explanation, if not of apology; for to any one who is accustomed to think of Thucydides as typically prosaic, and nothing if not purely historical, the epithet *Mythistoricus* may seem to carry a note of challenge, or even of paradox. But the sense in which the expression has here been used is quite consistent with the historian's much-talked-of 'trustworthiness', and, indeed, with the literal truth of every statement of fact in the whole of his work. It is possible, however, even for a writer of history, to be something much better than trustworthy. Xenophon, I suppose, is honest; but his honesty makes it none the easier to read him. To read Thucydides is, although certainly not easy, at any rate pleasant, because —trustworthiness and all—he is a great artist. It is the object of this essay to bring out an essentially artistic aspect of his work, which has escaped notice, partly because the history is so long that it is hard to take it in as a whole, and partly because the execution of the effect is imperfect, having been hindered by the good intentions with which Thucydides set out.

The history, as it stands, is the product of two hardly compatible designs. It was originally planned as a textbook of strategy and politics in the form of a journal; and it is commonly taken to be actually nothing more. But the work, in the course of its progress, began to grow, as it were of itself, out of this pedestrian plan into a shape with another contour, which, however, is broken by the rigid lines of the old plan, and discontinuous; much as a set of volcanic islands might heave themselves out of the sea, at such angles and distances that only to the eye of a bird, and not to the sailor cruising among them, would they appear as the summits of one and the same submerged mountain-chain. The present essay is mainly an attempt to chart these islands, leaving uncoloured blanks where the sea lies flat between them, and infringing none of the fishing-rights of the professed historian.

It is the intrusion of this artistic tendency—for a thing so unpremeditated can hardly be called a design—that justifies the epithet Mythistoricus. By *Mythistoria* I mean history cast in a mould of conception, whether artistic or philosophic, which, long before the work was even contemplated, was already inwrought into the very structure of the author's mind. In every age the common interpretation of the world of things is controlled by some scheme of unchallenged and unsuspected presupposition; and the mind of any individual, however little he may think himself to be in sympathy with his contemporaries, is not an insulated compartment, but more like a pool in one continuous medium—the circumambient atmosphere of his place and time. This element of thought is always, of course, most difficult to detect and analyse, just because it is a constant factor which underlies all the differential characters of many minds. It was impossible for Dante to know that his scheme of redemption would appear improbable when astronomy should cease to be geocentric. It is impossible for us to tell how pervasively our own view of the world is coloured by Darwinian biology and by the categories of mechanical and physical science. And so it was with Thucydides. He chose a task which promised to lie wholly within the sphere of positively ascertainable fact; and, to make assurance double sure, he set himself limits which further restricted this sphere, till it seemed that no bias, no preconception, no art except the art of methodical inquiry, could possibly intrude. But he had not reckoned with the truth that you cannot collect facts, like so many pebbles, without your own personality and the common mind of your age and country having something to say to the choice and arrangement of the collection. He had forgotten that he was an Athenian, born before Aeschylus was dead; and it did not occur to him that he must have a standpoint and outlook from which the world, having a long way to travel in a thousand or two thousand years, would drift far indeed. Thus it came about that even his vigilant precaution allowed a certain traditional mode of thought, characteristic of the Athenian mind, to shape the mass of facts which was to have been shapeless, so that the work of science came to be a work of art. And, since this mode of thought had, as we shall see, grown without a break out of a mythological conception of the world of human acts and passions, which is the world of history, I have given him the epithet Mythistoricus.

This essay, although its argument (of which a summary will be found in the Table of Contents) is continuous, has been divided into two parts which in a way reflect the twofold design of Thucydides' history. Having occasion to look into the question, how the Peloponnesian War arose, I felt, vaguely but strongly, that Thucydides' account of its origin is remarkably inadequate; and I came to form a very different theory of the real causes of the war. This theory I have stated in the first four chapters, because, although the subject seems to me to be of no great importance in itself, it led me to inquire further, why Thucydides has told us about this matter—and told us at considerable length—so exceedingly little that appears to us relevant. The rest of the book is an answer to this question. I found that the reason lay, not in the author's famous reticence—he thought he had recorded all we should want to know—but in the fact that he did not, as is commonly asserted, take a scientific view of human history. Rather he took the view of one who, having an admirably scientific temper, lacked the indispensable aid of accumulated and systematic knowledge, and of the apparatus of scientific conceptions, which the labour of subsequent centuries has refined, elaborated, and distinguished. Instead of this furniture of thought, to the inheritance of which every modern student is born, Thucydides possessed, in common with his contemporaries at Athens, the cast of mind induced by an early education consisting almost exclusively in the study of the poets.  No amount of hard, rational thinking—an exercise which Thucydides never intermitted—could suffice to break up this mould, in an age when science had as yet provided no alternative system of conception.  The bent of his poetical and artistic nurture comes out in the mythistorical portions of the work, which in the later chapters I have singled out and put together. The principle which informs and connects them is the tragic theory of human nature—a traditional psychology which Thucydides seems to me to have learnt from Aeschylus.  I have tried to show at some length how the form of the Aeschylean drama is built upon this psychology; and, finally, I have traced the theory of the tragic passions back into that dim past of mythological belief out of which it came into the hands of the Athenian dramatists.  So my original question finds its answer.  Thucydides never understood the origin of the war, because his mind was filled with preconceptions which shaped the events he witnessed into a certain form; and this form chanced to be such that it snapped the causal links between incidents, in the connexion of which the secret lies.

The Greek historians can be interpreted only by reference to the poets; and to understand the poets, we must know something of the mythological stage of thought, the fund of glowing chaos out of which every part of that beautiful, articulate world was slowly fashioned by the Hellenic intellect. There is, on the literary side, no branch of classical study which is not still suffering from the neglect of mythology. The poets are still treated as if, like an eighteenth-century essayist, they had a tiresome trick of making 'allusions' which have to be looked up in a dictionary.  The history of philosophy is written as if Thales had suddenly dropped from the sky, and, as he bumped the earth, ejaculated, 'Everything must be made of water!'  The historians are examined on the point of 'trustworthiness'—a question which it is the inveterate tendency of Englishmen to treat as a moral question; and, the certificate of honesty once awarded, their evidence is accepted as if they had written yesterday.  The fallacy which I have designated 'The Modernist Fallacy' was never, perhaps, so rife as it is now; and, but that I have no wish to be contentious, this essay might be taken as a polemic against it, in so far as I have argued that the thought of a most prosaic and rational writer of antiquity moved in an atmosphere which we should recognize to be poetic and mythical.

Since I make no claim to have added to the stock of detailed historical information, but only to have given a new setting to established facts, I have not thought it necessary to acknowledge the source of every statement. The material of the first four chapters is taken largely from Dr. Busolt's monumental *Griechische Geschichte*, or from well-known sources which Dr. Busolt's learning and industry have made easily accessible to any student. I have also found Beloch's work useful and suggestive. If I have, for the convenience of exposition, here and there expressed disagreement with a phrase from Professor Bury's *History of Greece*, I would not be thought insensible of the services rendered to scholarship by a student whose vast erudition has not blunted the delicate feeling for poetry revealed in his editions of Pindar.

My thanks are due to the Publishers for their unvarying courtesy and consideration. My friend, Mr. A. E. Bernays, of Trinity College, has kindly read the proofs and suggested corrections. I should like also to recognize with gratitude the wonderful promptitude and efficiency of the readers and staff of the Clarendon Press.

There remain two other debts of a more personal kind.

One, which I am glad to acknowledge in this place, is somewhat indefinite, but still profound. It is to Dr. Verrall, who, at a time when classical poetry in this country either served as an engine of moral discipline in the teaching of grammar or added an elegance of profane scholarship to the cultured leisure of a deanery, was among the first to show that a modern intellect could achieve a real and burning contact with the living minds of Greece.  From his books and lectures many of my generation first learnt that the Greeks were not blind children, with a singular turn for the commonplace, crying for the light of Christian revelation; and I am conscious, moreover, that in this present attempt to understand, not the syntax, but the mind, of Thucydides, I am following, for part of the way, a path which first opened before me when, in the breathless silence of his lecture-room, I began to understand how literary art could be the passion of a life.

The other obligation is to Miss Jane Harrison, to whom this book is dedicated in token that, but for the sympathy and encouragement she has given at every stage of its growth, this dream would have followed others up the chimney with the smoke.  Any element of value there may be in the mythological chapters is due, directly or indirectly, to her; and, grateful as I am for the learning which she has put unreservedly at my disposal, I am much more grateful for the swift and faultless insight which, again and again, has taken me straight to a point which my slower apprehension had fumbled for in vain.

F. M. C.

TRINITY COLLEGE,
  *January*, 1907.

# CONTENTS

## PART I. THUCYDIDES HISTORICUS

## PART II. THUCYDIDES MYTHICUS

### INTRODUCTORY

### VI. THE LUCK OF PYLOS

# PART I

# THUCYDIDES HISTORICUS

# CHAPTER I

## THE CAUSES OF THE WAR

THUCYDIDES prefaces the introductory Book of his history with the statement that he has recorded the grounds of quarrel between Athens and the Peloponnesians, 'in order that no one may ever have to ask from what origin so great a war arose among the Hellenes.'[1] Plainly he thought that his account, which follows, of the disputes and negotiations on the eve of the outbreak ought to satisfy posterity. He has told us all the ascertained truth which seemed to him relevant. But somehow we are not satisfied. We do not feel, after reading the first Book, that Thucydides has told us all that we want to know, or all that he knew and, if he had considered it relevant, might have told. So attempts have again and again been made to go behind his story. We are still troubled by the question which he thought no one would ever have to ask.

Our impression, as we review this preliminary narrative, sums itself into a sense of contradiction. The ostensible protagonists in the Peloponnesian War were Sparta and Athens—Athens as represented by Pericles. On the other hand, neither Pericles nor Sparta is provided with any sufficient motive for engaging, just then, in hostilities. Accordingly we find in the modern histories, which are necessarily based on Thucydides, conflicting statements of the type : 'Sparta, or Corinth, forced the war upon Athens,' and then again : 'Pericles saw that war was inevitable and chose this moment for forcing it upon Sparta.' So uncertain are we on the questions : who wanted this war, and why they wanted it.

[1] i. 23. 5.

Why, then, did Athens and Sparta fight? This very question seems to have puzzled contemporaries; for various accounts were already current when Thucydides wrote, and it was partly his object to correct vulgar opinion and readjust the perspective to his own view. Modern historians do little more than traverse the same ground in his footsteps and follow him to the same conclusion.

Besides Thucydides' own opinion, which we reserve for the present, three main views can be distinguished. These are: (1) that the war was promoted by Pericles from personal motives; (2) that it was a racial war—Ionian against Dorian; (3) that it was a conflict of political ideals—Democracy against Oligarchy.[1] The first of these is only a superficial account of the immediate cause. The other two are more reflective, pointing to causes of a wider and deeper sort, and touching the whole character and significance of the struggle. We will briefly discuss them in order.

(1) That Pericles had personal grounds for thrusting the war on Sparta, seems to have been the vulgar belief—the belief which Thucydides desired, above all, to refute. Pericles, said the gossips, was avenging the theft of three loose women[2]; he was afraid of sharing the fate of Pheidias, and so stirred up a general conflagration;[3] he wished to avoid rendering account of public moneys;[4] he acted from an ambitious desire to humble the pride of the Peloponnesians.[5] These and similar current scandals have found their way, through Ephorus and others, into Plutarch and Diodorus. Among the moderns, Beloch[6] inclines to revert to a view of this type. Pericles, finding his position at home shaken, was anxious to turn attention elsewhere. But it has been sufficiently replied that, though this motive might explain his socialistic

---

[1] 'The inevitable struggle between these rival powers widened into a conflict of race between Ionians and Dorians, and a party warfare between democracy and oligarchy.'—*Companion to Greek Studies*, Cambridge, 1905, p. 69. When a war is described as 'inevitable', we may be almost certain that its causes are not known.

[2] Arist. *Ach.* 524.          [3] Arist. *Pax*, 603.
[4] Diod. xiii. 38.          [5] Plut. *malig. Herod.* 6.
[6] *Griech. Gesch.* i. 515.

measures in home politics, the war was certain to be unpopular with a great part of the citizens, and could not, as conducted by Pericles, have any dazzling results at first.[1]

If there is any truth in this view, there must have been something in Pericles' situation more threatening and more difficult to meet than malicious prosecutions of his personal friends; or he could not have been driven to an expedient so desperate and (must we not add?) so unscrupulous. We will pass on, bearing in mind that contemporary Athens, as this scandal shows, believed that Pericles made the war, and was hard put to it to divine his reasons.

(2) Was it, then, a racial conflict of Ionian against Dorian? Thucydides, at any rate, nowhere suggests that racial antipathy was a main element. In fact, two nations do not go to war on such grounds; though, of course, when war has broken out, there will always be people wicked enough to inflame the prejudice and pride of blood. The Corinthians will call upon Sparta to help the Potidaeans 'who are Dorians besieged by Ionians'.[2] Brasidas will tell his troops that they are Dorians about to meet Ionians whom they have beaten again and again.[3] Especially will language of this kind be heard in Sicily, because there the diplomatic game of Athens is to stir up Ionian racial feeling against Syracuse, and to cover designs of conquest with the fine pretext of 'succouring our kinsmen of Leontini'.[4] Hermocrates brushes aside these plausible excuses. Let no one say, he urges, that, though the Dorians among us may be enemies to the Athenians, the Chalcidians are safe because they are Ionians and kinsmen to Athens. The Athenians do not attack us because we are divided into two races, of which one is their enemy, the other their friend.[5] Precisely; and the same holds of Athens and Sparta at home. We must find some more tangible motive for war than a difference of race.

(3) The third view is that the struggle was political. 'The war became in time a conflict of political principles: community of feeling and interest joined democrats on the one

---

[1] Delbrück, cit. Busolt, iii. 2. 819.    [2] Thuc. i. 124.
[3] Thuc. v. 9.    [4] Thuc. vi. 76 ff.    [5] Thuc. iv. 61.

side against oligarchs on the other.'[1] But though it may be true that the war *became so in time*, this will not account for the outbreak. The point is complicated, because 'oligarch' and 'democrat' meant very different things in different states, and at different times in the same state. We must recur to this difficulty later; here it is enough to observe that Sparta did not fight Athens because Athens was silly enough to have a democratic constitution. No one would maintain that. Nor had the Athenians any objection to the Spartan system of government—at Sparta.

It will hardly be believed, either, that each state fought to give Greece in general the blessings of a constitution like its own. Of course, we shall find one of them posing as a benefactor. 'The sympathies of mankind were largely on the side of the Spartans, who proclaimed themselves the liberators of Hellas'.[2] The words were sure to find willing ears among the oppressed subjects of Athenian 'tyranny'. But why, when Mytilene sent to Sparta *immediately before the war*[3] and offered to revolt, did Sparta refuse her aid? The similar pretensions of Athens in earlier days had not been more substantial. To the minor states 'freedom' meant autonomy. The Athenian allies, until they revolted, were allowed considerable latitude in self-government. An oligarchy of landowners was tolerated at Samos, till the revolt of 440. Mytilene had a moderate oligarchy, till the revolt of 428. But then these very facts show that Athens did not care enough for the abstract principle of democracy to fight for the recognition of it in other states. Neither she nor Sparta was so philanthropic. 'Each of the two supreme states', says Aristotle,[4] 'set up in the other cities governments on the model of its own—democracies in the one case and oligarchies in the other. In so doing they considered their own interests,

---

[1] Whibley, *Political Parties at Athens*, p. 33. Mr. Whibley, of course, only gives this as one factor in the situation, which it certainly was, *after* the war had broken out.

[2] Thuc. ii. 8. 4.

[3] Thuc. iii. 2 ; the offer was probably made after the revolt of Potidaea.

[4] Ar. *Pol.* vi. (iv.) 11. 1296 *a* 32.

not those of the cities . . . The result has been that the cities have lost even the desire for equality, and are accustomed either to seek empire or to bow to superior force.' It was not, in fact, a question of the ideal form of government. The Athenian Demos did not set up democracies in the spirit in which Plato instituted an aristocracy in Utopia; they supported the corresponding class in the allied states, because they had common interests and a class-sympathy of poor against rich. Similarly the Spartan oligarchy maintained the corresponding class in neighbouring states, but only *inside the Peloponnese*. They were not conscious of a disinterested mission to the rest of Hellas.

The struggle between democracy and oligarchy, where it existed, was in the main not a warfare between nations and cities, but an internal duel between two parties in one city. Each wanted to rule in its own way; each was prepared at any moment to invoke the aid of the national enemy. But neither at Athens nor at Sparta was there any such struggle going on at the beginning of the war. It was natural for the contrasts of Ionian and Dorian, democrat and oligarch, to be much in the air, because the nominal head of the Peloponnesian league happened to be Dorian and oligarchical, while Athens was Ionian and democratic. Argos was democratic and Dorian; and she was sometimes on one side, sometimes on the other. But did she join Athens in 461 because she was democratic, and Sparta in the present war because she was Dorian?

Neither the racial contrast nor the political provides either party with a definite and sufficient motive for embarking, just at this moment, on a conflict. We must look elsewhere.

Most of the modern histories come back to Thucydides' one explicit statement of his own view, and there rest content. 'The most genuine pretext, though it appeared least in what was said, I consider to have been the growing power of the Athenians which *alarmed the Lacedaemonians* and *forced* them into war.'[1] Thucydides holds (1) that the Spartans

---

[1] Thuc. i. 23. 6; repeated in i. 88, and explained 88-118. 2; alluded to by the Corcyreans in i. 33.

were *afraid* of Athens' growing power, and (2) that the war was *forced* on Sparta.

We shall recur later to the explanation which Thucydides gives of this alarm. It is sufficient here to note that the Spartans were reluctant to fight; the impulse did not come from them. This we believe to be true. Sparta was not an imperial or conquering state. The purpose of her elaborate and rigid military system was often misunderstood; even Aristotle speaks of it as designed for conquest. But its existence is otherwise explained by a glance at the economic and social conditions. The soil of Lacedaemon was owned by a few, very large proprietors.[1] Hence, while the country could have maintained fifteen hundred horse and thirty thousand hoplites, the total number fell to a thousand, and Sparta could not survive a single blow. Her fall at Leuctra was due to the paucity of her citizen population. The laws were framed to encourage the increase of the privileged class; and this tendency, combined with the growth of large estates, was bound to produce a very large number of poor.[2] Only the small and decreasing body of the rich enjoyed full citizenship. The Spartiates, says Isocrates,[3] enslaved the souls of the common people no less than those of their servants. They appropriated, he goes on, not only the best of the land, but also more of it than was similarly occupied elsewhere in Greece, leaving so little for the mass of the people, and that little so poor, that these could scarcely keep alive with grinding toil. The common folk were split up in tiny 'cities', less important than villages in Attica. Deprived of all a freeman should have, they were yet compelled to serve as attendants in war. Worst of all, the Ephors could execute them untried, in any numbers. Their condition was lower than that of slaves in other parts of Greece. The Ephors, we are told, on taking office regularly declared war on the Helots, so that to massacre them at any moment might be legal.

---

[1] Ar. *Pol.* ii. 9 furnishes this and the following particulars.

[2] Cf. Thuc. i. 141. The Peloponnesians are αὐτουργοί and have no wealth.

[3] *Panath.* 270. Isocrates' statements are, of course, rhetorical; but these seem to be true.

The danger of such a situation—the constant menace of revolt—did not escape the observation of Aristotle,[1] who further remarks that the Spartans plainly had not discovered the best method of governing a subject population. To meet this danger, and not for purposes of conquest, their military system was designed and maintained. Thucydides saw this. In 424, he says, the Spartans favoured Brasidas' expedition, because, now that the Athenians were infesting the Peloponnese, they wanted to send some Helots out of the way and so prevent a rising for which the occupation of Pylos gave an opportunity. '*Most of the Lacedaemonian institutions were specially designed to secure them against this danger.*'[2]

This sagacious observation had escaped most of Thucydides' contemporaries. They could not understand why a great military power should not be aggressive, and they put it down to the notorious 'slowness' of the Spartan character. 'Of all the Hellenes', so the Corinthians expostulate, 'you alone keep quiet.' 'Justice with you seems to consist in not injuring others and only defending yourselves from being injured.'[3] Elsewhere,[4] Thucydides himself falls into the same strain. In 411, he says, if the Peloponnesians had been more energetic, the whole Athenian empire might have fallen into their hands ; but the two peoples were of very different tempers, the one quick and adventurous, the other timorous and slow. The Spartans, he remarks again, were never disposed to make war except when compelled.[5]

This reluctance is easy to explain. Situated in an out-of-the-way corner of the peninsula, locked in by mountains and almost harbourless coasts, prohibited by law from commerce and industry, the Spartans never voluntarily and spontaneously attempted conquest outside the Peloponnese. They did not want an empire over-seas, and when they got one, could not hold it. Their ideal was a 'life of virtue', to be lived by a small class at the expense of a majority held down by ruthless repression and treacherous massacre. For

---

[1] *Pol.* ii. 9.  
[3] Thuc. i. 68.  
[2] Thuc. iv. 80.  
[4] Thuc. viii. 96.  
[5] Thuc. i. 118.

fear of the Helots, it was necessary to maintain a ring of 'oligarchies' on their land frontier. That was all their ambition. Living on a powder-mine, they had everything to fear, and nothing positive to gain, from hostilities with Athens. The moment war broke out their coasts were defenceless. The Athenians—as Demosthenes had the wit to see—had only to land a force on some remote point, like Pylos, easily defensible and capable of being provisioned from the sea, and the Spartans were powerless. What could they do when the oppressed serfs flocked into such a centre of revolt? Yet this obvious peril faced them from the first moment of war with the mistress of the seas. Naturally, they were reluctant, and 'not of a temper to make war except when compelled'. Thucydides is right when he says they were forced into the war.

But who forced them? Pericles, and the Athenian democracy? The term 'democracy' has fatally misleading associations, and it is not easy always to remember that the language used by contemporaries about political parties is vitiated by a constant source of error. The old names, Whig and Tory, oligarch and democrat, which stand for the aims of parties in one generation go on being used in the next, when the lines of cleavage have really shifted and parties are divided on quite other issues. A democrat was a revolutionary under Peisistratus, a radical under Cleisthenes, and in the time of Pericles a conservative.

In order to understand the position of Pericles it is necessary to glance back over the period occupied by this change. The history of Athens exhibits a series of upheavals from below, which end in the full realization of democracy. The power of the great landed families, who ruled Athens down to the Persian wars, had been broken by Cleisthenes, though representatives of the two chief houses, the Alcmaeonidae and the Philaidae, continue to play the leading parts for some time to come. Themistocles, half an alien by birth, had broken into the charmed circle and created a party of his own, which the aristocrats combined to oppose. His invention of Athenian sea power and his creation of the Piraeus were strokes of fresh and innovating genius. The policy they stood for was justified at Salamis and adopted in the next generation.

After the Persian wars men's minds were at first filled with the Eastern peril. The Philaidae, headed by Kimon, took up the anti-Persian ideal—war to the death with the barbarian. The ideal was identified with pan-Hellenism and friendship for Athens' yokefellow, Sparta. The men of Marathon, the victory of the aristocrat Miltiades, rallied round Miltiades' son. The men of Salamis, the democratic victory won by the upstart Themistocles, supported the leader of the opposite house. The upheaval in this generation was led by Pericles and Ephialtes. Family tradition associated the Alcmaeonid Pericles with the seafaring population of 'the shore'. But the sea power of Athens comes to mean something different from what it meant to the generation who had seen the Persian wars. The Eastern peril fades, to vanish at Eurymedon. The Delian league loses its *raison d'être* and passes from an 'alliance' into an 'empire'. To Pericles empire meant glory ($\tau\iota\mu\acute{\eta}$), the first of the 'three most powerful motives—glory, fear, profit', which the Athenians allege as compelling them to retain the position they had won.[1] In his speeches Pericles is always dwelling on the glory of Athens' rule. A genuine imperialist, he honestly believed that the School of Hellas was a benevolent and beneficent institution, and did his best to make it so. 'No subject complains of being ruled by such a mistress, no enemy of being injured by so glorious an antagonist.'[2] Thucydides, the son of Melesias, kept up the opposition on the antiquated lines, and attacked Pericles for using the allies' treasure for other ends than war with Persia. Thucydides was behind the times; he was ostracized, and left Pericles in undisputed supremacy.

Meanwhile, with the achievement of complete democracy, the constitutional struggle was over. The people had gained all they wanted. They did not desire complete equality of all classes. As the oligarchic writer[3] puts it, they did not

---

[1] ὑπὸ ⟨τριῶν⟩ τῶν μεγίστων νικηθέντες, τιμῆς καὶ δέους καὶ ὠφελίας, Thuc. i. 76.

[2] Pseudo-Xen. *de rep. Ath.* i. 3.　　　[3] Thuc. ii. 41.

want the offices on which the safety of the state depended; they knew it was better for men of substance to hold them. They only want, he sneers, the offices which carry wages. It is less unfair to say that they were content with their stronghold, the law courts. As for the oligarchs, they were no longer a party. The oligarchs from conviction were a hopeless minority who could only intrigue in secret and try to influence elections.

The reign of Pericles follows. What was there left for Athens to do? From Pericles' point of view, nothing. He is accused of being no great statesman, only a great politician; he had no 'original constructive idea'. We dispute this. He had an original idea, which has too rarely made its appearance in the history of mankind. The idea was that, instead of spending the treasure of the league on materials for a very improbable war with Persia, it was better to spend it on enduring monuments of perfect art, and that to make a beautiful thing is a worthier occupation than killing other people. An additional advantage gained by this use of the Fund was that he could thus provide employment for a large working population. Those who laboured in the building of those great memorials of Athens' glory had as good a claim, he said, to be supported from the treasury as men engaged on foreign service. Workers in all materials, in marble and bronze, ivory and gold, ebony and cypress; carpenters, masons, brassfounders, marblecutters, dyers, goldsmiths, painters, engravers, turners; merchants and sailors who brought the material by sea and by land, wheelwrights, waggoners, carriers, ropemakers, leathercutters, roadmakers, miners—every art had a whole army of labourers at work and plenty was universally diffused. The whole city, almost, was drawing his wages.[1]

A thoroughly idyllic picture. It is true that the allies, who paid the bill, were becoming restive, and the second of the three imperial motives—fear—was beginning to be felt at Athens. Naxos had been the first to revolt, and 'the first to be enslaved contrary to the terms of alliance'.[2] Samos

[1] Plut. *Per.* xii.  [2] Thuc. i. 98.

and Byzantium had called for stern repression. But the allies had weakened themselves by letting their navies go and contributing money instead of ships. Scattered on islands they had no common place of meeting, now that the congress of the league had fallen into disuse.[1] Pericles' policy towards them was 'to keep them in hand'—a phrase several times attributed to him and probably often on his lips.

What reason had Pericles for making war with Sparta? That is just the question which puzzled contemporaries; hence the scandals which we mentioned and dismissed. When historians cannot discover a motive, they say that he saw that war was 'inevitable' and hastened the moment. But war meant danger to the stability of the Athenian empire—the one cloud on his horizon. So long as there was peace, the allies could be 'kept in hand'; but with the outbreak of hostilities, the Athenian fleet would have other work to do. The chances of revolt would be enormously increased. When the cry for autonomy had once been raised, Sparta would come forward as the liberator of Hellas. The first duty of Athens was to maintain unimpaired the empire which was her glory. Then why plunge her into a war which was the one thing that could make the danger of losing that empire imminent? And what would become of the noble ideal of Athens as a centre of culture and of art, the lesson and the glory of all Greece?

Pericles had no more reason than Sparta for desiring war; and this is precisely the impression which we get from Thucydides. He tells us indeed that Pericles urged the Athenians into the war; but neither at the place where this statement occurs,[2] nor yet in the speech of Pericles at the end of the Book is any motive assigned for this course of action. We can only conclude that Thucydides was at a loss to understand what the motive could be. Yet some one must have desired the war; and if the two protagonists on whom our attention is commonly fixed are each without a sufficient motive, we must seek elsewhere. In what direction?

[1] Ps.-Xen. *de Rep. Ath.* ii. 2.          [2] Thuc. i. 127.

The clue is supplied when we take account of a certain point of Thucydidean method. The facts which Thucydides in his introduction promises to tell us are of two kinds : first, the events (ἔργα)—what actually was done in the war ; and besides these, only 'the accounts given of themselves by the several parties in speeches (λόγῳ) '. The history does, in fact, consist of two elements—descriptive narration and speeches —what was done and what was said. This arrangement involves a limitation important for our present guidance. The arguments, pretexts, explanations, which occur in the speeches must be such as could, and would, be used on formal occasions, by speakers addressing a particular audience for a particular purpose. Further the speakers are, almost always, *official* speakers, the leaders of parties or the representatives of states ; there is no room in the plan for any statement of the views and aims of minorities, or of the non-official sections of a majority. It may be that our secret lies in those dark places which the restrictions of this method compel Thucydides to leave in darkness.

# CHAPTER II

## ATHENIAN PARTIES BEFORE THE WAR

WHO were the people on the Athenian side who made the war and why did they make it? Who caused the 'alarm of the Lacedaemonians' and 'forced' them to fight? We must look behind the official utterances of Pericles, and attempt an analysis of the majority with which he worked. We must stop speaking of 'the Athenians', as Thucydides does; not every Athenian was a Pericles in miniature.

Much has been written about the state of parties at Athens during the war—the state reflected in the earlier extant comedies of Aristophanes. One point, however, of great importance, is easily overlooked. It is that the state of parties *during* the war must have been very different from what it was *before* the war. The annual invasions of Attica caused an influx of the rural population into Athens, and so altered the balance of parties. Aristophanes shows us only the later, transformed condition. To answer our question we must go back to the previous state of affairs. Further, we must avoid obscuring the whole discussion by the use of irrelevant terms, such as oligarch and democrat.

The unknown author of the tract *On the Athenian Constitution* [1] tells us in a few pages more about the Athenian Demos than we shall find in the whole of Thucydides, and he shows us how the difference of parties looked to an old-fashioned aristocrat. He uses three antitheses. (1) The *commons* (δῆμος) are opposed to the *men of birth* (γενναῖοι) —a reminiscence of the old days of patrician rule ; (2) the *base mechanics* (πονηροί, which seems to have some of its original meaning, 'working men') are opposed to the leisured and

---

[1] Ps.-Xen. *de Rep. Ath.*

educated classes, naïvely called 'the *best*' (οἱ χρηστοί or οἱ βέλτιστοι) ; (3) the *poor* (πένητες) are contrasted with the *rich* (πλούσιοι) or men of position and substance (δυνατώτεροι). It will be seen that the division is not constitutional—democrat against oligarch—but a division of class interest —poor against rich. This author, however, is criticizing the democratic constitution which gives too much power to the poor ; he is not considering mainly the division of parties from the point of view of war. The conditions of war bring out a different conflict of interests. The antithesis of country and town here becomes significant. It cuts across the division of rich and poor ; in the country rich and poor alike shared certain risks in war-time which set them against rich and poor alike in the town.

The same author,[1] when speaking of war, says (almost in Pericles' words, Thuc. i. 143) : ' If Athens were only an island, she could escape having her lands ravaged by invaders. As it is, the farmers and the rich (οἱ γεωργοῦντες καὶ οἱ πλούσιοι) dread the incursions of the enemy, whereas the people (ὁ δῆμος), having nothing to lose, live in security.' In this passage ' the people '—so shifting are these terms [2]—means the *town* poor, contrasted with the owners of land, whether large holders (πλούσιοι) or small farmers (γεωργοῦντες). In Aristophanes [3] the same class, the town demos, are called ' the poor '. It is from this antithesis of country and town that we must start.

The strength of the landed interest was, on paper, very considerable. Thucydides,[4] in describing the removal of the country folk into Athens, says that it was very painful, because the Athenians, more than any other Hellenic people, had always been accustomed to live on the soil. Although united by Theseus in a single πόλις, most of them (οἱ πλείους),

---

[1] Ps.-Xen. *de Rep. Ath.* ii. 14.

[2] Thuc. ii. 65, speaking only of the country population, uses δῆμος to mean the peasantry with small holdings, as distinguished from οἱ δυνατοί who have large estates.

[3] *Eccl.* 197 ναῦς δεῖ καθέλκειν· τῷ πένητι μὲν δοκεῖ, | τοῖς πλουσίοις δὲ καὶ γεωργοῖς οὐ δοκεῖ. Cf. Plut. *vit. Nik.* 9 οἱ εὔποροι καὶ πρεσβύτεροι and most of οἱ γεωργοί favoured peace.    [4] ii. 16.

down to the time of this war, resided from old habit in the country. They had just restored their country houses after the Persian invasion, and now they were called upon to forsake their ancient manner of life and leave the village which to them was a city.

The country people, as is implied when the term 'poor' is specially used of the town demos, were comparatively well-to-do. The larger owners worked their farms by slave-labour; and even the small holders would have one or two slaves.[1] They grew, probably, enough corn to supply their own needs, though not those of the town, which depended chiefly on importation. They sent fruit and vegetables to the Athenian market, and olive-oil across the seas. This class had little interest in commerce or in empire; and they had everything to lose by war, which meant the destruction of their olive trees.[2] If they were so numerous, why did they not prevent the war?

The answer is simple. Their leaders, the territorial aristocracy, had little political influence. 'Oligarchs' by tradition, they were suspected of laconism and of intrigues to subvert the democracy. The great majority of the country people were, like Aristophanes' Acharnians, peasants who took no interest in politics, and seldom or never came to Athens. Their hatred of the confinement of town-life is illustrated by Dikaiopolis' complaints:

> 'Looking in vain to the prospect of the fields,
> Loathing the city, longing for a peace,
> To return to my poor village and my farm,
> That never used to cry "Come buy my charcoal!"
> Nor "Buy my oil!" nor "Buy my anything!"
> But gave me what I wanted, freely and fairly,
> Clear of all cost, with never a word of buying
> Or such buy-words.'[3]

Many of the citizens, says Isocrates, did not even come to the city for festivals, but preferred to stay at home and enjoy the pleasures of the country.[4]

---

[1] Hence Thuc. calls the Peloponnesians by contrast, αὐτουργοί.

[2] A point frequently mentioned: Thuc. ii. 72, 75; Ar. *Ach.* 182, 232, 512; *Pax*, 628, &c.           [3] Ar. *Ach.* 32. Frere.

[4] Isocr. *Areop.* 52. Cf. Eur. *Or.* 918 ὀλιγάκις ἄστυ κἀγορᾶς χραίνων κύκλον,

The 'men of Marathon', now, as always, settled on the soil,
were a generation behind the townspeople, and hated the
new growth of the 'democratic' Piraeus. They cared for
the Empire only on its original, anti-Persian basis, and for
the Parthenon not at all. They did not want to exploit the
allies. By traditional sentiment they were not hostile to
the Spartans. They were out of touch with the new school
in politics, and so long as peace allowed them to stay quietly
on their farms, they were a negligible factor in political
combinations. In Aristophanes we only see them in much
altered circumstances, exasperated by being driven into the
town, and enraged against the invaders who had ravaged
their homes. The more sober and far-sighted joined the
peace party. Others in time would become assimilated to
the town-poor, and in the desperation of ruin would reinforce
the party of war. But all this was after the war had begun ;
before it broke out their numerical strength was not felt.
The country-folk, anyhow, were not the people who made
the war. To find them we must look to the town.

Athens was not one town, but two. The new factor in
fifth-century politics is the Piraeus. The port had been
created by Themistocles, who substituted for the exposed,
sandy bay of Phalerum the rock-defended harbour on the
other side of Acte. It had been fortified, and the new town
was laid out on the best modern principles by Hippodamus.
By the beginning of the Peloponnesian war it had become
the chief commercial centre of the Greek world. Even after
the fall of Athens its yearly export and import trade was
reckoned at 2,000 talents, and before the war it must have
been much greater. From 510 to 430 B.C. the population of
Athens and the Piraeus together is said to have increased
from 20,000 to 100,000. This increase must have been
chiefly due to the influx of a commercial and industrial
population into the Piraeus. The new-comers were, of
course, aliens. While a majority of the citizens were, as
Thucydides says, country people, a great majority of the

αὐτουργός, Supp. 420 γαπόνος δ' ἀνὴρ πένης, | εἰ καὶ γένοιτο μὴ ἀμαθής, ἔργων ὕπο |
οὐκ ἂν δύναιτο πρὸς τὰ κοίν' ἀποβλέπειν.

'resident aliens' must have been townspeople, engaged in industry or commerce down at the port. The strength of the alien element in the town population is often ignored in spite of the evidence.

The encouragement of alien immigrants dates from Solon,[1] who 'saw that Attica had a barren and poor soil and that merchants who traffic by sea are not wont to import their goods where they can get nothing in exchange, and accordingly turned the attention of the citizens to manufactures'. 'He ordered that trades should be accounted honourable.' His law for the naturalization of foreigners granted the citizenship only to such as transplanted themselves with their whole family to Athens, to exercise some manual trade. The intention was not to deter but to encourage immigrants, by the hope of civic rights, to settle permanently and start industries. This recruiting of the native population must have gone on steadily through the sixth and fifth centuries. Of course, foreign families who migrated to Athens before the Persian war would be quite Athenianized by the end of the fifth century. But the great influx must have been after the foundation of the Piraeus. From 480 to 450 Athens granted citizenship freely. Pericles, perhaps in alarm at this increasing infiltration of foreign blood, made the conditions of naturalization harder. But the unnaturalized alien was still, for industrial purposes, as free as the citizen, and had the protection of law. At the beginning of the Peloponnesian war there were 9,000 adult men in this condition, who, with their families, made up an alien population of 30,000. Although not politically on the same level, these people belonged to the same social class, and had the same interests as the other recent immigrants who had been admitted to citizenship. United with them they formed a solid body with definite ends to gain, and with the business man's practical sense of the means to gaining them.

How the native-born Athenians regarded them we know from the rhetorical outbursts of Isocrates. Reviewing the days of maritime empire under the democracy, he says,[2] 'Who

---

[1] Plutarch, *Solon*, xxii.          [2] *de Pace*, 79, 88, 89.

could endure the brutality of our fathers who gathered from all Greece the laziest rascals to man their triremes, and so excited the hatred of all Hellenes ; who ejected the best from other states, and divided their substance among the lowest ruffians in Greece!' 'They filled the public tombs with citizens, and the public registers with aliens.' 'A city will be happy, not when it collects a multitude of citizens at random from every nation in the world, but when it preserves above all the race of its original inhabitants.' So Xenophon [1] notes that the resident aliens include not only Greeks from other states, but many Phrygians, Lydians, Syrians, and barbarians of all sorts.

This growing mass of commercial, industrial, and sea-going people, in the harbour town, must have been a factor of great and increasing importance. We hear little about them, except expressions of contempt from the aristocratic authors whose work has come down to us. Their occupations excited the disgust of the true Athenian gentleman who, whatever Solon might prescribe, never could think of trade as anything but dishonourable and degrading. The last thing he would admit, even to himself, would be that this class could have a decisive influence on the policy of Athens. But we ought not to allow our own view to be distorted by the prejudice of our authorities. Some of the wealthier of the unenfranchised aliens, it is true, were highly respected, and mixed on equal terms with the Athenian aristocracy. The house of Kephalus, Lysias' father, seems to have been a centre of intellectual society. Men of this sort, though excluded from civic life, must have exercised considerable influence, and could make their interests felt indirectly, through their citizen friends of the same social class. They had, moreover, an economic hold on a large number of free artisans in their employ, whose wages were kept down by the competition of slave labour. Many of these workmen were citizens, and their votes counted in the Assembly for just as much as the votes of the aristocrats who regarded working men as 'incapable of virtue'. They were the sovereign Demos,

[1] de Vect. 11. 3.

and if they and their employers, whose interests were theirs,
knew what they wanted, they could be given a morning's
holiday to go and vote for it.

This, then, is the new force in Athenian politics, ignored
and despised by the upper-class writers whose works we know,
but bound, sooner or later, to make itself felt decisively.

What were their aims and ideals ?   We have no expression
of them from any member of the class itself ; but we can
infer enough from the statements of their opponents.   The
Empire, to them, meant thalassocracy—command of the main
arteries of trade ; it meant also the tribute of the allies, which
found its way into their pockets in wages or doles, and
served to keep them on the right side of the narrow line which
separated so many of them from starvation.   We get a
glimpse—one of the very rare glimpses in literature of what
we call economic considerations—in the tract already referred
to, *On the Constitution of Athens*.[1]   The writer is not making
one of the ordinary aristocratic attacks on the Demos.   He
recognizes that the Demos understands its own interests and
plays its game well ; only he thinks the game a base one, and
the players πονηροί.   'Wealth', he says, ' can belong only to the
Athenians among all Greeks and Barbarians.   For, suppose a
city is rich in timber for ship-building, how is it to dispose of
its timber, unless it prevails upon (πείθει) the power which
controls the sea ?   Or suppose it has iron, or bronze, or flax,
or any other commodity used in ship-building.   We import
these commodities, one from one place, another from another ;
and *we will not allow other States, who are rivals, to import
them, on pain of being excluded from the seas*.[2]   We sit at
home and all these things come to us by sea ; but no other
city has all these commodities at once.   One is rich in flax,
but its land is bare and timberless ; another has iron, but not
bronze, and so on.   Only at the Piraeus can you find them all.' [3]

---

[1] Ps.-Xen. *de Rep. Ath.* ii. 11.

[2] Οὐ χρήσονται τῇ θαλάττῃ—a reference to the Megarian decrees ?

[3] Isocrates *Paneg.* 42 says, Athens set up at the Piraeus an emporium in the
midst of Greece, such that there can be obtained all the commodities which
could scarcely be found singly in other states.

The class we are considering evidently regarded the Athenian navy as an instrument for controlling as they pleased the sea-borne trade in Greek waters. The third of the three imperial motives—profit—was dominant with them.

That Cleon's majority, after Pericles' death, was drawn chiefly from this commercial and industrial class, has always been recognized. Aristophanes speaks of them as tradesmen —leather-sellers, honey-sellers, cheese-mongers.[1] When Trygaeus[2] summons 'farmers, merchants, carpenters, workmen, aliens, foreigners, islanders' to help in drawing up the image of Peace, only the farmers answer the summons; none of the rest will stir a finger. But the evidence of Aristophanes of course refers to a later date, when the war had already run through its first stage.

The impression left by ancient writers is that no representatives of this party—no members of this class—came to the surface till after Pericles' death. For this impression Thucydides is chiefly responsible; in his mind, as in those of his contemporaries,[3] the death of Pericles closed an epoch. When that great personal influence was withdrawn, it seemed to them as if the demos had undergone a critical change. Until Pericles' death, says the author of *The Athenian Constitution*,[4] the leaders of the people were all respectable. The list runs : Xanthippos, Themistocles, Ephialtes, Pericles—Cleon, Cleophon. Cleon, we know, was a tanner ; Cleophon was a lyre-maker. What a fall, after the Olympian aristocrat ! But it was not so sudden a fall as it looks in this account ; Cleon was not the first of the 'dynasty of tradesmen'.[5] There was the oakum-dealer and bran-seller, Eukrates, 'the boar-pig from Melite,' who was condemned on the scrutiny of his accounts and retired into private life—' made a clean bolt to the bran-shop,' as Aristophanes puts it. Then there was the ' sheep-seller ', Lysicles, with whom, as Aeschines, the Socratic,[6] reported, Aspasia lived after Pericles' death. There

---

[1] *Knights*, 852 (425–424 B.C.).          [2] *Pax*, 296 and 508.
[3] Cf. Eupolis, *Demoi*, 15 (Mein. ii. 466), *Poleis*, 7 (Mein. ii. 510).
[4] *Ath. Pol.* 28.          [5] See Ar. *Knights*, 125 ff.
[6] Plut. *Per.* 24.

is no ground for believing that he was contemptible. Cleon was the next unofficial leader of the advanced section. We happen to know, from a comic fragment, that he began to attack Pericles as early as 431. He acted as prosecutor in a process against the generals in the winter 430–429. Thucydides,[1] in his first mention of him, calls him 'at that time by far the first in the people's confidence'. This is less than two years after Pericles' death; he must have laid the foundations of his influence long before.

Almost all we know of Cleon comes from Aristophanes or Thucydides. The earliest extant play of Aristophanes dates from some years after the beginning of the war. Thucydides does not mention Cleon till he has become the official leader and spokesman of the demos; Eukrates he never names; Lysicles is barely mentioned,[2] and then only as the officer in command of an unimportant expedition. It is easy for us to slip into the assumption that the class represented by these leaders, and by others who are now hardly more than names, only became important after Pericles' death. But when it is realized that before the war the country-people were not a factor in politics, we see that the majority which Pericles had to work with must have largely consisted of this same commercial and industrial class. The opposition he had to fear came not from 'oligarchs', who were a powerless minority, but from the advanced section of the demos itself, led by these low-born tradesmen whom Thucydides will not deign to mention.

We described fifth-century history at Athens as a series of upheavals. The last of these had raised Pericles to undisputed supremacy, and at the same time had brought the constitutional question to a settlement. Democracy was achieved; reform could go no further. But time does not stand still; a new generation is growing up under Pericles' feet, with new aims and new demands. A period of peace has

---

[1] Thuc. iii. 36; cf. iv. 21.

[2] Thuc. iii. 19. Lysicles fell in battle in the winter 428–427. Thucydides omits to give his father's name—in contempt, perhaps, of his low birth.

given a new impetus to commerce and industry; and the Piraeus
is swelling to a size that threatens to overbalance the old town
under the Acropolis.    This teeming population, largely of
alien birth or naturalized but yesterday, takes no stock of
the hereditary feuds of Alcmaeonids and Philaidae.    They
have nothing in common, either by tradition or interest, with
the autochthonous country-folk, who, on their side, despise
them as a 'seafaring rabble', an 'undisciplined and vulgar
mob'.    They know nothing of the obsolete, anti-Persian ideal
of the League; they care nothing for the Periclean ideal of
Athens as the School of Hellas.    The later part of Pericles'
career can only be explained if we see that the demos he had
to manage did not, most of them, share his exalted thoughts
or understand a word of his magnificent Funeral Oration.
Gradually and steadily they were getting out of hand.    They
extorted from him his socialistic measures.    When he spent
the allies' treasure on magnificent buildings, he was serving
two ends—his own end, the beauty and glory of Athens, and
his supporters' end, employment and maintenance out of
public funds.    By such dexterous compromises he could keep
them in hand, till some man of the people arose to tell the
demos that they could take as a right what was granted
them as a favour.    From the moment the sovereign people
wakes up to its own power, Pericles must either go under
or take the lead whither they will.    He must walk at the
head of the crowd, or be trampled under foot; but the crowd
is going its own way.

Whither?    What were the aims of this obscure, inarticulate
army of tradesmen and handworkers, leaders of commerce
and industry, merchants and sea captains?    We shall attempt
an answer in the next Chapter.

# CHAPTER III

## THE MEGARIAN DECREES

THERE is a remarkable discrepancy between Thucydides' account of the negotiations immediately preceding the war and all the other ancient accounts we possess. These other authorities agree in representing certain decrees against Megara, passed at Athens on the eve of the war, as having a critical effect in bringing it on. Thucydides, on the contrary, does not even record these decrees at the proper point, and only makes a few allusions to them which attract no special attention. The explanation of this discrepancy will, we hope, throw some light on our inquiry into the aims of the party which made the war.

The evidence of Aristophanes with regard to these decrees has much weight. We must, of course, handle the statements of a comic poet cautiously; but there is a kind of inference which we can draw with confidence. The inference we can draw here is that the audience which witnessed the *Acharnians* believed certain things. They may or may not have believed that Pericles acted from personal motives. That is unimportant; if they did, it merely shows that they did not understand Pericles, and that they could not imagine any serious motive he could have entertained. What is important is that they believed that the series of decrees against Megara had much more to do with the outbreak of the war than any ordinary reader, not on his guard, could possibly gather from Thucydides' account. We are sure of this, because Aristophanes' purpose here is serious; he wishes to allay a shortsighted rage against Sparta and convert the poor, exasperated peasants to the cause of peace. He would not further this purpose by giving such an account of the origin of the war as every one in his audience knew to be substantially false. It is one thing to represent the quarrel as arising ultimately out of the theft of three courtesans; no one would take that too seriously. But when it comes to describing how the actual outbreak occurred, we can imagine no motive for pretending that the boycotting of Megara was the principal point on which the negotiations turned, unless it really was so. In Aristophanes' account it is the *sole* point:—

> 'For Pericles, like an Olympian Jove,
> With all his thunder and his thunderbolts
> Began to storm and lighten dreadfully,
> Alarming all the neighbourhood of Greece;
> And made decrees drawn up like drinking-songs,
> In which it was enacted and concluded,
> That the Megarians should remain excluded
> From every place where commerce was transacted,
> With all their ware—like 'old care'—in the ballad;
> And this decree by sea and land was valid.
>     Then the Megarians, being all half starved,
> Desired the Spartans, to desire of us,
> Just to repeal those laws; the laws I mentioned,
> Occasioned by the stealing of those strumpets.
> And so they begged and prayed us several times;
> And we refused; and so they went to war.'[1]

If this sketch of the negotiations is not roughly correct, what is the point of it?

The impression here given by Aristophanes is confirmed by Diodorus, who, after stating that Pericles had private motives for desiring war, proceeds thus[2]: 'There was a decree at Athens excluding the Megarians from the market and harbours, and the Megarians appealed to Sparta. The Lacedaemonians at their instance sent envoys empowered by a resolution of the Council of the League to demand that the Athenians should rescind the decree and to threaten war if they refused. The Athenian Assembly met, and Pericles with his great eloquence persuaded the Athenians not to annul the decree, saying that to give way to Sparta against their interests was the first step to servitude. So he advised them to remove from the country into the town, and having command of the sea to fight the Spartans to the end.'

[1] Ar. *Ach.* 530 ff.  Frere.          [2] Diod. xii. 39.

Plutarch[1] goes a step further and expressly states that
'probably no other point would have involved the Athenians
in war, if they could have been induced to rescind the
decree against Megara. Pericles exerted all his influence
to prevent this, and by working up the Athenian people to
share his rancour against Megara, was the sole author of the
war'. 'He seems to have had some private grudge against
Megara.'

All these accounts agree in two respects. (1) They make
the Megarian decree the central point of the negotiations,
(2) They connect this decree with some unexplained personal
rancour felt by Pericles against Megara. On the other hand,
Thucydides, as we shall presently show at length, keeps the
measures against Megara in the background.

What was the history of these decrees? In 446 the
Megarians had risen and expelled the Athenian garrisons
which had for some time held their ports. The Megarian
colony, Byzantium, had joined in the Samian revolt. The
commercial interests of Megara in Pontus were threatened by
Athenian enterprise in that region. Megara had a very small
territory, and its population lived by industry and by the trade
which passed through. Athens was the nearest market; so it
was easy for the great sea power to put the screw on the
small one. The first decree against Megara dates, probably,
from before the summer of 433. Athens excluded Megarian
wares from the Athenian market on pain of confiscation.
This is the first of the two decrees which Aristophanes
mentions.[2] It was not moved by Pericles. Thucydides does
not record it.

The second decree was more stringent. After the conclusion of the alliance with Corcyra,[3] on the trumpery excuse
that the Megarians had cultivated some sacred land at Eleusis,
or received fugitive slaves, or what not, Pericles moved that
the Megarians should be excluded (not merely from the
Athenian market, but) from all ports in the Athenian empire.

[1] *Pericles*, 29.  [2] *Ach.* 515.
[3] Probable date, winter, 433–432.

This meant flat ruin to Megara; for she was shut out of Byzantium, an indispensable port of call on the Pontic route, and the central mart of the corn-trade on which she depended. Aristophanes'[1] picture of starvation at Megara is not overdrawn. Here is another incident—surely important enough, and falling well within his period—which Thucydides does not record in its place.

Thucydides also omits to mention a third decree—that of Charinos—which declared a 'truceless war' with Megara. This decree falls between the attack on Plataea in April, 431, with which the war opens, and the march of the Peloponnesian army.[2] Why do we hear nothing of it from the historian of the war?

Let us now look at the allusions to Megara which Thucydides does make.

(1) The Corinthians in their speech at Athens (i. 42) refer, in passing, to 'the ill-feeling which your treatment of the Megarians has already inspired'.

(2) At the congress at Sparta (i. 67) the Lacedaemonians summon their allies to bring forward their grievances against Athens. 'Others came with their several charges, including the Megarians, who, among many other causes of quarrel, stated that they were excluded from the harbours in the Athenian Empire and from the Attic market, contrary to the treaty.'

(3) In the negotiations which preceded the declaration of war (i. 139), the Lacedaemonians after making other demands 'insisted, above all, and in the plainest terms, that if the Athenians wanted to avert war they must rescind the decree which excluded the Megarians from the market of Athens and the harbours in the Athenian dominions. But the Athenians would not listen to them, or rescind the decree; alleging in reply that the Megarians had tilled the sacred ground and the neutral borderland and had received runaway slaves.' In the debate which followed 'some said the decree ought not to stand in the way of peace'.

---

[1] *Ach.* 535, 730 ff. ; *Pax*, 245, 481.
[2] In the interval between Thuc. ii. 2 and ii. 13.

(4) Pericles in his speech on this occasion[1] discusses the Lacedaemonian grievances, and refers to Megara in curious language: 'They tell us to withdraw from Potidaea, to leave Aegina independent, and to rescind the decree against Megara. *Do not imagine that we shall be fighting for a small matter if we refuse to annul this measure, of which they make so much, telling us its revocation would stop the war. This small matter involves the trial and confirmation of your whole purpose. If you give way about a trifle they will think you are afraid and make harder conditions.'*

(5) At i. 144 Pericles makes his counter-demand: 'We will not exclude the Megarians, if the Lacedaemonians will not exclude foreigners from Sparta.' The Athenians adopted these terms.

Even from these few allusions the truth peeps out, that the decree ' *of which they make so much, telling us its revocation would stop the war* ' was really, as it appears in Aristophanes, Plutarch, and Diodorus, the turning-point of the negotiations. But we venture to say that no one, reading the whole story in Thucydides and unacquainted with the other evidence, would gather this impression. Such a reader would be left with the idea that the decree was in itself, as Pericles calls it, ' a trifling matter,' exaggerated by the Spartans, and merely held to by the Athenians as a point of honour. He would never discover that there were *three* decrees, each more stringent than the last, or that the second was moved by Pericles himself, or that, by this 'trifling matter', Megara was reduced nearly to starvation.

The same design of keeping Megarian affairs in the background can be detected in Thucydides' treatment of the operations in that 'truceless war', the declaration of which he never records. At ii. 31 he mentions an invasion of the Megarid in full force, and observes that the invasion was repeated every year until Nisaea was taken. This incidental observation is repeated at iv. 66 (B.C. 424). But these invasions are not, like the Spartan invasions of Attica, recorded separately as they occurred, according to Thucydides' avowed

[1] Thuc. i. 140 ff.

plan of chronicling the events of the war. At ii. 93 we discover from a passing reference that the Athenians had established a fort in Salamis, opposite the Megarian coast, and kept three ships stationed there 'to prevent anything being conveyed by sea into or out of Megara'. We hear of this fort again at iii. 51, when the Athenians capture Minoa, to make the blockade more effective. From these hints we gather that all through the early part of the war Athens was following up her policy of bringing the severest possible pressure to bear on Megara. But why are we only given hints and summary allusions to the incidents of this truceless war?

One motive which might induce Thucydides to suppress Pericles' connexion with the attack on Megara has already been mentioned. From all the non-Thucydidean accounts it is clear that this attack was currently associated with some petty, personal rancour on Pericles' part. Thucydides, who knew that Pericles was incapable of plunging Athens into war for such motives, wished to contradict the scandal. For the same reason he keeps silent about the indirect attacks made upon Pericles through the persons of Pheidias, Anaxagoras, Aspasia. But this is hardly a sufficient explanation of the anomalies we have pointed out.

There is however one hypothesis which would provide a complete explanation. Thucydides, we remember, is bound by his plan of speech-writing to state only official policies ; he speaks of 'the Athenians' as if they were one united whole, with a single purpose. Suppose, now, that the attack on Megara, the boycotting decrees, and the truceless war, were part of a policy which had *not been originated by Pericles, but forced upon him against his will*. Suppose it was the policy of the class which furnished the bulk of his majority, the class we attempted to characterize in the last chapter—in a word, the policy of the Piraeus. Suppose that younger leaders, sprung from that class itself, were already threatening to outbid Pericles in the popular favour ; that Cleon, for instance, was telling the demos to take their own way and, if Pericles would not lead them, he would. How would Pericles meet this situation?

Imagine a statesman of aristocratic birth, with the ideals and prejudices of his class; mainly interested in culture, in art and philosophy; by temperament exceptionally sensitive and reserved; openly called a 'tyrant'—the 'new Peisistratus'. He owes his position—a position which the habits of a lifetime have made indispensable—to the favour of a class of working people, incapable of his aspirations, ignorant of his pursuits; largely of alien extraction and indifferent to his hereditary traditions; engaged in occupations which his own class despises as mercenary and degrading. He can keep them amused for a time with festivals, doles, and abundance of employment on public works; but what will happen when they become conscious of the power he has irrevocably put in their hands? A very little agitation will suffice to consolidate and marshal them in irresistible ranks. Someone—Cleon, let us say,—puts into their heads a wider policy than that of appropriating the allies' treasure in the form of wages.

The first step in this policy involves the coercion of Megara —why, we shall presently see. The policy is distasteful to Pericles; he will stand out against it as long as he dares; but even his influence cannot hold back the demos. The first decree against Megara is moved by somebody—his very name is lost— and carried. For Pericles to stand out longer would be to advertise all Greece that his influence is no longer supreme. He throws himself into the campaign against Megara with a vehemence which makes people think he must have some personal spite. Some young Megarians must have carried off a couple of Aspasia's women. So idle tongues run on scandal. Pericles is not sorry that his real motive is not divined by the gossips. He moves in his own person the second, more stringent decree. His upstart competitors are instantly silenced; the words are taken out of their mouths; their policy becomes the policy of the leader whom they hoped to displace. There is some disappointment of personal ambitions, which must wait for a better opening; Pericles cannot live for ever. But, politically, a signal triumph is won. Athens has taken the first step in the execution of a plan that was not matured in Aspasia's boudoir, but has been the theme of many back-parlour conferences in the wineshops along the quays. Its authors can well afford to go on working below the surface.

What was the rest of this plan? To find that out we must concentrate our attention on the point from which Thucydides diverts it. We must study the significance of Megara, and discover the purpose of a violent and sustained attack on that inoffensive little community.[1]

The town of Megara is in a tiny plain, dominated on all sides by barren hills. The country could, of itself, support only a very small population. Yet Megara had once been a great sea-power, founding her colonies far to the east and west, in Pontus and in Sicily. The Megarians, says Isocrates,[2] started with few advantages; they had no territory, no harbours, no mines; they were 'tillers of stones'; yet now they have the finest houses in Greece. Isocrates' explanation of this paradox well illustrates the blindness of the Greeks to economic causes. The prosperity of Megara is due, he tells us, to virtuous moderation ($\sigma\omega\phi\rhoο\sigmaύνη$)!

The Megarian territory fills most of the length of the isthmus which joins the Peloponnese and Northern Greece. The advantages of such a position, given the conditions under which commerce was carried on in the ancient world, have, until very recently, not been perceived. Thus Grote looked at the situation only through modern eyes.[3] 'The acquisition of Megara (in 461 B.C.) was of signal value to the Athenians, since it opened up to them *the whole range of territory* across the outer isthmus of Corinth to the interior of the Krissaean Gulf, on which the Megarian port of Pegae was situated, and *placed them in possession of the passes* of Mount Geraneia, so that they could arrest the march of

---

[1] In the next paragraphs I am following closely M. Victor Bérard's brilliant exposition of his 'Law of Isthmuses' in *Les Phéniciens et l'Odyssée*, i. p. 61 ff, and freely borrowing his evidence. Any reader of this fascinating book will see that all this section of my work is inspired by his discoveries.

[2] *de Pace*, 117.                 [3] Grote, iv. 408.

a Peloponnesian army over the isthmus and protect Attica from invasion.' This is a modern view; we naturally think of the isthmus as a *land*-link, ' opening up a range of territory'; we travel along it by the railway which takes us from Patras, through Corinth, to Athens. Our route by sea goes round the south of the Peloponnese, past Cape Malea. But, before the invention of steam, an isthmus, as M. Bérard has shown, is not only a link between two continents; it is of much more importance as a bridge between two seas. For the comprehension of ancient commercial routes, and of all that part of history which depends on them, it is essential to grasp M. Bérard's cardinal principle : *the route which follows the land as far as possible, and takes to the sea only when the land fails, was the cheapest, easiest, and safest.*

We will here adduce only one of M. Bérard's illustrations, because it is taken from Thucydides himself. Among the reasons which the historian gives for the great distress at Athens, caused by the occupation of Dekeleia, is the following: ' Provisions formerly conveyed by the shorter route from Euboea to Oropus and thence overland through Dekeleia, were now carried by sea round the promontory of Sunium *at great cost.*' [1] The road from Oropus by Dekeleia to Athens was an isthmic route. Now that steam has made us independent of winds, no one would dream of sending corn from Oropus to Athens by road ; and this land-route, which in the time of Dicaearchus [2] was still a flourishing caravan-track, ' well supplied with inns,' is now utterly abandoned. But before the introduction of steam it was easier, quicker, and cheaper than the sea-route round Sunium.

Now, if the isthmus of Dekeleia was of such vital significance to Athens, the isthmus of Corinth and Megara—as a glance at the map will show—must have been the most important bridge between two seas in the whole of central Greece. It was the gate of the Western Ocean. The other gate—the channel, to the south of the Peloponnese, round Cape Malea—was beset with terrors to the sailor. It is a

---

[1] Thuc. vii. 28 ἡ παρακομιδὴ . . . πολυτελὴς ἐγίγνετο.

[2] *Geogr. Gr. Min.* i. p. 100, quoted by M. Bérard, i. p. 73.

gap in a chain of islands—Kythera, Aegilia, Crete, Kasos, Karpathos, Rhodes—which block the southern entrance of the Aegean. In the channels between these islands strong currents and violent winds naturally prevail, and Malea is not the least dangerous point. It was here that Ulysses was swept from his course ' by the stream of the sea and the north wind '.[1] Herodotus tells how the Corcyreans were prevented from sending their fleet to help the Greeks at Salamis by the Etesian winds at Malea.[2] The Athenians in 424 were afraid that they could not revictual their fleet at Pylos in Messenia. 'They feared lest the winter should overtake them at their post, seeing that the conveyance of provisions round the Peloponnese would be quite impossible. Pylos itself was a desert, and *not even in summer could they send round sufficient supplies.* The coast was without harbours.'[3] During the four winter months, we read elsewhere,[4] it was not easy even to send a message by sea from Sicily to Athens.

Such were the dangers, in the time of sailing-ships, of what is now the regular sea-route to the Piraeus. The possessors of the Corinthian and Megarian isthmus were the gainers. For this point we have the explicit evidence of Strabo,[5] who says: ' Corinth was called (by Homer) "the rich", because of its *emporium*, situated as it is on the isthmus and possessing two harbours, one on the side of Asia, the other on the side of Italy. This made the exchange of merchandise between these regions easy. In the old days the passage to Sicily was not good for sailing (εὔπλους), and the open seas were dangerous, especially off Malea, because of the meeting of winds there (ἀντίπνοιαι). Hence the proverb, " When you pass Malea, forget your home." Hence it was convenient for merchants both from Italy and from Asia to avoid the passage round Malea, and to bring their merchandise to Corinth. By land, likewise, the tolls on what was exported from or imported into the Peloponnese went to those who held the entrance (τὰ κλεῖθρα).'

---

[1] *Od.* ix. 80. Most of these references are taken from M. Bérard, i. p. 82 ff.
[2] Herod. vii. 168.
[3] Thuc. vi. 27.
[4] Thuc. iv. 21.
[5] Strabo viii. 378.

Strabo gives another instance of the same phenomenon: the wealth of Krisa, near Delphi, was due to its position on an 'isthmus'. Krisa was not a port; it lay inland on a spur of the mountains commanding the road up the gorge from the harbour of Itea to Delphi. The prosperity of its inhabitants, according to Strabo,[1] 'was due to the heavy *tolls* (τέλη) which they exacted from those who came to the shrine from Sicily and Italy.' The position of Krisa is analogous to that of Dekeleia; it commands an isthmic route across Phokis to Thebes and the Euboean seas. The importance of Delphi itself was probably due to its being situated on this ancient commercial artery. In the early days when Euboea was colonizing Sicily we may be fairly sure that the communication with the west followed this line.

Thucydides'[2] testimony about Corinth agrees with that of Strabo. 'Corinth, being seated on an isthmus, was naturally from the first a centre of commerce; for the Hellenes within and without the Peloponnese, in the old days when they *communicated more by land than by sea*, had to pass through her territory to reach one another. Her power was due to wealth, as the testimony of the ancient poets shows, when they call her "rich". And when the Hellenes *began to take more to the sea* Corinth acquired a fleet and kept down piracy; *and as she offered an emporium both by sea and land, her revenues were a source of power.'*

Consider, now, the feelings of the merchants, down in the Piraeus, with the great stream of traffic between Sicily and Italy in the west and Asia Minor and the seas and islands to the east, flowing both ways across the isthmus, under their very eyes. The Piraeus had captured the bulk of the eastern trade formerly carried on by Euboea, Aegina, Megara. The only great field for further expansion was in the west, and Corinth held the gateway. Every vase that the Athenian potteries exported to Italy, every cheese that came from Syracuse to the port of Athens, had to pay toll to the keepers of the isthmus. Attica was cut off from the western seas by

---

[1] Strabo ix. 418.  [2] Thuc. i. 13.

Boeotia, the Megarid, Corinth. The weak point in this chain was Megara, which possessed, moreover, a port on each sea— Pegae on the west, Nisaea on the east—with a road over the pass joining them. What would become of the riches of Corinth, when the Piraeus had established an alternative channel for the trade across the isthmus? And so we read [1] that, in 461, 'Athens obtained the alliance of Megara, which had quarrelled with Corinth. Thus the Athenians gained *both Megara and Pegae, and built long walls from Megara to Nisaea, and garrisoned them. And from this above all arose the intense hatred of Corinth for Athens.'

Yes! and we can guess the sort of hatred. It is not the hatred of Dorian against Ionian, or of oligarch against demo-crat; it is the hatred of the principal trader with Italy and Sicily against her most dangerous rival, the Piraeus.

'Corinth you hated; so did she hate you!' [2]

The war which followed the seizure of Megara by Athens in 461 presents some remarkable analogies with the later Peloponnesian war.

(1) It began with a quarrel between Corinth and Megara, whose territory forms the bridge between the Aegean and the West. Athens was allied with Megara. The later war begins with a quarrel between Corinth and Corcyra, which is ' conveniently situated for the voyage to Italy and Sicily'.[3] Athens is allied with Corcyra.

(2) In the earlier war Athens secured at once Megara, Pegae, and Nisaea.[4] At its conclusion, owing to the untimely revolt of Euboea, she was compelled to surrender them.

The later war opens with a series of drastic measures against Megara, followed up by yearly invasions, and the capture of Minoa, and later of Nisaea and Megara itself. At a critical moment, Cleon sacrifices the chance of peace by an exorbitant demand for the cession of *Pegae and Nisaea*, together with other places, none of which had been in Athenian hands in this war. The negotiations broke down.[5]

---

[1] Thuc. i. 103.  [2] Ar. *Eccl.* 199. Κορινθίοις ἤχθεσθε, κἀκεῖνοί γέ σοι.
[3] Thuc. i. 36.
[4] Thuc. i. 111, an Athenian fleet was at Pegae till 454.  [5] Thuc. iv. 21.

(3) In the earlier war Sparta held aloof at first, intervening only when Boeotia was conquered.

In the later, Sparta is not concerned in the outbreak of war at Corcyra. She only comes in under strong pressure from Corinth, on whose port (as the Corinthians point out) the interior of the Peloponnese is economically dependent.[1]

(4) The most striking analogy of all is the following. During the earlier operations, with all Greece on her hands, Athens suddenly undertook a very large and costly expedition —to Egypt!

In the thick of the Peloponnesian war, 'with her suburbs,' as Isocrates says, 'in the enemies' hands,' Athens undertook a still larger and costlier expedition to Sicily—an expedition prepared for, years before, by small expeditions sent out to foment civil and racial discord among the Sicilian states.

Each of these enterprises was a disastrous failure. With regard to the Egyptian expedition, we are told that it was a 'fatal coincidence that Athens' forces were divided. With her full strength she might have crushed the Peloponnesians'.[2] The Sicilian expedition, we suppose, must have been another fatal coincidence. But, perhaps, if we look in the right quarter, we may find in both undertakings some evidence of calculation and design.

The upshot of the earlier war, the net gain of Athens when all her other gains had been lost, was the extinction of Aegina, who had hitherto been a strong naval and commercial power, and now had joined Corinth. Athens blockaded the island, and reduced it; the Aeginetans' fleet was surrendered and they became tributaries. Aegina, we note, is situated in an eastward-facing gulf; her trade must have been chiefly in Aegean waters and the Levant. Had she any commercial connexion with Egypt? When King Amasis, who, as Herodotus tells us,[3] was partial to the Greeks, established Greek settlers at Naukratis, he granted lands to those who wanted to trade along the coast, so that they might erect temples.

---

[1] Thuc. i. 120.   [2] Bury, *History of Greece* (1900), p. 355.
[3] Herod. ii. 178.

The most famous of these shrines was the Hellenion, a joint foundation of several states, which had the right to appoint governors of the emporium. Three states had separate temples : the Samians had a temple to Hera ; the Milesians, to Apollo ; the *Aeginetans*, to Zeus.

Aegina, then, was one of the three states whose interests in Egyptian commerce were large enough for her to maintain a separate sanctuary for her settlers there. Of the other two, Miletus was ruined by the Persian wars, and her trade was transferred to the Piraeus ; Samos had become a tributary of Athens. Aegina remained. Is it a very hazardous inference that there was some connexion between the war in Greece and the expedition to Egypt—that it was not a mere fatal coincidence ? If one of the objects of Athens was to capture the Egyptian trade, that would explain these simultaneous operations at both ends of the chain. She failed of her other objects because she tried too much at once; but she succeeded in extinguishing Aegina.

With this instructive parallel before us, may we not conjecture further that the Sicilian expedition was not an incomprehensible vagary of the wild and self-interested Alcibiades, but was part of the original scheme of the party which promoted the Peloponnesian war ? If Sicily had been from the first the distant objective, the nearer objective was not Sparta, but Corinth. And Corinth was to be attacked through Megara, which provided the desired avenue to the West.

This is the supposition required to complete our hypothesis —the supposition that Sicily was in view from the first. Not in Pericles' view ; it was no part of the official programme, as he saw it, and hence it does not appear in Thucydides' story till he is out of the way. Pericles did not want to conquer Sicily, but some other people did ; and they were the people who forced on Pericles the violent measures against Megara.

We reserve for the next chapter some considerations which tend to show that Thucydides' narrative, in its earlier part, obscures important facts relating to the designs on Sicily.

# CHAPTER IV

## THE WESTERN POLICY

THE commercial relations of Athens with the West dated from early in the sixth century; the black-figured Attic vases found their way to Etruria before 550. But Athens had no colony of her own in Italy or Sicily. After the fall of Chalkis, however, and the loss of her marine (about 506), Athens succeeded to her position, and the Chalkidian colonies looked to her for support against Syracuse. The occupation of Naupactos in 459 was regarded as a menace to Corinthian connexions with the West. Athenian commerce was growing in that quarter; the Attic vases of the fifth century completely oust Corinthian ware in Etruria. There was also a considerable export to Campania, and a somewhat smaller trade with Sicily. Athens imported corn, pigs, and cheese from Sicily, metal-ware from Etruria, and woven stuffs from Carthage. 'All the pleasant things of Sicily and Italy were brought together at Athens.'[1] They were paid for partly in pottery and partly in Attic silver. The Euboic-Attic standard was already in use in most Sicilian states at the end of the sixth century.

Politically, the relations of Athens with the Western Greeks can be traced as far back as the middle of the fifth century. We hear of an embassy from Egesta, asking for help against Selinus, in 454–3 ; but Athens, just then weakened by the loss of the Egyptian expedition, could do nothing. She was invited to share in the settlement of New Sybaris in 453. The first important step was the foundation of Thurii, for trade with Campania and Etruria (443). Pericles tried to give the enterprise a panhellenic character; but Thurii was soon

---

[1] Ps.-Xen. *de rep. Ath.* ii. 7.

a centre of purely Athenian influence in Southern Italy. It became rich and prosperous.

The founding of Thurii is not mentioned by Thucydides in his account of the fifty years between the Persian war and the Peloponnesian. We might have expected some notice of it in a work which leads up to the great effort after expansion in the West. But, if this omission is curious, his silence on another incident is much more remarkable. Just on the eve of the war, Syracuse and her Dorian neighbours were fighting with Leontini, the other Ionian colonies, and the Italian Locrians. Athens concluded an alliance with Leontini, and another, in the same year, with Rhegium.[1] Of these treaties, made about the time when the two Athenian squadrons were dispatched to Corcyra, Thucydides says not a word, until he comes to the embassy of Leontini, six years later, in 427. Even there we have only the merest allusion: ' So the allies of Leontini sent to Athens, *in accordance with an old-standing alliance* and because they were Ionians, and induced the Athenians to send a fleet.'[2] That is the only reference which is to be found in the history; so long as Pericles is on the scene there is complete silence about his colonial policy in the West, complete silence about political relations with Sicilian and Italian states.

The part played by Pericles in the alliance with Corcyra is also utterly effaced in the long story of the negotiations.[3] We are given speeches by the Corcyreans and by the Corinthians, but no utterance of the Athenian statesman. The conclusion of the alliance is narrated in very summary language, as follows:[4] ' The Athenians heard both sides, and two meetings of the Assembly were held. At the first they inclined to the arguments of the Corinthians; but at the second they changed their minds. They would not go so far as an offensive and defensive alliance with Corcyra, for if they did

---

[1] CIA. iv. 1, 33 a, p. 13. CIG. 74 = CIA. i. 33. Both treaties are dated in the archonship of Apseudes (433–2).

[2] Thuc. iii. 86 κατά τε παλαιὰν ξυμμαχίαν καὶ . . .          [3] Thuc. i. 22–44.

[4] Thuc. i. 44.

so a demand from Corcyra that they should co-operate against
Corinth would involve them in a breach of their treaty with
the Peloponnesians. They concluded, however, a defensive
alliance. War with the Peloponnesians appeared to be
inevitable in any case, and they did not want to let Corcyra,
with her strong navy, join Corinth. Their plan was rather
to embroil the two states more and more with one another, so
that when war came Corinth and the other naval powers
might be weaker.'[1] In the next chapter Thucydides plunges
straight into the story of the naval operations off Corcyra.

Now, in all the twenty chapters, of which the last has
just been quoted, there is no mention of Pericles; we hear
only of 'the Athenians'. Who effected the change of feeling
at the second assembly, when Athens was converted to the
Corcyrean side? Why have we no account of this second
meeting, like the long account of the Mytilenean debate, at
which a similar conversion was effected? Surely at this
critical point in the story of the quarrel which led to the
war, Thucydides has missed an opportunity of explaining
somewhat more fully why Athens allied herself with Corcyra.
At least he might have told us in three words whose policy
it was, even if he could not tell us whether this decisive
step had any bearing on larger schemes, whose schemes they
were, and what Pericles thought of them. He has, however,
given us just the bare minimum of enlightenment on these
points.

In the above translation of i. 44 we have omitted a short
sentence at the end which comes in as a sort of afterthought.
It is this[2]: 'And further it seemed to them that the island
(Corcyra) was conveniently situated on the coasting-route
to Italy and Sicily.' These words refer to one of the numerous
arguments urged in the Corcyreans' speech. Corcyra, they
say, 'is conveniently situated for the coasting voyage to
Italy and Sicily, so as either to prevent a fleet from coming

---

[1] One short sentence, to which we shall return in a moment, is omitted
here.

[2] i. 44. 3 ἅμα δὲ τῆς τε Ἰταλίας καὶ Σικελίας καλῶς ἐφαίνετο αὐτοῖς ἡ νῆσος ἐν
παράπλῳ κεῖσθαι.

from those countries to the aid of the Peloponnesians *or to help a fleet from here on its way thither*, and is very useful, generally.'[1] The point is then immediately dropped.

These two sentences, where they stand in the long story of the negotiations, are exceedingly inconspicuous; but when we have noticed them we are set wondering why they are there at all, if it is true, as Grote for instance says, that the Athenians *began* to conceive designs on the West seven or eight years after the outbreak of the war. Assertions of this sort are made, against all other ancient testimony, on the authority of Thucydides alone; but when we look closely, have they even that authority? What is the point of the two short sentences quoted above? Every one seems content to remark that the Corcyreans only mean—as indeed they say—that they could hinder help coming from Sicily to the Peloponnesians. But that is not all; why do they add '*or help a fleet from here on its way thither*'? This tiny, inconspicuous clause has no meaning unless some one at Athens was already contemplating a transference of the scene of war to Sicilian waters. The argument was addressed to the Athenians; and, together with the other consideration, that the second and third naval powers in Greece would be weakened by division, it decided them to form an alliance with Corcyra. A series of expeditions to the West were actually made by Athens, and the Corcyrean democrats did what they could to facilitate their passage. The conclusion is irresistible that here, as in other instances, the fidelity of Thucydides has preserved an indication of critical importance.

So long as we assume that when Thucydides says 'the Athenians', he means Pericles, that Pericles and his majority were completely agreed in their ideals and policy, and that Thucydides' version of Pericles' policy is correct and complete, we must, in the teeth of a whole series of indications and testimonies, go on asserting that 'Athens' had no designs on the West until Pericles was dead. But these current

---

[1] i. 36. 2 τῆς τε γὰρ Ἰταλίας καὶ Σικελίας καλῶς παράπλου κεῖται, ὥστε μήτε ἐκεῖθεν ναυτικὸν ἐᾶσαι Πελοποννησίοις ἐπελθεῖν τό τε ἐνθένδε πρὸς τἀκεῖ παραπέμψαι, καὶ ἐς τἆλλα ξυμφορώτατόν ἐστι.

assumptions will not account for the fact that Thucydides completely effaces the action of Pericles in regard both to the Megarian decrees and to the Corcyrean alliance. We suggest that when Thucydides says 'the Athenians', he means the Athenians and not Pericles, because 'the Athenians' had a policy of their own, which Pericles adopted only when his hand was forced. The historian conveys the correct impression, that the policy in question was not originated by the nominal leader of the demos.

He gives us another indication in the speech in which Pericles lays down his plan of campaign[1] : Harass the Peloponnesian coasts; abandon the country and move into town, so as to turn Athens into an island. 'I have many reasons for expecting victory, *if you will not extend your empire during the war*, or go out of your way to encounter unnecessary risks. I am more afraid of our own mistakes than of the enemy's strategy.'[2] Why was this warning needed, unless some extension of empire was already in contemplation ? The acquisition of Megara *alone* can hardly be meant, since Pericles himself had moved the second Megarian decree.

Thus, when we take enough trouble to collect and analyse the indications which Thucydides' accuracy has preserved, we can extract from the historian himself a confirmation of our other authorities. Diodorus supports our conclusion. Speaking of the Leontine embassy of 427 he says[3] : 'The Athenians had *long before* (καὶ πάλαι) been coveting Sicily for the excellence of the country, and they now concluded an alliance with Leontini because they really desired to conquer the island. For, some years before, when Corinth was fighting Corcyra, the *demos* preferred the alliance with Corcyra *because it was conveniently situated for the voyage to Sicily.*[4] The Athenians had command of the sea, many allies, and much treasure; and they hoped to conquer the Lacedaemonians, and, after becoming leaders of all Greece, to gain possession of Sicily.' That is how a later historian,

---

[1] Thuc. i. 140 ff.     [2] i. 144.     [3] Diod. xii. 54.

[4] διὰ τὸ τὴν Κέρκυραν εὐφυῶς κεῖσθαι πρὸς τὸν εἰς Σικελίαν πλοῦν.

who, though little more than a compiler, had sources of information closed to us, read the story of the Corcyrean negotiation. His reading agrees exactly with ours.

Plutarch's witness is on the same side. Speaking of the moment after the Egyptian disaster of 449 and before the 'Sacred War' of 448 he says,[1] 'many were *already* possessed by that fatal passion for Sicily which later was inflamed by Alcibiades and his friends. Some dreamed even of Carthage and Etruria.' Here Plutarch dates these designs from seventeen or eighteen years before the war. Again, he says[2] 'the Athenians were coveting Sicily *while Pericles was still alive*, and after his death they attacked her and sent their so-called relief expeditions to prepare the way for the great expedition against Syracuse'.

The only reason which modern historians have for refusing to accept these statements is the silence of Thucydides, whose hints escape them. But with reference to the further stage of this policy—the attack on Carthage—we can estimate the value of an argument based on his reticence. In this case we have not the mere opinion of a late writer but the indisputable evidence of a contemporary.

Thucydides does not mention Carthage till he comes to the year 415, when he says that Alcibiades hoped to be the conqueror of Sicily and Carthage.[3] In his speech at Sparta,[4] Alcibiades asserts that the Athenians meant to attack Sicily first, then the Greeks in Italy, and finally Carthage herself. Hermocrates, addressing the Sicilians in conference, advises them to send for help to the Carthaginians. '*An Athenian attack on their city is nothing more than they expect; they live in constant apprehension of it.*'[5] Here, once more, Thucydides preserves just one indication that his story is incomplete. But for this sentence, he would have left us to suppose that the designs on Carthage originated in the wild brain of Alcibiades. This impression has already been conveyed, and

---

[1] *vit. Per.* 20.          [2] *vit. Alkib.* 17.

[3] vi. 15.                [4] vi. 90.

[5] vi. 34 οὐ γὰρ ἀνέλπιστον αὐτοῖς, ἀλλ᾽ αἰεὶ διὰ φόβου εἰσὶ μή ποτε ᾿Αθηναῖοι αὐτοῖς ἐπὶ τὴν πόλιν ἔλθωσι.

the language here is not explicit or striking enough to dispel it.

We happen to know, however, that an attack on Carthage was not first conceived in 415. In the *Knights* of Aristophanes[1] the elderly trireme addresses her sisters—

> Ladies, have you heard the news? In the town it passed for truth
> That a certain low-bred upstart, one Hyperbolus forsooth,
> Asks a hundred of our number, with a further proposition
> That we should sail with him *to Carthage* on a secret expedition.

The date of this play is 424—nine years earlier than Thucydides' first mention of Carthage. The question at the moment was between the recall and the reinforcement of the fleet in Sicilian waters, which had been sent out in 427 and was actually recalled in the summer of this year 424–423. The above passage makes it clear that Hyperbolus had demanded a strong reinforcement, and further that designs against Carthage were already in the air. Thucydides never mentions Hyperbolus till viii. 78, where he records his assassination, and he says nothing of the proposal mentioned in the *Knights*. He has, in fact, done as much to connect the larger plans of Western conquest with Alcibiades as he has done to disconnect them from Pericles. We shall try to show later how it comes about that the conquest of Sicily is kept out of sight so long as Pericles lives, kept in the background while Cleon holds the stage, and brought to the front with Alcibiades. We do not deny that this project did come more and more to the front as the war proceeded ; all that we have argued is that it was in the background before Thucydides allows us to see it at all.

The objection may be made : If the conquest of Sicily was in view from the first, why did not the great expedition take place earlier than 415 ?

There are several answers. At first Pericles was there to prevent it. He could not avoid adopting the policy of war with Corinth and the Peloponnesian league ; but, by adopting it, he triumphantly secured his own position, and so long as his

influence lasted he could restrict the Athenians to his own
defensive scheme and make them listen to his warning:
'do not extend your empire during the war.' Then came the
plague, upsetting all calculations and decimating Athens. The
revolt of Lesbos soon followed and diverted attention to
dangers within the empire. Yet even so, in the very year of
this revolt (427), with the treasure running out, the rich
burdened by the war-tax, the peasantry ruined by invasion,
the crowded city ravaged by plague—in the midst of all this,
an advanced squadron of twenty ships was sent to stir up
discord in the Sicilian states. 'Athens,' says Grote,[1] 'began
operations on a small scale in Sicily, probably contrary to the
advice of both Nikias and Kleon, neither of them seemingly
favourable to these distant undertakings.' On whose advice,
then? Grote does not say. 'Athens,' writes a more recent
historian,[2] 'again takes the maritime offensive, but the operations lack any connexion and design, in the absence of a simple
and conscious purpose.' Is there a lack of purpose and design?
Let us glance at the main course of the war.

On Pericles' plan, the war, but for accidents, might have
gone on for ever. The Spartans invade Attica for two or
three weeks every year, ravage the country unchecked, and
retire. The Athenians conduct biennial invasions of the
Megarid, ravage the country unchecked, and retire. The fleet,
in the sailing season, is sent round the coast of the Peloponnese,
makes descents unchecked, and retires. The two combatants
are like blindfolded boxers delivering in the dark blows which
neither hurt nor can be parried. This was what Pericles and
his Spartan friend Archidamus intended; they both hoped that
the combatants would get tired of these annual picnics.

But as soon as Pericles is out of the way things take
a different turn. Vigorous offensive action *at the mouth of
the Corinthian gulf* is crowned by the brilliant victory of
Phormio. These naval operations are connected with an
attempt to detach the whole of *Acarnania* from the Athenian
alliance. Observe how, at once, the centre of interest is
shifted to the second stage in 'the coasting voyage to Italy

---

[1] *History of Greece*, v. 210.     [2] Busolt, *Griech. Gesch.*, iii. 2, p. 1053.

and Sicily' in which Megara was the first stage and Corcyra
the third.    Then the revolt of Lesbos creates an unforeseen
diversion.   But when that is disposed of, we read of the
establishment of the democracy and of Athenian influence
in *Corcyra* ; the capture of Minoa—a substantial step in the
coercion of *Megara*, which is still invaded twice yearly ;
a preliminary expedition to *Sicily* ; Demosthenes' campaigns
in *Leucas* and *Aetolia* ;   a second expedition to *Sicily* with
instructions to settle affairs at *Corcyra* on the way.   Then comes
a second diversion—the Pylos episode.   The negotiations
which follow break down because Cleon demands the cession
of *Nisaea and Pegae* (the Megarian ports), Troezen and *Achaea*.
An invasion of *Corinthian* territory is followed by the capture
of the long walls of *Megara* and *Nisaea*.   There is an intrigue
with the Boeotian demos, by which Athens is to secure
*Siphae*, the port on the Corinthian gulf.   More operations
follow in *Acarnania*, including the capture of Oeniadae.
The third and most serious diversion is effected by Brasidas'
unprecedented winter-march to Amphipolis, the loss of which
brings the Ten Years' War to a close.

Is there no design in this series of attacks at various points
along the route across Megara, down the Corinthian gulf,
round the corner of Acarnania to Corcyra, on to Italy and
Sicily ?   Or are we right in thinking that as soon as the people
interested in the establishment of commercial connexions along
this route have a free hand, there is plenty of evidence in their
plan of war for a simple and conscious purpose ?

Our main contention is simply that this scheme dates from
before the beginning of the war, and was only temporarily
delayed by Pericles, who always disapproved of it.

There is one more passage [1] to which, in concluding, we
ought to call attention.   It is the chapter where Thucydides
reviews the career of Pericles and contrasts him with his
successors.   Written after the fall of Athens, it is one of
the latest additions to the early part of the history.

[1] ii. 65.   The Sicilian disaster and the fall of Athens are mentioned in
§ 12.

'So long as Pericles ruled Athens in the times of peace, he led her wisely and brought her safely through, and in his days she reached the height of her greatness. When the war broke out, it is clear that, here again, he was right in his estimate of her power. He survived the declaration of war two years and six months; and after his death his foresight with respect to the war was still more clearly apparent. He had told the Athenians that all would be well if they would be quiet, keep up their navy, and *not try to add to their empire during the war* or run their city into danger. But the Athenians did everything he told them not to do: they engaged in *a policy which seemed to have nothing to do with the war* from motives of private ambition or private gain,[1] with disastrous consequences to themselves and their allies. Success would only have meant glory or profit to individuals; failure meant ruin to Athens. The reason was that Pericles, since his position was assured by his acknowledged worth and wisdom, and he was proved transparently clear of corruption, controlled the multitude in a free spirit. Instead of being led by them, he led them; he was not seeking to acquire power by ignoble arts, for, on the strength of his known high character, he already possessed it; consequently, he did not speak to please the multitude, but was able to oppose and even to anger them. Accordingly, whenever he saw that they were elated with unmeasured arrogance,[2] he spoke and cast them down into fear; and again, when they were unreasonably afraid, he tried to restore their confidence. So came about what was nominally a democracy, but really a reign of the first citizen.

'His successors, however, were more on an equality with one another, each struggling to be first; and they were inclined to flatter the people and to sacrifice the public interests. Hence came many errors—errors for a great city with an empire; above all, the Sicilian expedition, though in this

---

[1] ἄλλα ἔξω τοῦ πολέμου δοκοῦντα εἶναι ... ἐπολίτευσαν,—the Sicilian expedition. 'Private ambition' was Alcibiades' motive; 'private gain' that of the commercial party.

[2] παρὰ καιρὸν ὕβρει θαρσοῦντας.

instance it was not so much that they made a mistake of judgement in estimating the strength of those whom they assailed,[1] as that the men who sent out the expedition, instead of taking thought for the needs of a distant army, were engaged in private quarrels for the leadership of the people. So they kept no vigilant eye on the fortunes of the fleet, and at home for the first time introduced civil commotion.'

We do not wish to minimize or brush away the words: 'instead of being led by them, he led them'—words which seem to contradict the hypothesis we have put forward. But it is fair to point out that Thucydides is reviewing the whole of Pericles' career, not speaking only of the last five years of it. He *ends* with the words, 'So came about what was nominally a democracy, but really a reign of the first citizen.' The reign of Pericles was established ten years before the war, when his last opponent, Thucydides, son of Melesias, was ostracized. The historian is contrasting the career as a whole with the thirty years that followed. It is fair also to remark that a statesman who is described as 'not saying pleasant things', 'opposing the people even to angering them,' 'casting them down when they were elated by un-measured arrogance,' was certainly one whose aims and policy were likely to differ from those of his supporters. The hypothesis which we have put forward merely involves that, although all that Thucydides says is true of Pericles while his position was undisputed, in the last few years of his life he *chose to lead the people rather than be led by them.*

The main point of the contrast, what seemed to Thucydides the great difference between Pericles and his successors, is that Pericles had no private ends to serve. His position was assured; he was indifferent to money. The later leaders—especially Alcibiades—had to win a position; they sought

---

[1] This remarkable sentence has the air of a cool revision of the judgement expressed in vi. 1 : 'Most of the Athenians had no idea of the size of Sicily and the numbers of its inhabitants, and did not know they were undertaking a war not much less serious than the Peloponnesian war.' That was written when Thucydides' mind was full of conceptions hereafter to be analysed.

glory and power. Others—especially the dynasty of tradesmen —sought profit. Hence, where they flattered, Pericles ruled; while they were ambitious or sordid, he was 'free' (ἐλεύθερος), above ambition and above gain. That this is a true picture there is no reason to doubt; we only question whether it is quite complete.

Thucydides, contrary to his custom, anticipates the death of Pericles in his narrative by more than a year.[1] He has just before given us a glimpse of his behaviour when the tide of popular indignation had risen against him, and in the last speech he shows us the stately figure erect and calm above the storm. Then, as if he could not bear to let any later troubles or even death itself come between us and this impression, he drops the curtain on the close of Pericles' life. Whatever stood here in his original draft, he has substituted for it the sober and final tribute of a reverent admiration.

The historian, when he watched the opening events of the war and set about his task, could not foresee the Sicilian expedition. He was not in the confidence either of Pericles or of Cleon and the other, more obscure, captains of the commercial party, who formulated, in their secret conclaves, the policy of the Piraeus. They were clever enough not to show their full hand to any outside observer. The first move in the game was the decree against Megara, the significance of which was seen by Pericles but by no one else. What made it finally impossible for any one else to see it, was Pericles' action in taking the anti-Megarian policy out of the hands of its originators, and adopting it as his own. Thucydides knew that he could not be acting from personal spite; but the decrees and the sustained attacks by which year by year they were followed up could only be interpreted by one who took them in connexion with the whole series of operations along the route to the West. At the outset,

---

[1] ii. 65. The death of Pericles occurred in September 429, and its proper place in chronological order would be at ii. 95.

the only people who had an inkling of the larger scheme were : the leaders of the commercial party, who originated it ; Pericles, who adopted the first manœuvre in order to thwart, if possible, the rest of the plan ; and (probably) the democratic leaders at Corcyra, the men whose arguments and pretexts will be found in the Corcyrean envoys' speech.[1] These envoys, not realizing, perhaps, how delicate the situation was at Athens, had tactlessly dropped a phrase which stuck in Thucydides' head because it puzzled him. They had said something about Corcyra being a convenient station on the voyage to Sicily and Italy. What could this have to do with a war between Athens and Sparta ? Yet Thucydides vaguely felt that this consideration weighed with the majority who voted for alliance with Corcyra ; and so with his punctilious fidelity he puts down exactly what he knew: 'And further it seemed to them that the island was conveniently situated on the coasting-route to Italy and Sicily.'

The policy of the Piraeus came to the surface only after Pericles' death ; it did not finally and fully emerge till the great expedition of 415, and by that time Thucydides' opinion about the origin of the war was already formed, and much of his First Part was written. In the lapse of eighteen years the memory of the outbreak had faded. Looking back, he sees the figure of Pericles, exalted by distance and consecrated by time. How great was that free and generous spirit, in contrast with the selfish ambition or low covetousness of the men who had taken his place! The Sicilian expedition was their work ; seeking glory or private gain, they involved Athens in 'a policy which seemed to have nothing to do with the war'. To Thucydides, from first to last, the Sicilian enterprise was an irrelevant diversion imported into the war between Athens and Sparta— the war as designed by Pericles ; and he attributed it to motives which, as he rightly insists, Pericles could not have entertained. Hence he never saw its connexion with the Megarian decrees—a link without which the origin of the Peloponnesian War was an insoluble enigma.

[1] i. 32–6.

# CHAPTER V

In the foregoing chapters we have put forward a theory of the causes of the Peloponnesian War. If that theory is well founded, the causes were such as Thucydides could not have known. This is certainly a sufficient reason for his not having told us what they were; but it does not explain why he did not look for the origin of the war in the quarters where we have looked for it, or how he came to regard his account as complete and satisfactory. He says that his description of what immediately preceded the outbreak is written in order that no one may ever have to ask 'out of what so great a war arose'—the very question, it might seem, which we have spent four chapters in trying to answer. Whether the answer we found is the right one or not, what is certain is that some answer is wanted. Our next question is: why was Thucydides content with his First Book, and why are we not content with it?

There are on the surface indications of a wide divergence between his conception of his task in writing history and our conception of it, between what he offers and what we demand. Can we trace this divergence down to its source? Putting our own, very different, hypothesis along-side of Thucydides' introductory Book, and taking it (whether right or wrong in points of detail) as at least the expression of a typically modern view, can we explain the contrast between the two accounts? This is a wider and more interesting inquiry than the search for the origin of a particular war between two ancient cities; it should take us to the centre of Thucydides' general view of history and of the historian's aim and office.

What, precisely, does Thucydides undertake to tell us ?—
that is the point from which we must start.   The answer lies
in his own prefatory statement of his scope and method.[1]
In the first place, he undertakes to state the plain truth about
what happened.[2]   In the second place he divides his subject-
matter—the truths he means to record—under two heads :
speeches (λόγοι), and the events (ἔργα) of the war.   The passage
is so important for our purpose that we will give it in full :

'As to the accounts given of themselves by the several
parties in *speeches*,[3] either on the eve of war or when they
were already engaged, it would be hard to reproduce the
exact language used, whether I heard it myself or it was
reported to me by others.   The speeches as they stand represent what, in my opinion was most necessary to be said by
the several speakers about the matter in question at the
moment, and I have kept as closely as possible to the general
sense of what was really said.   Of the *events*—what actually
was done in the war,[4] I have thought fit not to write from
any chance information, nor yet according to any notion
of my own, but to record those at which I was present, or
which I heard of from others, with the greatest possible
accuracy of investigation.   To discover these facts was labori-
ous, because those who were present at the various events
differed in their reports of the same occurrences, according
to the state of their memories or as they sympathized with
one side or the other.'

Observe that in this very careful account of what the history
is to contain, there is not a word about *causes*.   Each episode
in the military operations is to be described just as it happened ; we shall be told no more than an eyewitness might
have seen on the spot.   Besides this, we are to listen to the
'accounts' given, the arguments used and pretexts alleged,
by politicians and the representatives of states—no more
than the audience at the assembly or at a congress of allies
might actually have heard.   The history as we have it does

---

[1] i. 20-2.        [2] τῶν γενομένων τὸ σαφές, i. 22. 4.

[3] i. 22 ὅσα μὲν λόγῳ εἶπον ἕκαστοι.

[4] τὰ δ' ἔργα τῶν πραχθέντων ἐν τῷ πολέμῳ.

consist, almost entirely, of these two elements. But why has Thucydides deliberately adopted such an extraordinary method ? Why, in particular, does he say nothing about causes, but put us off with the *ex parte* 'accounts' of interested persons, as publicly and formally stated with a view to persuading other interested persons ? Here on the threshold we find, between his notion of an historian's business and ours, as wide a gulf as can be conceived. How could he think that it was enough to tell us what ' the Corinthians ' or ' the Athenians ' alleged, instead of what were the real, underlying causes of this war ?

The method adopted by Thucydides was to a certain extent imposed upon him inevitably by the circumstances in which he wrote. A brief account of these will throw some light on the peculiarities of the work as we have it, and will help us to determine how far these peculiarities are shaped by external accident, and how far they result from the author's conception of history.

The work was intended to cover the whole twenty-seven years of the Peloponnesian War. The eight books we have— all that ever was written—actually cover twenty years. They are divided into two nearly equal parts, of which the second is unfinished.[1] Part I contains the Ten Years' War. Part II begins with a fresh introduction in which the author for the first time remarks that the Ten Years' War turned out to be only the first episode in a struggle of which it was all along prophesied that it should last thrice nine years—the only one of the many oracles which was fulfilled. From this remark, occurring where it does, it is plain that Part I must have been far advanced before Thucydides knew how long the war was to continue. Careful search, moreover, has detected in it here and there several expressions which a thorough revision would have removed, and it may be concluded that, although considerable additions were made later, it was never rewritten as a whole. The second Part is

---

[1] The division occurs at v. 20. The introduction to Part II begins at v. 26; chapters 21-5 forming a connecting link.

incomplete; Book VIII ends abruptly and is throughout in an unfinished condition. On the other hand, Books VI and VII (the Sicilian Expedition) are perhaps the most perfect part of the work.

We may infer with certainty that Thucydides having begun to write, as he says himself,[1] so soon as the war broke out, worked at the history, as occasion offered, all through the twenty-seven years of war and after his restoration from exile at its close, until death ended his labours.

About his manner of working there can be little doubt. He evidently kept a sort of diary, recording the bare events, with details of time and place, as he heard of them. The entries form an annalistic thread, running through the whole, on which the fuller narrative could be constructed. In some places they actually remain embedded in the expanded story, which in other instances has replaced them.[2] With this chronological framework as a basis, he would write up the more elaborate descriptions whenever he met with an eye-witness who could supply the necessary details, and the account would, no doubt, be carefully revised, if fresh information came in later from another source. From the circumstance that the unfinished Book VIII contains only short notes of the contents of speeches, whereas the narrative is in parts fairly full, it is not rash to conclude that in many cases the finished speeches of the earlier books were the last additions to the narratives which they accompany.

His choice of incidents for fuller treatment was, of course, in part dependent on the chance of his meeting with some one who possessed the necessary information. Apart from this, he appears to have selected typical episodes, such as the siege of Plataea, the victory of Phormio, Demosthenes' campaign in Aetolia, the capture of Sphacteria, Brasidas' great march to the North, the siege of Syracuse. Each of these military

---

[1] i. 1. 1.

[2] See, for example, ii. 19. 1, where the formal record of the invasion is left in the middle of the detailed description of it. On a close scrutiny it will be seen that chapters 18 and 19, which precede and follow it, are slightly inconsistent, and must have been written at different times.

achievements had some peculiar circumstances which made the operations interesting to contemporaries—though not always in the same degree to us—from the point of view of strategy and tactics. A few episodes, of which the most remarkable is the Corcyrean sedition, are treated in the same way on account of their political significance. The description of the plague at Athens is for the instruction of physicians. In all these cases, which together make up the greater part of the work, the intention is that which is stated in the introduction. 'I shall be satisfied if the facts are pronounced to be useful by those who shall desire to know clearly what has happened in the past and the sort of things that are likely, so far as man can foresee, to happen again in the future.'

Such was the plan originally laid down for himself by Thucydides. He was not reviewing his whole period in focus and perspective after a sufficient interval of time, but he was obliged to compose at odd moments, determined by the accidents of opportunity and scattered over a period of thirty to thirty-five years. During all the first part of his labours he was writing concurrently with the events he recorded, often in the dark as to their relative importance, their bearing and connexions, and necessarily ignorant of their remoter consequences. All he could do at first was to keep his journal, and now and then to work up a detached episode. The result could not for a long time possess more unity than the collected volumes of a monthly review; no general tendency or trend of events could be discerned, no shadow cast before the unknown issue.

But these considerations of outward circumstance, while they account for many of the features which make the work so unlike a modern history, leave our present question untouched. However much he might be in the dark about the causes of the war when he began to write, however impossible it may have been for the darkness to be dispelled later, the strange thing is that he should have thought that he had dispelled it. It is stranger still that in describing the contents of his book he should have altogether omitted to mention *causes*, and laid down a plan of writing which, if adhered to, would exclude any discussion of them.

Another ancient historian, Polybius [1], has told us explicitly what class of things he considers are the 'causes' of a war. In his superior and priggish way, he speaks with contempt of men who cannot distinguish the '*beginning*' (ἀρχή), or first overt act of hostilities, from the '*cause and pretext*' (αἰτίας καὶ προφάσεως). 'I,' he says, 'shall regard the first attempt to put in execution what had already been determined, as a "beginning"; but *I shall mean by "causes"* (αἰτίας) *those decisions and counsels which precede and lead to such attempts; I mean considerations and states of mind and calculations, and the things which bring us to make a decision or form a purpose.*' A *pretext* is an alleged 'cause'. Polybius illustrates his use of terms from the war of Antiochus, of which the '*cause*' (αἰτία) was the anger of the Aetolians; the *pretext* (πρόφασις) was the liberation of Greece; the *beginning* (ἀρχή) was the descent of Antiochus upon Demetrias. The whole passage is in a didactic tone; Polybius is evidently pleased with his powers of discrimination.

With this in mind let us look at the passage [2], where Thucydides for a moment goes beyond his prescribed limits and expresses his own opinion about the 'cause' of the Peloponnesian War. We shall find all the three terms distinguished by Polybius.

'The Athenians and Peloponnesians *began* (ἤρξαντο) by breaking the thirty years' truce which they had made after the capture of Euboea. Why they broke it—their grievances and differences (τὰς αἰτίας καὶ τὰς διαφοράς), I have first set forth, that no one may ever have to inquire from what origin (ἐξ ὅτου) so great a war arose among the Hellenes. *The most genuine pretext, though it appeared least in what was said,*[3] I believe to have been the increasing power of Athens, and

---

[1] iii. 6–7.

[2] i. 23. 4. We shall discuss later the digression (i. 88–118) where this statement is repeated and the grounds of the Spartans' fear are explained.

[3] τὴν μὲν ἀληθεστάτην πρόφασιν, ἀφανεστάτην δὲ λόγῳ.

the alarm which they gave to the Lacedaemonians, and so forced them into war. But the *grievances publicly alleged* [1] by each side for breaking the truce and going to war were as follows.' Then he passes at once to the description of civil strife at Epidamnus, of her appeal to Corinth, and so forth.

The first point in this passage to which we would draw attention is a point of disagreement between Polybius and Thucydides. Polybius carefully distinguishes between a 'cause' (αἰτία) and a 'pretext' (πρόφασις). The *pretext* of the war of Antiochus was the liberation of Greece—an avowed, but not a true, 'cause'; its (true) *cause* was the Aetolians' anger. Now Thucydides, we note, inverts the use of these terms. The alarm of the Lacedaemonians, which Polybius would call a 'cause' (true, but not avowed), Thucydides calls 'the most genuine *pretext*, though it appeared least in what was said'. When he comes to the 'grievances publicly alleged'—what Polybius would call 'pretexts' (avowed, but not true), he calls them αἰτίαι.

We could hardly have better evidence that Thucydides draws no clear distinction between an αἰτία and a πρόφασις. No respectable writer who had such a distinction in his thoughts could speak of a 'most genuine *pretext* (πρόφασις) which appeared least in what was said'—which, in fact, was least of all a pretext. Jowett, in rendering this phrase, instinctively substitutes the modernism: 'the real, though unavowed, *cause.*' Hobbes is less modern and renders it faithfully: 'the truest *Quarrell*, though least in speech.' [2]

---

[1] αἱ δ' ἐς τὸ φανερὸν λεγόμεναι αἰτίαι.

[2] Mr. Forbes, in his edition of Thuc. i, translates: 'For (and this was the truest cause, though least was said about it), &c.' (p. 28). In his glossary p. 166) he says 'πρόφασις is twice used emphatically for the *real*, as opposed to the *pretended*, motive or cause', citing i. 23 and vi. 6. He adds a note: 'The idea in these places probably is "if they had openly said what they really meant"; of course πρόφασις cannot *mean* "real motive". Cf. Dem. *de Cor.* 156 (201), probably an imitation of Thucydides, ὅτι τὴν μὲν ἀληθῆ πρόφασιν τῶν πραγμάτων . . . ἀπεκρύπτετο.' αἰτίαι Mr. Forbes renders 'grievances' (p. 28); but slips into using 'causes' on p. 75: 'Thucydides has thus far' (up to chap. 88) 'been explaining the avowed causes of the war. He now goes on to the real cause—the alarm of Sparta . . .' On i. 146 he translates πρόφασις by 'cause', without comment.

Thucydides, in fact, throughout his first book uses the words αἰτία and πρόφασις interchangeably.[1] In Polybius αἰτία is perhaps more nearly equivalent to 'reason' (in the psychological sense), than to 'cause'. In Thucydides it does not mean 'cause' at all, and should seldom be translated 'reason'. It means 'grievance'. There is in Thucydidean Greek no word which even approaches the meaning and associations of the English 'cause', with its correlative 'effect'.

This truth is recognized as a linguistic fact; but surely it is something more. It implies that when Thucydides sat down to write his first Book, he never so much as asked himself the question which we have asked and tried to answer: 'What were the causes of the war?' The questions he did ask were: What was the 'beginning' (ἀρχή)—the first act of war? and: What were the grievances, quarrels, pretexts of the combatants?—τίνες ἦσαν αἱ αἰτίαι; The answers to these two questions he regards as containing a complete account of that 'out of which' (ἐξ ὅτου) the war arose. The combatants 'began', he says, by breaking the treaty of thirty years' peace; the grievances, accusations, and pretexts occupy the rest of Book I (except the digression, 88–118). But that is all which he attempts to tell. We ought to give up speaking of the first Book as being about the causes of the war; it is much truer to say that there is hardly a word about causes in it from beginning to end. Thucydides has not told us the causes, and one reason for this omission is that he never raised the question, and never could raise it, in distinct and unambiguous terms.

The first Book is not an analysis of causes, but the story of a quarrel. Thucydides approaches his subject in the same

---

[1] Compare iv. 85. 1, where Brasidas says, of his expedition to Acanthus, ἡ ἔκπεμψίς μου . . . γεγένηται τὴν αἰτίαν ἐπαληθεύουσα ἣν ἀρχόμενοι τοῦ πολέμου προείπομεν, 'Αθηναίοις ἐλευθεροῦντες τὴν 'Ελλάδα πολεμήσειν, and § 6 τὴν αἰτίαν πιστὴν ἀποδεικνύναι. Here αἰτία is used to mean a pretext or alleged ground of quarrel which (in the speaker's view) was always genuine, but needed to be proved genuine by corresponding action. i. 55. 2 αἰτία δὲ αὕτη πρώτη ἐγένετο τοῦ πολέμου τοῖς Κορινθίοις ἐς τοὺς 'Αθηναίους, ὅτι . . . ἐναυμάχουν: i. 118. 1 ὅσα πρόφασις τοῦδε τοῦ πολέμου κατέστη, referring to the same events.

way that Herodotus approaches his in the opening chapters,
where he recounts the earlier stages in ' the quarrel for which
the Greeks and barbarians fought'.[1] That feud began with
the rape of the Argive princess, Io, by some Phoenician
traders. Certain Greeks retaliated by carrying off Europa,
daughter of the King of Tyre, and so 'squared the account'.
Next time the aggressors were the Greeks, who sailed to
Colchis and carried away Medea. Then Alexander, son of
Priam, bent on vengeance, made a prize of Helen. Diplomatic
protests failing, the Trojan war followed, Priam's kingdom
was overthrown, and thenceforth the barbarians regarded the
Greeks as enemies. The expeditions of Darius and Xerxes
were conceived as reprisals for the expedition of Agamemnon.

Similarly, the first book of Thucydides traces the feud
between Athens and ' the Peloponnesians'. Seen in that
light, the structure and contents of the book become natural
and intelligible : accusations and pretexts and *ex parte*
statements, which are ridiculously out of place in a discussion of causes, are just what we expect in the story of a
quarrel. The speakers are like litigants in a process ; one
party states its grievances, the other attempts refutation.
Thucydides seems to take it as his primary duty to put
forward both cases fairly, and to leave the reader to judge.
He does not, like a modern historian, assume the judicial
position himself, treat the allegations as so much (almost
worthless) evidence to be ' summed up', and then attempt
an independent investigation of the causes which these
allegations were partly designed to conceal.

We may observe a further psychological consequence en-
tailed by this manner of approaching the subject : Thucydides'
thoughts, being bent on the earlier stages of the quarrel, are
fixed solely on the past. Now, the policy of commercial
expansion to the West, which we have ascribed to the Piraeus,

---

[1] δι' ἣν αἰτίην ἐπολέμησαν, Herod. i. 1. Compare the story of the feud
between Athens and Aegina (Herod. v. 82) which opens thus : ἡ δὲ ἔχθρη ἡ
προοφειλομένη ἐς 'Αθηναίους ἐκ τῶν Αἰγινητέων ἐγένετο ἐξ ἀρχῆς τοιῆσδε. Similarly
the earlier stages in the quarrel between Persia and Scythia are resumed
(Herod. iv. 1) to explain Darius' invasion.

lay wholly in the future.  It was not a 'grievance' on either side; and no one who was looking for grievances could possibly come to think of it.  Hence the alliance with Corcyra, for instance, instead of being regarded as a step in the execution of this policy, is treated from the Corinthians' standpoint, as an interference on the part of Athens in a private feud between Corinth and one of her colonies.  The situation of the island on the route to Italy and Sicily, which to us is the significant fact, is, as we have seen, barely mentioned, in a couple of sentences, without any emphasis or explanation; it has nothing to do with any grievance.

But, if the bulk of this first Book is not about causes, there remains the one statement that 'the most genuine pretext was the Spartans' fear of the increasing power of Athens'.  Although Thucydides has no word for cause, a 'most genuine pretext' means one which is based on some genuine, real feeling; and this feeling we may describe, though he cannot so describe it, as a *cause*.  We remark here an agreement between the two passages we quoted from Thucydides and Polybius: both alike find the 'reason', or 'genuine pretext', of a war in a *feeling*, a state of mind, attributed to one of the nations involved.  The *anger* of the Aetolians was the reason (αἰτία) of the war of Antiochus; the *fear* of the Lacedaemonians is the 'most genuine pretext' for this war.  The digression in chapters 88–118 is intended to explain this fear, by describing the growth of Athens.  We will glance through it, in order to note from what point of view the description is written.

Thucydides goes back to the retreat of the Persians. When the invaders were gone, the Athenians set about restoring their desolated homes and rebuilding their walls (89).  The Lacedaemonians, urged by their allies and fearing the new growth of the Athenian navy, send envoys to dissuade them from fortifying their city.  The diplomatic manœuvres by which Themistocles hoodwinked the Spartans until the walls were built are told in detail (90–1).  The Spartans concealed their anger and disappointment (92). The Piraeus is founded and fortified as a refuge in case of

another barbarian invasion (93). The tyranny of Pausanias
drives the allies to prefer the supremacy of Athens (95), who
takes tribute of them, under colour of intended reprisals upon
Persia, though they remain autonomous and meet for deliberation in a common assembly (97). Naxos was the first to revolt
and the first to be 'enslaved contrary to the convention' (98);
the turn of others came later. The fault lay partly with the
Athenians' severity in exaction, partly with the negligence of
the allies (99). Various Athenian successes are recorded (100).
The revolted Thasians induce the Spartans secretly to promise
an invasion of Attica, which is prevented only by the great
Helot rising (101). Kimon is sent to help the Lacedaemonians
in crushing the rebels at Ithome, but he is received with
suspicion and sent back with insulting discourtesy. 'This
was the first open difference' between the two states. Athens
renounces the Lacedaemonian alliance (102), and 'being now
at feud with Sparta' settles the banished Messenians at
Naupactus, and allies herself with Megara. Her occupation
of this city and of its ports, Nisaea and Pegae, is 'the beginning of the Corinthians' intense hatred of Athens' (103).

Then follow the Egyptian Expedition and the war with
Corinth, and later with Sparta; the battles of Tanagra and
Oenophyta; the reduction of Aegina; the failure of the
Egyptian Expedition (104–110). After some minor operations
a five years' truce is concluded between the Peloponnesians
and Athens. Kimon (the last representative of the anti-
Persian ideal) falls, in an 'Hellenic' war against Asiatics,
at Cyprus (112). Then intestine strife breaks out again in
Greece; Athens is worsted and restores the places she has
held in the Peloponnese (115). The revolt of Samos and
Byzantium is crushed (117).

Thucydides returns to his main narrative in these words:[1]
'And now, a few years later, occurred the affairs at Corcyra
and Potidaea above narrated, and all that came to be a
pretext for this war.' The transactions mentioned in the
digression occupied fifty years, 'in which, while the Athenians
established more firmly their mastery over their empire and

[1] i. 118.

themselves advanced greatly in power, the Lacedaemonians, perceiving it, only made slight attempts to prevent them, and for the most part of the time remained inactive ; for they had never been quick to go to war, if they were not compelled ; and in part they were hindered by wars at home; until at last the power of Athens was clearly rising high and they were laying hands on the Peloponnesian league. Now the Lacedaemonians could bear it no longer; they decided that they must set to their hands with energy and pull down the strength of Athens, if they could, by embarking on this war.'

In so far as this digression is more than a mere chronicle intended to correct the current dating of the events, it is clearly an account of how the 'difference' arose between Athens and Sparta and the breach widened into an irreparable feud. In the Persian wars the two states had stood together against the Eastern invader ; but no sooner was the danger past than anger and suspicion broke out through the deceitful policy of Themistocles.  So the feud began, and its course is traced through the 'first open difference', and the wars that followed, down to the latest ' grievances ' which occupy the rest of the book.  The phase of this process which especially interests Thucydides is the change that came over the character of the Athenian league.  He belonged by family tradition to the old school which took for its motto, Unity in Hellas and War to the death with the barbarian, and in the transition from an 'alliance' to an 'empire' and from an empire to a 'tyranny' he read the defection of Athens from this ideal, which Kimon, his kinsman and hero, had championed to the end.  Thinking on these lines, his attention was fixed on the nominal heads of the two leagues, Athens and Sparta.  The first Book might have been very different if he had studied rather the Piraeus and Corinth, and sought causes instead of grounds of quarrel.

We must now recur to the point of agreement we noted between Thucydides and Polybius.[1]  Thucydides has told us

[1] See above, p. 61.

why a certain 'pretext' was 'the most genuine', and this pretext, we notice, is a feeling of fear attributed to a nation as a whole; just as the 'reason' which Polybius finds for the war of Antiochus is the anger of the Aetolians. Polybius, moreover, expressly limits the term αἰτία, in connexion with the history of a war, solely to *psychological* 'reasons'—to feelings and other states of mind which immediately precede action, 'whatever brings us to make a decision or form a purpose.' With this limitation Thucydides seems tacitly to agree, when he finds the genuine pretext in the *fear* of the Spartans, and attributes their inaction (in so far as it was not due to accidental hindrances) to the slowness of their national *temperament*. It appears to us to be characteristic of ancient historians in general, that in so far as they look for causes of human events, they look, apart from supernatural agencies, solely to *psychological* causes—the motives and characters of individuals and of cities.

In the present instance, we ought not to overlook the fact that Thucydides is writing from the Athenian side, and consequently tends to regard 'the Peloponnesians' or at least the several states (Sparta, Corinth, &c.) as *units*. Thus, he tells us of the 'fear of *the Lacedaemonians*', and 'the intense hatred of *the Corinthians*'; but Archidamus and Brasidas are the only two individuals on the Peloponnesian side whose motives are even dimly apprehended. He evidently knew nothing about the state of politics and the prominent personalities at Corinth. On the other hand, in his own city he takes account of two elements: the national *character* of 'the Athenians' as a whole, and the character and *motives* of leading men, Pericles, Cleon, Alcibiades, Nikias, and so on. This is perfectly natural. The Athenian people met as a body in the ecclesia, and its character could be observed there directly, as well as traced in its collective action; but its motives become articulate only in the 'demagogue', the 'spokesman of the people', or in the representative sent on a mission to a foreign state. When they are formulated in the 'pretexts' of individual leaders, they are inevitably associated with their personalities and private ambitions. The disinterested ideal of Athens' glory is impersonated in Pericles ; her restless covetousness ($\pi\lambda\epsilon o\nu\epsilon\xi\iota\alpha$) in Cleon ; her ambition of conquest in Alcibiades. Now all these peculiarities of Thucydides' narrative are psychological accidents which ought to be discounted in criticizing his evidence. With respect to the origin of the war, in particular, we see how the unconscious preoccupations they involve would prevent Thucydides from seeing that Pericles and his majority were not at one, that the motives which actuated the men who voted for his proposals were not necessarily identical with the motives which were expressed in his 'pretexts', or with his own private motives. The secret was not to be found in Pericles' speeches, nor yet in the national character of 'the Athenians'.

The exclusive concentration of the ancient historians on the motives and characters of men and of states is the key to the divergence we noticed between their histories and ours. We are not content with 'causes' of this sort only ; we were not satisfied, for instance, to attribute the prosperity of Megara to virtuous moderation. When Solon (according to Plutarch [1]) observed that merchants are not *accustomed* to bring their wares to places where they can get nothing in exchange, he was stating a truth not as we should state it. We look for a different sort of explanations and we express them in different terms.

Thus, in constructing our hypothesis about the origin of the war, instead of looking for states of mind such as fear, ambition, virtuous moderation, we sought for the causes alike of the Peloponnesian war, of the Sicilian expedition, and of the prosperity of Megara in what we call an economic and topological situation. We did not look, primarily, into the breasts of Pericles, Cleon, and Alcibiades and study their characters and personal motives, but we consulted population statistics and the map of Greece. When we had observed the rise of a commercial population in the Piraeus, and noted that Corinth was well situated to control the stream of trade from Sicily across the isthmus, it occurred to us that Megara was on the same isthmus and presented the

[1] See above, p. 19.

only weak point which the Piraeus, with designs of expansion westward, could attack. The result was that, whereas there was no possible connexion between such isolated psychological facts as the alarm of the Spartans, the personal ambitions of Cleon and Alcibiades, and the virtuous moderation of the Megarian people, the connexion between the elements and factors in the 'situation' we considered was obvious. Hence we could perceive that the whole war, the Sicilian enterprise, and the attack on Megara, could all be traced to one and the same set of causes, which governed the entire train of events. The personal motives of individuals only came in as a secondary factor, modifying the details of what seemed in itself an almost inevitable process.

Similarly we are inclined to go beyond Solon's acute observation of the habits of merchants. Solon's way of putting it was that merchants are not *accustomed* to give anything for nothing; he remarks it as a fact of human nature. Our language is different because we tend to abstract from the psychological aspect, and to formulate, instead, a general law, which says nothing about the natural preferences of merchants, but speaks of a necessity that exports should balance imports. So long as the preference of merchants was alone considered, the foundation of economic science could not be laid. Thus we find Plato still ignorant of a law which Solon, a practical man, was on the verge of discovering.[1]

The great contrast, in fact, between ancient and modern history is this: that whereas the moderns instinctively and incessantly seek for the operation of social conditions, of economic and topological factors, and of political forces and processes of evolution,—all of which elements they try to bring under laws, as general and abstract as possible; the ancients looked simply and solely to the feelings, motives, characters of individuals or of cities. These, and (apart from supernatural agencies) these only, appeared to them to shape the course of human history.

---

[1] Socrates, in the *Alcibiades* (i. 122 E), argues that the Lacedaemonians must be exceedingly rich, because silver and gold come into the country from all quarters of Greece and never go out again (industry and export trade being forbidden by Lycurgus' constitution).

The contrast reveals a profound divergence of ultimate views as to the position of man in the universe, and here at last we reach the central point of the position. No historian can be completely criticized until we have taken account of his philosophical attitude. For an ancient historian, whose standpoint is so remote that we cannot safely assume any common ground, the inquiry is imperative. Our previous discussion furnishes the point of departure: we have to consider what philosophic doctrine is tacitly and unconsciously implied, when it is tacitly and unconsciously assumed that the only 'causes' which it is relevant to discuss in the history of a war are the immediate motives and passions of individuals or of personified states.

When we have brought the question to this issue, the answer is not far to seek. The latent implication is that *every motive is a first cause, or is determined solely by character*.[1]

If we would understand Thucydides, we must not regard a human action as partly caused by innumerable influences

---

[1] This doctrine is implicit in rationalist Greek thought till the fourth century, when it first becomes explicit in the Aristotelian doctrine of free will. We cannot go at length into this question; but briefly the doctrine is as follows. A man's action is caused by his desire of some end. That, of course, is true; but the next step is false. This step is the assertion that the end in question—the object of desire—is the *cause* of the desire. A man thinks of some result he wishes to attain: how can he bring it about? He thinks of the means to it; beginning from the 'end'—the last effect to be caused—he traces the chain of means backwards till he reaches the first means—some action which it is immediately within his power to perform. This last link in his chain of thought is the first link in the chain of execution. He performs the action; it is a *beginning* (ἀρχή) which starts the series of means leading back again to the desired result. The two processes of reflection and execution form a closed circle, which ends where it began, in the object or 'end' desired. The 'end' is called a 'final cause'; the action and the desire which prompts it are the '*beginning of motion*' (ἀρχὴ κινήσεως). Man is the original source and parent of his acts, ἀρχὴν ... γεννητὴν τῶν πράξεων ὥσπερ καὶ τέκνων, Ar. *Eth. Nic.* γ iii. 15 and v. 5. To this we may add, with Aristotle, that the activity is conditioned (not caused) by character, and the account is then complete. We are here following Aristotle's statement of the point which concerns us without taking account of any modifications first introduced by Aristotle. We are only considering what is assumed by men who might have been his grandfathers.

of environment, and by events that happened before the agent was born, right back into an immeasurable past; nor must we think of it as a single point in the total state of the world at a given moment, which state can be completely accounted for only by the total state at the previous moment, and so on. We must think of it as springing then and there out of the man's passions and character, and rid our minds, moreover, of the notion of *law* as applying to human actions and events. The fundamental conception which all our thought about the world implies must be banished—the conception, namely, that the whole course of events of every kind, human or non-human, is one enormous concatenation of causes and effects stretching forward and back into infinite time, and spreading outwards over immeasurable space, a concatenation in which every link is necessarily connected with all the rest, however remote. The world upon which the Greek looked out presented no such spectacle as this. Human affairs—the subject-matter of history—were not to him a single strand in the illimitable web of natural evolution; their course was shaped solely by one or both of two factors: immediate human motives, and the will of gods and spirits, of Fortune, or of Fate. The rationalist who rejected the second class was left with the first alone—the original and uncaused acts of human wills. That is why Polybius expressly limits the term ' cause' (αἰτία) in relation to history to one class of things — motives. Thucydides takes the limitation for granted.

On this all-important point we part company with many recognized authorities. We will quote a typical statement from Professor Gomperz' brilliant review of Greek thought :—

' There is hardly any pair of contemporaries who offer a more glaring contrast than Herodotus and Thucydides. Barely a score of years divided their works from one another, but a gulf of centuries seems to yawn between their temper and inspiration. Herodotus creates throughout an entirely old-fashioned impression ; Thucydides is a modern of the moderns. He made a clean sweep of the political and religious bias, the legendary and novelistic sympathies, and the primitive beliefs, rarely mitigated by the light of criticism, which marked the elder historian. The gaze of Thucydides is primarily fixed on the political factors, on the actual relations of forces, on the natural foundation, so to speak, of historical phenomena. He looks for their springs, not in the dispensations of supernatural beings, nor yet, except in a moderate degree, in the caprices and passions of individual men. Behind those he always sought for the universal forces that animated them, for the conditions of the peoples, and the interests of the states. . . . It was his constant endeavour to describe the course of human affairs as though it were a process of nature informed by the light of inexorable causality.' [1]

This passage is perhaps unguarded in expression, and it seems somewhat ungracious to fasten upon details; we take it only as a typical instance of what seems to us a fallacy very prevalent in modern histories of ancient thought. What lies behind the positive statements in Professor Gomperz' paragraph is the very different and merely negative proposition that Thucydides records nothing which is not consistent with a scientific conception of the world—that he tacitly rejects supernatural causes. Let us admit, for the present, that this is true. The fallacy consists in passing from this negative statement to the assertion, implied throughout the paragraph, that the void left by the rejection of supernaturalism was filled by modern science.

The chief point in which we differ from Professor Gomperz arises over his last statement, that Thucydides endeavoured to describe the course of human affairs as though it were a process of nature informed by inexorable causality. This is precisely what we have seen reason to deny. Human affairs have, for Thucydides, not even an analogy with processes of nature; much less are they identified with one of the processes of nature; much less, again, is their course informed by inexorable causality. Man, isolated from, and opposed to, Nature, moves along a narrow path, unrelated

---

[1] Gomperz, *Greek Thinkers* (E.T.), i. 503. We are sorry to quote this interesting work only to express disagreement.

to what lies beyond, and lighted only by a few dim rays of human 'foresight' (γνώμη), or by the false, wandering fires of Hope. He bears within him, self-contained, his destiny in his own character[1]; and this, with the purposes which arise out of it, shapes his course. That is all, in Thucydides' view, that we can say; except that, now and again, out of the surrounding darkness come the blinding strokes of Fortune, unaccountable and unforeseen. We shall try to prove later, in detail, that Thucydides' history can only be understood when we start from some such conception as this. If we presuppose the very modern view—it is not yet a century old —that human affairs are a process of nature indissolubly woven into one world-process by causal law, we shall be misled at every turn.

And, besides rejecting this general conception, we must beware of saying that Thucydides looked for such entities as 'political factors', 'relations of forces', 'the natural foundation of historical phenomena,' 'universal forces which animate men.' We are not merely objecting to forms of words; we are protesting against the attribution to Thucydides of the whole class of categories and conceptions and modes of thought of which these and similar phrases are the expression. It is precisely in respect of these conceptions that modern history differs from ancient. They have been imported, but yesterday, from Darwinian biology and from branches of mathematical and physical science which in fifth-century Athens were undiscovered, and which, if they had been discovered, no one would have dreamed of bringing into connexion with human history. Perhaps the importation has not been all to the good. A combination of political forces is a bloodless and inhuman entity, and in the manipulation of these mechanical categories we seem to lose touch of the realities they conceal —the pulse and play of warm, live passions, the beating hearts of men who suffer and aspire. We are sometimes put off with phrases instead of explanations; and the language of cogs and pulleys fails, sometimes, to illuminate the workings of the spirit.

---

[1] Ἦθος ἀνθρώπῳ δαίμων, Heracleitus, frag. 119 (Diels.).

Further, not only has History proper been invaded by these abstract sciences, but also—and partly as a consequence— a number of ancillary sciences, fast growing up round the old method of narrating human actions, are parcelling out the field occupied by the ancient descriptive science of Politics. Collectively, they may be called Sociology. The best established of them is Economics, which studies the phenomenon known to the Greeks by the moral term, πλεονεξία, 'covetousness,' that vice of human character which makes a man want to 'have more' than his neighbour. It was in ancient days the topic for a chapter in Ethics or for a character sketch, like those of Theophrastus, of 'the covetous man'. Now it is studied in almost complete abstraction from anything psychological. The fluctuations of the money market are traced in columns of figures and in curves on a diagram.

The laws which Economics attempts to establish, the categories of its ideal constructions, the abstract methods of this science and of others like it, find their way into History. The modern historian deals in vague entities, in groups and tendencies and the balance of forces. Further, he is always aware of a vast accumulation of ordered knowledge in the background. The comparative method and the survey of evidence drawn from remote lands and from unnumbered centuries have taught him to take nothing for granted, and to seek for connexions between phenomena which his ancestors never dreamed of correlating.

The course of human events, then, is to be thought of as shaped by the wills and passions of individual men or of cities, not as a part of what lies around it and beyond. And what does lie beyond? For Thucydides, the answer is: the Unknown. This was the only answer possible to a man of his temperament, a man whose spirit needed, above all, what was clear and definite.[1] Like a few other enlightened men of his time, he had rejected every systematic explanation of the world that he could think of. Supernatural causes—the will

---

[1] 'Klarheit und Bestimmtheit ist das Bedürfnis seines Geistes,' Classen, Thuc. i, *Einl.* p. xlvi.

of personal gods and spirits—these men denied. Thucydides ought not, perhaps, to be described as a sceptic; the word has come to suggest a certain hardness of intellect and a degree of positive antagonism which are not, we think, characteristic of his mind. It is better to call him an agnostic, not of the dogmatic sort who know so much about the unknown that they confidently assert it to be unknowable; but of the sober, unprejudiced kind, whose single desire is to reach, and to observe religiously, the limits of what is known. Vulgar superstition is nothing to him, except at the few points where it stands in the path of knowledge; there he can treat it with cool irony. He could respect the piety of Nikias and love the man, while gravely condemning his credulity in one fatal matter where it blinded him to a definitely ascertained fact. He will note with grave severity how, in time of stress, men who profess religion fall short of their ideals; but for his own part he seems to stand aside, rejecting, we may imagine, with more scorn than ignorant faith would deserve the philosophizing compromises and senile allegorizings of an age too sceptical, and not quite sceptical enough, to be at ease with itself. In his attitude towards religion (which must not be confounded with the quackeries of strolling oracle-vendors) there is never a trace of lightness or irreverence.

The men of the enlightenment were agreed in rejecting religion; but Thucydides had gone yet further in agnosticism than most of them, and rejected also the 'philosophical' schemes of the universe. With his strong and steady desire for literal, certain truth, knowing by experience how hard it is to get a consistent account of things actually seen and done from the men who saw and did them, he had not much respect for philosophies which, when science was still a blind and babbling infant, professed to reveal how the universe came into being.

Well-meaning efforts have been made to furnish him with a belief in some providential government of the world. But there is not a shadow of proof that he recognized the

'Mind' of Anaxagoras any more than the Zeus of Aeschylus. Indeed, his avoidance of the word νοῦς (to which he prefers γνώμη) may indicate a definite wish to renounce the philosophic theory associated in his day with the term. From Anaxagoras and other 'philosophers' he accepted a few results of scientific observation—about eclipses, earthquakes and the like—all that had yet been won from the vast field of the unknown by the first inroads of knowledge. That is the extent of his debt to 'philosophy', in the way of positive results; all it had done for him otherwise was of a negative sort. Since Parmenides had declared the sensible world to be an illusion, agnosticism in one form or another had taken possession of many thoughtful minds. It is only in this way that Thucydides owed to philosophy his marvellous sense of the limits of certain knowledge.

If we would put ourselves at the point where Thucydides stood when he began his task, we must perform an almost impossible feat. To rid our minds of religious and metaphysical beliefs which are not identical with our own is comparatively easy. What is exceedingly difficult but equally necessary, is to throw off the inheritance to which we are born, of concepts distinguished and defined by a vast and subtle terminology, logical, metaphysical, scientific, created by Aristotle, refined by the schoolmen, and enlarged by centuries of discovery. Thucydides lived at the one moment in recorded history which has seen a brilliantly intellectual society, nearly emancipated from a dying religion, and at the same time unaided by science, as yet hardly born. Nowhere but in a few men of that generation shall we find so much independence of thought combined with such destitute poverty in the apparatus and machinery of thinking.[1] The want of

---

[1] It is not easy for us to realize how impossible it was to think clearly in a language which did not supply, as modern languages do, a refined and distinct terminology. When Thucydides' contemporary, Democritus, wrote: 'By convention sweet, by convention sour; in truth atoms and void,' he *meant*, we say, something of this sort: that the primary qualities of matter are objectively real, while the secondary are only subjective. But to offer this proposition, or anything like it, as a paraphrase of the Greek is utterly uncritical. It is to disguise the fact that the Greek word (νόμῳ) rendered

scientific categories, and above all of the cardinal conception
of law as applying to human actions, makes a gulf between
Thucydides and ourselves immensely greater than any which
his want of superstitious beliefs makes between him and
Herodotus. We must rid our minds of scientific terminology,
as well as of religion and philosophy, if we are to appreciate
the unique detachment of Thucydides' mind, moving in the
rarest of atmospheres between the old age and the new.
Descartes, for all his efforts, was immeasurably less free from
metaphysical preoccupation; Socrates appears, in comparison,
superstitious.

When we have made all these deductions, and swept away
as much as we can of our furniture of thought, we are left in
presence of a reflective and very observant mind, whose interest is concentrated on human acts and motives. Its peculiar
note is a feeling for truth which, exalted as it is, has less
of passion in it than of austere regard. All the character
of the man is in the famous passage where he rebukes, without condescending to name him, the inaccuracy of Herodotus.
'There are many facts, not falling into oblivion through lapse
of time but belonging to our own day, about which the
Hellenes in general are misinformed. They believe, for instance, that the Lacedaemonian kings have not one vote each
but two, and that they have a 'Pitanate regiment', which in
fact never existed. So little pains do most men take in the
inquiry for the truth; they will sooner turn to the first story
that comes to hand.'[1]

Of all the indictments of Herodotus this is the most grim
and the most just. We could defend him from the accusa-

---

'subjective', is deplorably ambiguous, and means 'legal', 'conventional,'
'artificial,' 'unnatural,' 'arbitrary,' and a number of other things. Enough
remains of the controversies of the time to show that this ambiguity lay,
not in language only, but in thought. These ideas, all covered by one word
in the only tongue known to the Greeks, were simply not distinguished,
and to import a distinction by assigning one meaning to the word to the
exclusion of the rest is to commit the fallacy into which Professor Gomperz
seems to us to have fallen.

[1] Thuc. i. 20; Hdt. vi. 57; ix. 53.

tion of 'malignity'; we could palliate his superstitions and romancings; but we cannot deny that in respect of these two irreducible little facts, which may possibly be of some use to a modern antiquary, but were then utterly insignificant, he was careless. The kings of Lacedaemon had only one vote; the Spartan regiments were not territorial. He might have ascertained the truth, and he did not.

Deeply interested in human character, punctiliously accurate, an agnostic not of the militant order but by way of patient, rational conviction, Thucydides found a congenial field only in the history of a contemporary war waged between the states he knew by men whom he had seen and heard. Here were facts which could be found out, and laboriously sifted, and set down for the instruction of posterity. Just how much can be found out and set down he is careful to define in the passage from which we started in this chapter; we can now see why the field it limits is so restricted, the renunciation so austere. If the creative faculties of man could be severed from the receptive, if science could first banish art and next cast out of herself all hypothesis and generalization, then the historian might reduce himself to the compass of Thucydides' programme: '*the accounts given of themselves by the several states in speeches, when they were on the eve of war or later when they were engaged*'; and '*the events—what was actually done in the war*'.

The events are matter of observation: the only difficulty is to get an accurate account from eyewitnesses. Besides 'what was done', nothing seems relevant except the immediate motives of the agents. These can be ascertained only in two ways. We may infer from a man's behaviour what his feelings are; but such inferences are a leap into the dark, and although Thucydides of course could not avoid making them, he openly states them as rarely as possible. Safer, to his mind, was the method of keeping, here also, to observed facts: namely, the reasons publicly alleged, the 'accounts' given of their actions by the agents themselves. If these can be faithfully and literally reported, posterity may perhaps

see more light through the words than Thucydides could
be sure of seeing. It is to this magnificent sense of the
historian's duty to truth that we owe those indications, inexplicable to the man who recorded them, significant only to
a modern observer, on which we can base our hypothesis
about the origin of the war.

The time for investigating causes, and making hypothetical
constructions was not yet. We must constantly remind ourselves that Thucydides seemed to himself to stand on the very
threshold of history. Behind him lay a past which, in comparison with ours, was unimaginably meagre. From beyond the
Grecian seas had come nothing but travellers' tales of the Eastern wonderland. Within the tiny Hellenic world itself, the
slender current of history flashed only here and there a broken
gleam through the tangled overgrowth of legend and gorgeous
flowers of poetry, whose shoots and pushing tendrils had
gained even upon the great Persian war-time of fifty years
before, so that the figure of Xerxes was fading already to join
the shades of Priam and Agamemnon in the world of dreams.
The creator of history would set himself no more ambitious
task than to save from the dissolving fabric of human fact
a few hard stones, unhewn, and fit only to serve for a
foundation.

# PART II

# THUCYDIDES MYTHICUS

## INTRODUCTORY

In the last chapter we tried to define Thucydides' starting-point, to take stock of his equipment, and to see his undertaking as he must have seen it in prospect. When, however, we observe the impression left on our minds by the work as a whole, we find that this impression contains an element which is not accounted for by the author's avowed method and design. If Thucydides had steadily adhered to what must have been his original plan—a mere journal of the war, threading a disconnected row of illustrative episodes—the history would have had no more artistic value than just the sum of values of its several parts; but this does not correspond to the impression actually conveyed. We are vaguely, but unmistakably, conscious of an artistic effect of the whole—an effect imperfectly executed, tentative, more than half lost in broken lights and formless shadows, but certainly something more than a series or aggregate of distinct impressions.

We are further aware that this artistic unity is closely bound up with the worth and beauty of the book, and with its appeal to a modern mind. The antiquarian interest of the story is no greater than that of Polybius' narrative or Xenophon's. The utility which the detailed record of battle and campaign was intended to possess—how obsolete and meaningless this must be to a world whose armoury of slaughter is enriched with siege-gun and ironclad! The political philosophy of the city state may be neglected by the modern socialist. The observations upon human nature are less subtle than those of an ordinary novelist of to-day. A certain nobility of thought, a considerable skill in the presentation of character and in narrative—what more than these would be left? If contemporaries were warned that

the history would be 'rather unattractive', what attraction
would it retain for us to-day? Yet it does attract and move
us strangely; and this appeal is a thing to be reckoned with
and explained.

The results of our inquiry, if they are true, will be of some
literary interest, and they also have a bearing on the moral
character of Thucydides. The current interpretation of that
part of the history which deals with Cleon leaves a dark
cloud hanging over its author,—a cloud which well-meaning
defenders have tried, but never quite successfully, to dispel.
It cannot, we think, be denied that Thucydides hated and
despised Cleon. We have no right to complain of that; for one
man may hate and despise another with very good reason;
and we need not think much the worse of either. The moral
question touches not the man, but the historian. Has he
misrepresented the facts about Cleon *because* he had a
'personal grudge' against 'an able, but coarse, noisy, ill-bred,
audacious man?'[1] If he has done so, and for that motive,
what are we to say of an historian who began his work with
an austere profession of fidelity to truth, and then distorted
his narrative, concealed facts, and insinuated detraction, with
the deliberate purpose of discrediting a politician who had
been instrumental in causing his own banishment? Yet this
is what is implied in the current hypothesis, that Thucydides
was actuated by a personal grudge. But why do we let him
off with this mild phrase, instead of branding the man for
a hypocrite, to be ranked among the lowest, as having sinned
against the light? If we do let him off, it is because the
history as a whole leaves an impression inconsistent with this
account of the matter. It is not the work of a man capable
of consciously indulging the pettiness of personal spite, but
of one who could tell the story of his own military failure,
which cost him twenty years of exile, without a syllable of
extenuation. Throughout the book there is a nobility of
tone, a kind of exalted aloofness, which makes some of his

[1] Bury, *Hist. of Greece* (1900), p. 456.

grave judgements sound as if the voice of History herself had spoken.

In the following pages we hope to show that Thucydides' incomplete presentation of fact in this part of the history is due, not to a personal motive, but to the influence of a principle of design which was never formulated, because he certainly did not contemplate it in prospect when he began his work, and probably to the last never found out how pervasive and profound had been its operation.

We believe, moreover, it is possible to lay our finger on the place where this new principle first definitely modifies the narrative. It is at the beginning of Book IV, in the story of the occupation of Pylos. In the next chapter we shall proceed at once to this episode, and try to bring to the surface this underlying principle which in later chapters will be further illustrated and explained.

There is always something ungracious, something, almost, of impiety, in the office of criticism. A work of art is not meant to be taken to pieces; analysis is like a mischievous child dismounting a delicate machine. When it comes to poetry, our instinct revolts and cries out to us, for the sake of all that is beautiful, to leave it alone. But in the interpretation of an age far removed from ours, with a cast of thought and a tradition of artistic workmanship long fallen into disuse, we are faced with a cruel dilemma. If we analyse, some volatile and evanescent spirit is released and is not to be recaptured; if we refrain, we may miss the very qualities which the artist himself valued most highly. The generation is gone which was bred to the same intellectual heritage and met the lightest hint with native comprehension. For us only the strong effort of imaginative sympathy can reconquer the lost ground.

# CHAPTER VI

## THE LUCK OF PYLOS

THE first episode in the History which presents features apparently inexplicable on the supposition that Thucydides is working on his avowed plan, and certainly not fully explained by any hypothesis yet advanced by modern criticism, is the story of the occupation of Pylos. We shall first give an outline of the narrative, in which we shall merely summarize or abbreviate, refraining, with all the Thucydidean caution we can muster, from throwing any colour over it. We shall include those parts of the story in which the unexplained factor is evidently at work, excluding details which present no difficulty. A few introductory words are necessary to describe the situation which immediately precedes our episode.

The History has reached the opening of the seventh year of war (B. C. 425). In consequence of the check which the Peloponnesian arms had suffered in Acarnania, following upon the failure of Demosthenes' daring plan of campaign in the same region, a lull had fallen. The first heat of conflict was over; at Athens, as at Sparta, discouragement had strengthened the party of peace. Year by year the suffering peasants must crowd into the plague-stricken city, when word came that the irresistible army of invasion was mustering at the Isthmus; and year by year trudge sadly back to find the seared vestiges of ruin in trampled cornfield, in uptorn vine and olive, and blackened homestead. In the early summer evenings, when the invader had crossed the pass above Acharnae, knots of ragged and dejected figures would gather on the northward slopes of the Acropolis, and

you might have heard husky voices debating whose farm
was that, which was marked by the ugly red glow, yonder,
on the foot-hills of Parnes.   The *Acharnians* of Aristophanes
was produced at the Lenaean Festival in February of this year.
The poet's genial sense of the clean healthfulness and beauty
of life on the country farms in happier days had enforced the
strong sanity of his appeal.  He attempted to turn the current
of blind exasperation against the invader into the channels
that made for peace.   It is no good, he told the poor fellows,
to grind your teeth at the wicked Spartans; the thing to do
is to stop the war.   Some of the real Acharnians must have
been convinced; for the good Nikias and his friends were
returned in some force at the elections in April.   True, the
war-party had insisted that the operations in Sicily must
be seen through, and forty ships were sent to relieve the
small squadron already in the western seas.   But Sicily was
far away; and it was understood that this expedition was
to 'put an end to the war in that region', and to give the
fleet the benefits of exercise.[1]   From this point we will take
up the text of the narrative and follow it closely with just
the necessary abbreviation.[2]   We shall draw attention in the
notes to certain expressions which the reader is asked to bear
in mind.

The fleet sailed for Sicily under the command of Eurymedon
and Sophocles, with orders to put in by the way at Corcyra,
where the democratic and philathenian party who held the
capital were reduced nearly to starvation by the depredations
of the exiles ensconced on Mount Istone.   With the fleet went
Demosthenes, who 'though since his retreat from Acarnania
he held no official command,[3] was at his own request instructed
to make use of the fleet, if he so wished, about the coasts of
the Peloponnese'.

As the squadron rounded the southern promontory of

---

[1] iii. 115. 4.

[2] iv. 2 ff.  The passages within inverted commas are translated without
abbreviation or addition.

[3] He was general elect, but would not enter on office for some months.

Messenia, news came that a Peloponnesian fleet had stolen a march on them and was already at Corcyra. Eurymedon and Sophocles were anxious to push on. Demosthenes, however, ' urged them to put in first at Pylos and do what was necessary before proceeding on their voyage. The generals objected, but it so chanced that a storm came on which drove the fleet into Pylos.[1] Demosthenes began at once to urge that the position should be fortified; this, he said, was the object he had had in view when he accompanied the fleet. He pointed out that there was great abundance of timber and stones, and that the position was naturally strong, while the country for a considerable distance round was, like the place itself, uninhabited. Pylos is about forty-six miles from Sparta, and lies in the land which was formerly Messenia; it is now called Koryphasium by the Lacedaemonians. The generals replied that there were plenty of desert promontories round the Peloponnese, which Demosthenes might occupy if he wanted the public money to be wasted. But Demosthenes thought that this particular spot had special advantages. There was a harbour at hand,[2] and the Messenians, whose ancient home this had been and who spoke the same dialect as the Lacedaemonians, could do them much harm from such a base; and further they would be a trusty garrison.

' The generals would not listen to him; no more would the soldiers, when he proceeded to impart his plan to the officers. Hence, the weather being unfit for sailing, he was compelled to remain idle; until the soldiers themselves, having nothing to

---

[1] iv. 3. 1 ἀντιλεγόντων δὲ κατὰ τύχην χειμὼν ἐπιγενόμενος κατήνεγκε τὰς ναῦς ἐς τὴν Πύλον. The large and deep bay of Navarino is partly closed by the narrow island of Sphacteria which lies, with a length of 2¾ miles, along its mouth, leaving a narrow channel to the north, and a wider to the south. The north channel is dominated on its further side by the deserted peninsula of Pylos, the circumference of which is naturally defended by inaccessible cliffs except for a small distance at the north end (where a sandy isthmus joins it to the mainland), and for a somewhat longer extent on its south and south-west shores.

[2] The anchorage was close to Pylos at the north-west corner of what is now the lagoon of Osmyn Aga. At this date the lagoon was navigable and formed an inner chamber north of Navarino Bay, and partly cut off from it by a sand-spit.

do, were seized with an impulse [1] to fortify the position. So they set about the work ; and, being unprovided with iron tools for stone-cutting, they brought rocks which they picked out and put together as they happened to fit. Where mortar was required, for want of buckets, they carried the mud on their backs, bending double to form a resting-place for it, and locking their hands behind, to keep it from falling off. By every means in their power they hurried on, so as to complete the parts most open to attack, before the Lacedaemonians should arrive, the position being in most places so strong already that no wall was needed. The Lacedaemonians were just then celebrating a festival [2] ; and, besides, when they heard the news they made light of it, thinking that, when they did go out, they could easily take the place by assault, even supposing the Athenians would wait to meet them. They were also somewhat delayed by their army being still in Attica. In six days the Athenians finished the fortification on the land side and at other points where it was most required. They then left Demosthenes with five ships to defend it, while the greater part of the fleet hastened on their voyage to Corcyra and Sicily.' [3]

'The Peloponnesian army in Attica, on hearing of the occupation of Pylos, retreated homewards in haste; for the Lacedaemonians, and especially King Agis, saw that this occupation touched them closely ; and further, the invasion having been made early, while the crops were still green, they were running short of provisions for the soldiery, and bad weather had come on with a severity unusual at that season, and distressed the expedition. Thus many things coincided to hasten their retreat and to make this invasion very short. They had stayed in Attica only a fortnight.'

When the army reached home, the Spartiates raised the country-side and started to the rescue of Pylos. The rest of

---

[1] iv. 4. 1 ὁρμὴ ἐνέπεσε περιστᾶσιν ἐκτειχίσαι τὸ χωρίον. We omit περιστᾶσιν, the meaning of which is doubtful.

[2] iv. 5. 1 ἑορτήν τινα ἔτυχον ἄγοντες. Ἔτυχον denotes the *coincidence* of two events with the implication that the coincidence was undesigned, or accidental. Often this implication is not *felt* at all.

[3] iv. 5. 2 ταῖς δὲ πλείοσι ναυσὶ τὸν ἐς τὴν Κέρκυραν πλοῦν καὶ Σικελίαν ἠπείγοντο.

the Lacedaemonians were slower to move, having but just returned from another expedition. They sent round a summons to their allies in all quarters, and recalled their fleet from Corcyra. It 'reached Pylos, unperceived by the Athenian fleet at Zakynthos'.[1] On their approach Demosthenes sent two of his five ships to summon 'Eurymedon and the Athenians in the fleet at Zakynthos' to come to him, as Pylos was in danger. They came in all haste. The Lacedaemonians were preparing for a combined attack by sea and land, 'expecting to capture with ease such hastily constructed works, defended by so small a garrison.' They intended to block the fairway of the two entrances to the harbour with lines of ships, so as to exclude the Athenian fleet,[2] 'unless indeed they should have taken Pylos before' it arrived.

---

[1] The fleet of Eurymedon, last mentioned as leaving Pylos for Corcyra and Sicily. Zakynthos is the first port of call on the route northwards, about seventy miles from Pylos.

[2] There has been much controversy on the question which were the two channels to be blocked. My own opinion is (1) that in this part of the narrative 'the harbour' means the present lagoon of Osmyn Aga; (2) that the sand-spit separating this lagoon from Navarino Bay reached nearly to Pylos, leaving only one narrow entrance just under Pylos; (3) that the two channels to be blocked were the two *approaches* to this entrance, viz. the Sphagia channel, between the north end of Sphacteria and the south shore of Pylos, and the channel between the north-east corner of Sphacteria and the end of the sand-spit. The object of blocking both these approaches, instead of the one entrance (between Pylos and the sand-spit), was obviously to keep open communications with the Spartans on the island. If the entrance only had been barred, they would have been isolated. I also believe that Thucydides' informant in the first narrative (the siege of Pylos) was one of the defenders of Pylos, who would naturally mean by 'the harbour' the lagoon, just under Pylos, which was his centre of interest; and that the informant in the second narrative (the capture of Sphacteria) was a different person, much better at describing localities, who had personally fought over the island on the day of its capture. His centre of interest was Sphacteria, and by 'the harbour' he indisputably meant Navarino Bay, where the Athenian fleet then was. Thucydides never found out that there were really two harbours, owing to the curious duplication of the sites : two harbours, each with two approaches, in the one case at the two ends, in the other on the two sides of one end, of the same island. The only new point in this view is the identification of the two channels; the rest is taken from the valuable papers of Mr. Grundy (*J. H. S.* xvi) and Mr. Burrows (*J. H. S.* xviii).

They landed a strong party on the island of Sphacteria, to prevent the enemy from occupying it. Pylos, which had no landing-place towards the open sea, would thus be completely isolated. They thought 'they would probably carry the position by siege, without a sea-fight or any danger, as it was unprovisioned and had been occupied with little preparation'.

Demosthenes drew up his three remaining ships under shelter of a stockade at the south-east corner of his defences. The sailors he armed as best he could, mostly with shields of wicker-work. 'For there was no means of providing heavy armour in an uninhabited spot; and even these arms they only obtained from a thirty-oared privateer and a light boat belonging to some Messenians who just then arrived on the scene.[1] These Messenians proved to include about forty heavy-armed men, whom Demosthenes used with the rest.'

Then follows a detailed account of Brasidas' unsuccessful attempt to force a landing on Pylos by running his ships ashore. The description concludes with the reflection: 'It was a singular turn of fortune [2] that Athenians should be on land, and that land Laconian, repelling an attack from the sea by Lacedaemonians; while Lacedaemonians on ship-board were trying to effect a landing on their own soil, now hostile to them, in the face of Athenians. For in those days it was the great glory of the Lacedaemonians to be an inland people superior to all in land fighting, and of the Athenians to be sailors and the first power by sea.' This observation is echoed again after the battle which followed between the two fleets in the harbour. The Peloponnesians had at the moment neglected the precaution of closing the entrances.[3] The Athenian fleet, reinforced by a few guard-ships from Naupactos and three Chians, sailed in and knocked them into bits, following up the pursuit to the point of attempting to tow off from the shore some ships which had not been launched.

---

[1] iv. 9. 1 Μεσσηνίων . . . οἳ ἔτυχον παραγενόμενοι.  ὁπλῖταί τε τῶν Μεσσηνίων τούτων ὡς τεσσαράκοντα ἐγένοντο.

[2] iv. 12. 3 ἐς τοῦτο περιέστη ἡ τύχη ὥστε . . .

[3] iv. 13. 4 οὔτε ἃ διενοήθησαν, φάρξαι τοὺς ἔσπλους, ἔτυχον ποιήσαντες.

The Lacedaemonians ran down into the water to save them, and a fierce struggle ensued. Thus 'the usual methods of warfare of the two combatants were interchanged. For in their excitement and dismay the Lacedaemonians were (one might almost say) fighting a sea-battle from land, while the Athenians as they were winning and were desirous to follow up their present good luck to the furthest point fought a land-battle from ships'.[1] So ended the first round of hostilities at Pylos.

In shortening the above narrative we have intentionally brought into prominence a series of suggestions which are anything but conspicuous in the long story as it stands in the text. We have cut away the mass in which they are embedded and left them clumsily sticking out, so that no one can miss them. Probably thousands of readers have passed them without attention, and yet carried away just the impression which they ought to convey. That impression is that the occupation of Pylos—the first step to the most decisive success achieved by Athens in this war—was *the most casual thing in the world.*

The fleet, bound as it was for Sicily, with instructions to call on the way at Corcyra, where it was urgently needed, would never have put in at Pylos, if a storm had not ' *by chance* '[2] driven it to shelter. The generals in command could not imagine why the position should be occupied; and when Demosthenes tried to convince the troops, he failed. It was owing to the accidental continuance of bad weather that from sheer want of something to do ' *an impulse seized* ' the soldiers to fortify the place. The undertaking was so unexpected that no tools had been provided; the walls were patched up somehow with rocks and mud. They had time to finish it because the Lacedaemonians at home were *just then* celebrating a festival. A singularly happy improvisation on

---

[1] iv. 14. 3 βουλόμενοι τῇ παρούσῃ τύχῃ ὡς ἐπὶ πλεῖστον ἐπεξελθεῖν.

[2] Observe that the note of accident is clearly sounded at the outset in κατὰ τύχην (not ἔτυχε) and below in ὁρμὴ ἐνέπεσε. Later the fainter suggestion of ἔτυχον suffices to sustain it.

the part of Fortune; but there is more to come. Just when reinforcements and a supply of arms are urgently needed by the extemporized garrison, a couple of piratical craft come bearing down the wind from the north. They turn out, oddly enough, to be Messenians with forty hoplites aboard and—how very fortunate!—a supply of spare arms. When, finally, the Peloponnesians at the critical moment neglect a precaution vital to their plan, and leave the garrison of Sphacteria cut off on the island, we feel that Fortune has filled the cup of the Athenians almost overfull. To crown all, in her whimsical way, she reverses the rôles of the combatants, and sets the sailors fighting on land and the landsmen by water.

We observe, too, that if Fortune favoured the Athenians, they were also helped by an extraordinary series of stupid mistakes on the Lacedaemonian side. When the news first reached Sparta, the Lacedaemonians at home could not see, what Agis saw clearly enough, that the capture of Pylos was a serious incident. They also thought they could easily capture the position; though they might have remembered that Sparta was notoriously incompetent in siege operations, and that the revolted helots, who were not backed by the first sea-power in the world, had, in a similar extemporized stronghold at Ithome, held them at defiance. When they saw the position, they were equally confident of taking it with ease. They expected to exclude the Athenian fleet by closing the entrances, and so to avoid a sea-battle altogether. They landed troops on the island, and then by neglecting to close the entrances left them cut off—and this, though they knew the Athenian fleet was close at hand and were expecting its arrival. When it did arrive, their own fleet was not even clear of the beach and arrayed for battle. This series of blunders is hardly less remarkable than the series of accidents on the Athenian side.

We may admit, however, that it is not incredible that Spartans should be exceedingly stupid. The difficulty arises over that part of the narrative which is more concerned with the Athenians. Can we accept this as a simple and natural account of what really happened? The moment we turn back on it in a critical mood, we find that it is full of obscurities, gaps, incoherencies, which cry out for explanation. When we look still closer, we remark two further points. One is that some of these obscurities can be removed by careful comparison of one part of the narrative with another, so that we can piece together an hypothesis to fill the gaps, from evidence supplied by Thucydides, *but not used by him* for this obvious purpose. The other is that we have not here, as at other places in the History, a mere odd assortment of obscurities; but all the omissions contribute to one effect. What is left out is whatever would explain the motives and designs of the principal actors; what is put in and emphasized is every accident and every blunder of the enemy, that favoured the occupation. There is hardly a sentence in the whole story which is not so turned and so disposed as to make us feel that design counted for nothing and luck for everything. Let us look at some of the questions which these omissions and incoherencies leave unanswered.

First, we may ask whether it is credible that Demosthenes should not have explained sooner to Eurymedon and Sophocles 'the object he had in view when he accompanied the fleet'. The details of this plan are not disclosed till the latest possible moment in the narrative. When he first asked the generals to put in at Pylos, he is said to have requested them 'to do what was necessary before proceeding on their voyage'. They refused. Then followed the storm and drove them into Pylos. Not till this note of accident has been sounded are we allowed to know 'what was necessary'. Then, as if the sight of Pylos for the first time suggested the plan, Demosthenes points out the natural strength of the position. The generals, as if they had never had such a plan before them, say that there are plenty of desert promontories, if Demosthenes wants to waste the public money on occupying them. Demosthenes urges that this one has special advantages, and produces his trump card—the Messenians. In the next sentence we are told that he failed to convince any one whatever. By this arrangement of the story, Demosthenes' design is before our minds for the least possible time. It is not disclosed until in the first place it is firmly fixed in our thoughts that the fleet is hastening to Corcyra, and in the second place Fortune has intervened decisively to hinder its journey; and when it is disclosed, it is immediately (as it were) effaced again by the statement that the disclosure had no effect on any one. We are left with the impression that Demosthenes had not explained the whole thing to the generals *before the storm occurred*, and pressed on them all the advantages he mentions later. No wonder they objected to doing 'what was necessary'.

In the second place, if the generals were so blind to the possibilities of the place that they regarded the occupation as a waste of public money, we may naturally ask what occurred to make them change their minds and allow Demosthenes, after all, to remain? A Peloponnesian fleet of sixty sail, as against their own forty, was already in their path. Why did they detach five ships and leave them with Demosthenes, while they 'hastened on their voyage to Corcyra and Sicily'? Did Demosthenes appeal to the irregular commission which licensed him to 'use the fleet, if he wished, about the coasts of the Peloponnese'? But, if he did so, he was overruled; for we are definitely told that no one would listen to him. No; the occupation of Pylos was the purest of accidents. The building of the defences was a schoolboy frolic, begun (in schoolboy language) for a lark, to break the tedium of kicking heels and whistling for a wind. It kept them amused for six days, till the gale dropped. For all we are told, besides this piece of mudlarking, nothing whatever occurred in the interval to change the opinion of the responsible officers. Yet, without a syllable of explanation, we learn that they detached five ships—one-eighth of their strength—to garrison the deserted promontory, and themselves 'hastened on their voyage to Corcyra and Sicily'. Did they expect that Demosthenes with no provisions [1] and a small, insufficiently armed force would hold Pylos till they came back, or did they mean to leave their fellow citizens, for whose lives they were

---

[1] iv. 8. 8 σίτου τε οὐκ ἐνόντος.

responsible, to a certain fate ?　What would they say to the Athenian people when they returned from Sicily ?

When we read on, however, we learn from a side-allusion to ' the Athenian fleet at Zakynthos ' that, so far from ' hastening to Corcyra and Sicily ', they were, after at least ten days' or a fortnight's interval,[1] still only seventy miles away, at the nearest port of call.　This change of plan is not even directly recorded, much less explained.　Yet it means that the generals pitched their sailing orders to the winds, left Corcyra to the imminent peril of starvation or capture by assault, and endangered the advanced squadron in Sicilian waters which they were sent to reinforce.　Examples were not wanting to warn them that in such circumstances, a failure or even a reverse, meant certain prosecution and death, if ever they set foot again in Athens.　Yet they took the risk—all because of the mudlarks !

Our purpose, however, is not to attack the veracity of Thucydides, but to understand his method.　Without enlarging upon the obscurities of this episode, we have said enough to prove that some explanation is needed.　It is now clear that the story of Pylos, from first to last, is so treated as to convey the suggestion that it was all *a stroke of luck*.　It is also clear that, unless Eurymedon and Sophocles were out of their minds, some elements in the situation of a less fortuitous nature have been omitted or left almost out of sight.

Almost, but not entirely.　The reader may have felt that, although the narrative indicates no connexion between the two references to the Messenians, some connexion there must have been.　One of the exceptional advantages of Pylos to Demosthenes' mind was that it was the ancient home of the Messenians, whose knowledge of the local dialect would give them peculiar facilities for distressing the Spartans.　The point is just mentioned and dropped.　Six chapters later, a Messenian privateer with arms and reinforcements arrives in the nick of

---

[1] The time needed for news to reach Sparta and be forwarded to Agis in Attica ; for the withdrawal of the army of invasion, and *after that*, for word to be sent to the Peloponnesian fleet at Corcyra, and for these to come south.

time. These Messenians were (though Thucydides does not mention it) the exiles whom the Athenians had established at Naupactos, their naval base near the mouth of the Corinthian gulf. We remember now that in the previous year Demosthenes had been co-operating with these very Messenians in the Aetolian and Acarnanian campaigns. Moreover, in one of the battles he had employed them to play off a trick on his Doric antagonists.[1] The accent of his Messenian friends was now again to come in useful. And when the sentinel on Pylos reported that a couple of sail were standing in from the direction of Naupactos, we fancy Demosthenes was not surprised when they turned out to have forty hoplites aboard and a stock of spare shields in the casemates. Can we avoid the inference that the selection of Pylos was not so casual after all, that Demosthenes had learnt all about the possibilities of the position from his Messenian allies the year before? Further, must we not conjecture that Eurymedon, not daring to leave more than five ships behind, since the Peloponnesian fleet would almost certainly be recalled south and meet him, sent an urgent message to Naupactos, describing the position of Demosthenes and telling the Messenians to send a fast ship with such reinforcements and spare arms as they could produce without a moment's delay. The conjecture is confirmed by the later statement [2] that some guardships from Naupactos joined the fleet while still at Zakynthos. Eurymedon may have meant to wait there within call till Demosthenes' force should have been replaced by a sufficient garrison of Messenians, and then to reunite his fleet and proceed to Corcyra and Sicily. But why are we left to fill all these blanks by conjecture?

---

[1] iii. 112: 'At the first dawn of day he fell on the Ambrakiots, who were still lying where they had slept, and who so far from knowing anything of what had happened, thought his men were their own comrades. For Demosthenes had taken care to place the Messenians in the front rank and *desired them to speak to the enemy in their own Doric dialect*, so putting the outposts off their guard, since it was still dark and their appearance could not be distinguished.' This connexion has, of course, been remarked by other writers.

[2] iv. 13. 1.

Moreover it is implied that Demosthenes *knew* that the Athenian fleet was still close at hand when he needed to be rescued; and this seems to prove that when Eurymedon and Sophocles left him, they arranged with him that they should stop at the nearest possible port. If that is so, to describe Eurymedon's fleet on leaving Pylos as 'hastening to Corcyra and Sicily' is, at least, misleading. But here, at any rate, there can be no intention to mislead, since the contradiction with what follows is patent. We can only conclude that Thucydides' mind is for some reason so bent on regarding the occupation of Pylos as a mere casual episode in a 'voyage to Corcyra and Sicily', that this phrase slips out at a place where the context certainly contradicts it by implication. Such a lapse, in so careful a writer, is by itself sufficient evidence of a preoccupied mind.

We have here, in fine, a narrative which is unlike any earlier part of Thucydides' story. Hitherto he has told a plain tale, lucid, intelligible, natural. Now we find an episode in which facts of cardinal importance for the understanding of the events are left unmentioned, and indispensable links are wanting. If the missing facts and connexions were within the author's knowledge, why are they omitted? If they were not, we might at least expect that he would avow his ignorance and draw some attention to the blanks, instead of passing over them as if he were unconscious of their existence.

The question then is this: Why has Thucydides represented the occupation of Pylos as the merest stroke of good luck, undertaken with the least possible amount of deliberate calculation, and furthered at every turn of events by some unforeseen accident?

The simplest of all answers would be that as a matter of fact so it was. Accidents do happen; and there certainly was a considerable element of luck. No one can foresee the occurrence of a storm. The festival at Sparta was a coincidence—though we note by the way that it was not a festival sufficiently important to prevent the army of invasion from being absent in Attica. The Messenian privateer might conceivably have come by accident—though the supply of spare arms on so small a vessel is certainly odd. And so on. But all this does not explain the blanks and incoherencies we have noticed; and it is fair to add that every additional accident increases the strain on our belief. As soon as we reject this first answer, we have admitted that Thucydides— for whatever reason—is not telling the story just as it happened and just as we should tell it. There is some unexplained factor at work, something of which we have not yet taken account.

The solutions that have been offered, when the problem before us has been faced at all, fall under two heads. We are told either that Thucydides is 'moralizing' on the uncertainty of war, or that he is actuated by some personal feeling of 'malignity' and indulging it in detraction. The first of these hypotheses is, in our opinion, a grave charge against him as a man of sense; the second is a still graver charge against his moral character.

It is true that the uncertainty of war is one of the most frequent topics in the speeches; and small wonder that it is so. Thucydides' generation lived through a life-and-death struggle waged almost continuously for twenty-seven years. A nation at war is always, more or less, in a fever;[1] when the nation is intelligent and excitable by temperament, and the war is close at home, the fever will run high. For these twenty-seven years no Athenian mind was ever quite at rest. Not a record or document of this period but we find in it the mark of this unhealthiness, of nerves on the strain with watching, of the pulse which beats just too fast. Every capricious turn of good or ill luck in the struggle sent a thrill through their hearts. But, can we think that Thucydides would deliberately distort the facts of the occupation of Pylos, solely in order to illustrate the truth that accidents will happen? The question hardly needs an answer. No man of common intelligence could say to himself, 'In order to

[1] Cf. ii. 8 ἥ τε ἄλλη Ἑλλὰς ἅπασα μετέωρος ἦν ξυνιουσῶν τῶν πρώτων πόλεων.

show how uncertain are the chances of war, I will describe
a series of events *not just as they happened, but with the
causal links, which would show that the events were not
fortuitous, disguised and almost suppressed.'* There were
plenty of real instances of good and ill luck. What need
of this perverse invention of a spurious one?

Plainly, then, this is not a case of ' moralizing '; there is
some other reason; and so we fall back on the hypothesis
of ' malignity '. The malignity could only be directed either
against Cleon, whose exploit at Sphacteria followed on the
occupation of Pylos, or against Athens. There is, on this
supposition, some personal grudge, against the hated political
opponent, or against the city which banished Thucydides.

With regard to Cleon, this hypothesis will not fit the facts.
The occupation of Pylos was the exploit not of Cleon, but of
Demosthenes. For Demosthenes, the only soldier of genius
whom the Athenians could match with Brasidas, Thucydides
consistently shows a marked admiration. The capture of
Pylos was his master-stroke, and there was no motive for
belittling the achievement. Cleon does not appear till
later, when he goes to the scene of action and co-operates
in the capture of Sphacteria. Malignity against him might
be fully satisfied either by representing that subsequent
operation as favoured by fortune or by attributing all the
skill involved in its success to his colleague, Demosthenes.
Thucydides actually does both these things—whether from
malignity or because he thought it was true, is no matter
for our present problem. But a personal grudge against
Cleon could not be satisfied, or be in question at all, in the
earlier narrative of the seizure of Pylos.

Was it, then, a grudge against Athens that moved him?
Did he hate the city which condemned him to banishment
for his failure at Amphipolis, and desire to represent—or
rather to misrepresent—her most successful feat in the war as
a mere stroke of luck? This, we believe, is an hypothesis
which is now, reluctantly and with many attempts at pallia-
tion, allowed to pass current. It cannot be so easily and
certainly dismissed as the other suggestions. It is a possible

motive—possible, at least, to some men—and it would account for those facts we have hitherto considered. We cannot at this point finally disprove it; the facts which it will not account for have yet to be discussed. But we do not believe that any one who knows Thucydides is really satisfied with imputing to him a motive which, candidly described, is dishonourable, ignoble, mean. The imputation does not fit in with our general impression from the rest of the History. If there is any one who is satisfied with it, we will ask him to read once more the story of the retreat from Syracuse. Were those pages written by a man who hated Athens and triumphed in her fall?

We cannot think of any other motive which could have induced Thucydides deliberately to represent as fortuitous a series of events which we, after some reflection, can see to have been in great measure designed. We next observe that the supposition of 'malignity' is itself based on the tacit assumption that Thucydides is writing from the same stand-point, and handling his story on the same methods, as a modern historian. If a modern had written the narrative of Pylos, we could say with the highest degree of moral certainty, that the distortion was deliberate and the motive must be at least dishonest, if not ignobly personal. Hence we assume, unconsciously, that Thucydides' motive must have been of this sort. In our eagerness to hail him as 'a modern of the moderns', we thought we were paying him a compliment; but now the epithet turns out to carry with it a most damaging accusation. If we decline to regard Thucydides as a modern, and recur to our thesis that, being an ancient, he must have looked at the course of human history with very different eyes from ours, it seems that an alternative explanation may yet remain.

The suggestion which we would put forward is that Thucydides thought he really saw an *agency*, called 'Fortune', at work in these events. When we say 'chance favoured the designs of Demosthenes',[1] of course we mean, not that any of

---

[1] Bury, *Hist. of Greece* (1900), p. 429.

the accidents had no natural cause, but only that they were such as could not have been foreseen. But have we any ground for saying that this, and nothing more, was what Thucydides would have meant ?[1]

We will, for the moment, leave the notion of Fortune without precise definition. It is enough to take a belief in Fortune as meaning a belief in any non-natural agency, which breaks in, as it were, from outside and diverts the current of events, without itself being a part of the series or an effect determined by an antecedent member of it. Now, we have already pointed out that human actions are not to be fitted into such a series. Their only causes—if we are to speak of causes at all—are motives, each of which is itself uncaused by anything preceding it in time; all human motives are absolute 'beginnings of motion'. A view of the universe in which this irruption of free human agency is tacitly assumed is at any rate illogical if it denies the *possibility* of similar irruptions into the course of Nature by non-human agencies.

But we can go further than this. We observed that Thucydides had no word at all for 'cause' in our sense. From the fact, among others, that instead of discussing the causes of the war, he thought he had completely accounted for its origin when he had described the grievances (αἰτίαι) of the combatants, it appeared that it was not only the word that was missing, but the concept. Having no clear conception of cause and effect, he cannot have had any clear conception of a universal and exclusive reign of causal law in Nature. In criticizing Professor Gomperz we denied that Thucydides conceived the course of human affairs as 'a process of Nature informed by inexorable causality', or as having anything in common with such a process. We may now further deny that he could have thought of the *processes of Nature themselves* as informed by causality, in our modern sense—the sense, namely, that every event has a place in one total series of all

---

[1] That Thucydides would have meant just what we mean is commonly *assumed*, as for instance by Mr. Forbes, Introduction to Book I (p. xxxii): 'Chance (that is, the operation of unknown causes) is strong, the future is hard to foresee, hope is dangerous ; we must look facts in the face, whether we like them or not, and " think it out ".'

events, and is completely determined by previous events, and so on backwards into infinity; and that this is true of the future as well as of the past. By an αἰτία, in nature as in man, Thucydides does not mean a member of such a series, but a *free* agency, a '*beginning* of motion', an incursion of fresh original power. If this is so, there was nothing whatever in his view of the universe to exclude the *possibility* of extraordinary intervention on the part of some undefined non-human powers. We shall presently see that his language elsewhere implies that such a possibility was admitted by him.

That Thucydides had, on the contrary, a quite definite notion of causal law is commonly taken for granted, or actually asserted. M. Croiset,[1] for instance, after contrasting Thucydides with his predecessors, continues: 'De là sa conception de l'histoire. Si les faits sont liés par des lois permanentes et nécessaires, la connaissance des causes et des effets dans le passé peut faire prévoir le retour des mêmes effets, produits par les mêmes causes, selon la règle des choses humaines (κατὰ τὸ ἀνθρώπειον).' This passage suggests that Thucydides based his conception of history on a belief in permanent and necessary laws, connecting events *in such a way that from a sufficient knowledge of the present state of the world the future could be predicted with certainty.* If this is true, it of course excludes the operation of Fortune.[2] Let us, however, examine the passages to which M. Croiset refers in his note, as the foundation of the above statement.

The first is as follows: 'For recitation to an audience, perhaps the absence of the "mythical" will make these facts rather unattractive; but it will be enough if they are judged useful by those who shall wish to know the plain truth of what has happened *and of the events which, according to the course of human things, are likely to happen again, of the*

---

[1] Croiset, *Hist. de la lit. grecque*, iv. 113.

[2] We may note, by the way, that if Thucydides thought this, he had discovered a truth of which Aristotle was ignorant. The whole Aristotelian doctrine of Possibility rests on the logical thesis that propositions which refer to future events (e. g. 'there will be a battle to-morrow') are neither true nor false, because, unless the future were undetermined, 'nothing would happen by chance' (ἀπὸ τύχης) and all deliberation would be futile.

*same, or much the same, sort as these.*'[1]  What Thucydides
here has in his mind, we know from the other passage to
which M. Croiset refers.[2]  Thucydides is there explaining
why he gives an account of the outbreak of plague at Athens.
'Others may say, each according to his judgement, whether
he be physician or layman, from what it probably arose,
and assert that whatever he considers were the agencies of
so great a change, *were sufficient to acquire power to (produce) the transformation.*[3]  But I shall say what it was
like when it happened ; and I shall set forth *the things from
which, if it should ever come on again, one who considers
them might best be able, knowing them beforehand, to
recognize it without fail.*  I fell ill myself, and I saw with
my own eyes others suffering.'

Thucydides will record the *symptoms* of the plague, from
personal observation, so that posterity may recognize the
disorder if it should break out again.  This is all he thinks
useful.  He hints that the guesses of physicians are not
worth much more than those of laymen, about the 'agencies
responsible' which they consider were '*sufficient to acquire
power* to (produce) such a transformation'.  Had the man
who wrote that phrase anything in his mind remotely resembling the modern notion of cause and causal law ?  The
phrase is the very contradiction of it.  The notion it conveys
is that of an unknown, probably an unknowable, something,
responsible for the plague, and from time to time *acquiring*
enough power to produce an outbreak.  Thucydides rejects
all attempts to scrutinize the nature of this something, and
does not even directly commit himself to a belief in its
existence.  He will confine himself to describing what he
actually saw and suffered.  He hints that other people,

---

[1] i. 22. 4 . . . καὶ τῶν μελλόντων ποτὲ αὖθις κατὰ τὸ ἀνθρώπειον τοιούτων καὶ
παραπλησίων ἔσεσθαι.

[2] ii. 48. 3.

[3] λεγέτω . . . τὰς αἰτίας ἅστινας νομίζει τοσαύτης μεταβολῆς ἱκανὰς εἶναι δύναμιν
ἐς τὸ μεταστῆσαι σχεῖν.  The editors suspect interpolation in this portentous
phrase ; but there is no reason to doubt the text.  αἰτία cannot be rendered
'cause' without misleading.  It is something held 'responsible', and
credited with *power*.

doctors and laymen alike, would do well to follow his example. The doctors would see in the plague the operation of something 'divine' [1]; laymen would more definitely ascribe it to the onslaught of malignant spirits or offended gods. Some undoubtedly connected it with the curse which attached to the Almaeonid Pericles.[2] Others again would murmur that they had always said harm would come of allowing the homeless peasants to camp out in the Pelargikon, against the warning of an ancient oracle.

In the former passage, likewise, Thucydides is not thinking of 'necessary and permanent laws' in the sequence of events. He is merely reflecting that other wars will happen in the future. Other 'events of the same, or *much the same*, sort' will occur, 'according to the course of human things'.[3] This last phrase is ambiguous. It might mean 'so far as man can foresee', 'in all human probability'—a phrase which is least likely to be on our lips when we have in our thoughts a clear conception of non-human 'inexorable causality'.

We are too apt to take the few sound observations of nature, made by the Greeks at that date, as a proof that they conceived nature as universally ruled by law. Thucydides notes, for instance, that 'it seems (or, is thought) to be possible for an eclipse of the sun to happen only at the time of a new moon'[4]; and again, that when the moon is

---

[1] Mr. Forbes (*Thuc.* I, Introd. p. xxvii) rightly observes that 'a remarkable passage in Thucydides' contemporary, the physician Hippocrates, shows that we must not argue too hastily from a rejection of superstitious explanations of particular phenomena. Speaking of a malady prevalent among some of the Scythians, he says : οἱ μὲν οὖν ἐπιχώριοι τὴν αἰτίην προστιθέασι θεῷ, καὶ σέβονται τούτους τοὺς ἀνθρώπους καὶ προσκυνέουσι, δεδοικότες περί γε ἑωυτῶν ἕκαστοι. ἐμοὶ δὲ καὶ αὐτῷ δοκεῖ πάντα τὰ πάθεα θεῖα εἶναι καὶ τἆλλα πάντα, καὶ οὐδὲν ἕτερον ἑτέρου θειότερον οὐδὲ ἀνθρωπινώτερον, ἀλλὰ πάντα ὁμοῖα καὶ πάντα θεῖα· ἕκαστον δὲ ἔχει φύσιν τῶν τοιούτων καὶ οὐδὲν ἄνευ φύσιος γίγνεται. . . .'

[2] See ii. 58, 59, where, just after describing the severity of the plague, Thucydides says that the Athenians, hard pressed at once by (1) the war, and (2) the plague, (1) blamed Pericles for the war and (2) thought their misfortunes had come on them 'on his account' (δι' ἐκεῖνον). Cf. ii. 64. 1.

[3] 'Nach dem Laufe menschlicher Dinge'—Classen, *ad loc.*

[4] ii. 28 νουμηνίᾳ κατὰ σελήνην, ὥσπερ καὶ μόνον δοκεῖ εἶναι γίγνεσθαι δυνατόν, ὁ ἥλιος ἐξέλιπε.

eclipsed, it is full.[1] He inferred, moreover, that eclipses could not, as superstitious men like Nikias supposed, give prognostications of coming events. But between an isolated observation and inference of this sort and a general conception of law in nature there was a gulf which many centuries of labour had yet to fill. In the case of earthquakes, Thucydides had no sufficient series of observations on which to base an inference. Consequently, with admirable good sense, he records, without expressing or implying any belief or disbelief of his own, the one fact of which he was certain, namely, that 'they were said and thought to be signs of coming events'.[2]

Again, when he is insisting in his introduction that the Peloponnesian War was the greatest in recorded history, he thinks it worth while to point out that it was not inferior to previous wars in the number of earthquakes, eclipses,[3] droughts, famines, plagues, and other such convulsions of nature which accompanied it. Similar phenomena had been reported of previous wars, but this hearsay was too scantily confirmed by ascertained facts. ' *It now became not incredible*,' he says, '*for all these things came upon the Greeks at the same time with this war.*'[4] An unprejudiced reader of this passage must draw several conclusions. In the first place Thucydides feels no distinction between famines and plagues on the one hand, and eclipses, earthquakes, and droughts on the other. To us it seems easy to connect the former class with a state of war, and absolutely impossible to connect the latter. Second, he saw no reason

---

[1] vii. 50.

[2] ii. 8. 3.

[3] His putting in 'eclipses' shows that he did not understand why the sun is not eclipsed at *every* new moon, or the moon *every* time it is full. He thought eclipses were *more frequent* at times of war and did not know why. Cf. Plut. *Nic.* xxiii ὁ γὰρ πρῶτος σαφέστατόν τε πάντων καὶ θαρραλεώτατον περὶ σελήνης καταυγασμῶν καὶ σκιᾶς λόγον εἰς γραφὴν καταθέμενος Ἀναξαγόρας οὔτ' αὐτὸς ἦν παλαιὸς οὔτε ὁ λόγος ἔνδοξος ἀλλ' ἀπόρρητος ἔτι καὶ δι' ὀλίγων καὶ μετ' εὐλαβείας τινὸς ἢ πίστεως βαδίζων.

[4] i. 23. 3 τά τε πρότερον ἀκοῇ μὲν λεγόμενα, ἔργῳ δὲ σπανιώτερον βεβαιούμενα οὐκ ἄπιστα κατέστη, σεισμῶν τε πέρι . . . . ταῦτα γὰρ πάντα μετὰ τοῦδε τοῦ πολέμου ἅμα ξυνεπέθετο.

in the nature of things why events of either class should not be more frequent at times of war in Greece, and he thought the evidence pointed to the fact that they were. Third, if he was thinking at all of any sort of *causal connexion* between wars and (for instance) droughts, he must have attributed droughts to causes of a sort which find no place in modern science. Fourth, he shows his usual good sense in merely recording that these occurrences apparently came *at the same time* (ἅμα), without committing himself to any specific connexion between them. In fine, he shows a completely scientific spirit, and also an equally complete destitution of a scientific view of nature. In the former respect he is superior to the man who sacrifices to a volcano or prays for rain. In the latter he is not so far advanced as a modern peasant who is just educated enough to feel that there *can* be no connexion between his seeing four magpies and some one else having a child. Thucydides will not *worship* the inscrutable agencies responsible for convulsions of Nature; but he cannot rule out the hypothesis that such agencies exist and may ' acquire power ' to produce the convulsions coincidently with a war in Greece. He refrains from dogmatizing on either side; regarding, we may suppose, the current belief that malevolent spirits were responsible for such outbreaks,[1] as an incautious and unverified explanation.

M. Croiset has, in our opinion, slipped into a fallacy which is so common in the written history of thought that it seems to deserve a name of its own. We will call it the Modernist Fallacy. It takes several kindred shapes. In the present case, its formula is as follows: ' If a man in the remote past believed a certain proposition, he also believed all that we

---

[1] Porph. *de Abst.* ii. 40 ἐν γὰρ δὴ καὶ τοῦτο τῆς μεγίστης βλάβης τῆς ἀπὸ τῶν κακοεργῶν δαιμόνων θετέον, ὅτι αὐτοὶ αἴτιοι γιγνόμενοι τῶν περὶ τὴν γῆν παθημάτων, οἷον λοιμῶν, ἀφοριῶν, σεισμῶν, αὐχμῶν καὶ τῶν ὁμοίων . . . The belief, seriously entertained by this intelligent writer, has, of course, flourished to our own time in civilized countries. We remember an article in the *Spectator*, in which the writer argued that an earthquake in the West Indies was designed by God to stimulate seismological research. Neither the editor nor the readers seem to have been conscious of any difficulty or impiety in this opinion.

have since discovered to be implied in that proposition.'
Thucydides believed—who ever did not?—that events of
'the same, or much the same, sort' recur. Therefore, he must
have had a full and conscious belief in permanent and necessary laws of cause and effect, conceived as we conceive
them.

Thucydides' notion of Fortune may be more closely defined
by comparison and contrast with the opinions of the hardest
and clearest thinker among his contemporaries. Socrates,
according to his friend Xenophon,[1] believed that omens were
signs from the gods or 'the spiritual' (τὸ δαιμόνιον), and
recommended the use of divination to determine actions of
which the future results could not be foreseen. Those who
refused to employ divination in such matters were, he said,
as much 'possessed by an evil spirit' (δαιμονᾶν) as those who
did employ it in cases where ordinary human judgement
(γνώμη) would have sufficed. He 'demonstrated' that men
who supposed that the movements of the heavenly bodies
happened 'by some sort of constraints' (τισὶν ἀνάγκαις) were
fools. He asked (as Thucydides might have asked) whether
'they thought they had by this time a sufficient knowledge
of human things, that they should turn to think about such
matters, neglecting what is human and theorizing about the
divine'. Could they not see that it was impossible for men
to discover such things? Those who most prided themselves
on their theories disagreed with one another like so many
madmen quarrelling over their various delusions. Did they
expect, when they knew about divine things and by what
sort of constraints[2] they happen, to be able to make winds
and rains when they pleased? Or were they content merely
to know how these things happened?

The language here attributed to Socrates is religious; he
speaks of 'the divine' and 'the spiritual' (demonic). His
view is that human events are determined partly by 'foresight' (γνώμη) and partly by the agency of gods or spirits.

---

[1] Xen. *Mem.* i. 1.

[2] Ἀνάγκαις as the context shows, means 'constraints', such as a magician
claims to exercise in rain-making.

Foresight must be used to the utmost; but when it fails, we ought to resort to divination, the only means of discovering the intentions of the other set of agencies. Thucydides, when he is expressing his own opinions, does not speak of 'the divine', but merely of Fortune (Τύχη). But both men are alike in contrasting the field of ordinary human foresight (γνώμη) with the unknown field, which lies beyond it, of inscrutable, non-human powers, whether we call these gods and spirits or simply Fortune. This antithesis is more frequently in Thucydides' thoughts than any other except the famous contrast of 'word' and 'deed'. The two factors—γνώμη, human foresight, purpose, motive, and Τύχη, unforeseen non-human agencies—divide the field between them. They are the two factors—and the only two—which determine the course of a series of events such as a war; neither Socrates nor Thucydides thinks of natural law. One speaker after another in the History dwells on the contrast between a man's own γνώμη over which he has complete control, and Fortune over which he has no control at all.[1] Men may be ruined by fortune (ταῖς τύχαις), but if they are steadfast in purpose (γνώμαις), they have shown themselves true men.[2] Pericles[3] says that human designs and the issues of events alike take a course which is hard to discern; 'and hence we commonly regard Fortune as responsible for whatever falls out contrary to calculation.' Of the plague, Pericles says[4] that it was the only thing that had so far happened in the course of the war 'beyond any man's expectation'. He knows he is hated the more because of it;[5] but this is not fair unless he is to be given credit for unforeseen success as well. 'Divine things (τὰ δαιμόνια) must be borne as a matter

---

[1] iv. 64. 1 e.g. (Hermocrates) μηδὲ μωρίᾳ φιλονικῶν ἡγεῖσθαι τῆς τε οἰκείας γνώμης ὁμοίως αὐτοκράτωρ εἶναι καὶ ἧς οὐκ ἄρχω Τύχης : vi. 78. 2 οὐ γὰρ οἷόν τε ἅμα τῆς τ᾽ ἐπιθυμίας καὶ τῆς Τύχης τὸν αὐτὸν ὁμοίως ταμίαν γενέσθαι.

[2] i. 87. 2 (Peloponnesian generals).

[3] i. 140. 1 ἐνδέχεται γὰρ τὰς ξυμφορὰς τῶν πραγμάτων οὐχ ἧσσον ἀμαθῶς χωρῆσαι ἢ καὶ τὰς διανοίας τοῦ ἀνθρώπου· δι᾽ ὅπερ καὶ τὴν Τύχην, ὅσα ἂν παρὰ λόγον ξυμβῇ, εἰώθαμεν αἰτιᾶσθαι.

[4] ii. 64.

[5] Owing to the Alcmaeonid curse, see p. 101.

of necessity.' He does not argue that the plague *cannot* be his fault ; he speaks of it as a 'divine thing' which he could not be expected to foresee. He *may*, of course, be talking down to his audience ; in using the phrase τὰ δαιμόνια he probably is doing so. But what proof is there that he did not think of the outbreak as a stroke of some unknown power, which it would be rash to call by any more definite name than 'Fortune' ?

There is no need to multiply instances. An examination of all the important passages where this contrast occurs [1] has convinced us that Thucydides does not mean by 'Fortune' simply 'the operation of unknown (*natural*) causes', the working of ordinary causal law in the universe. He is thinking of extraordinary, sudden interventions of non-human agencies, occurring especially at critical moments in warfare, or manifest from time to time in convulsions of Nature. It is these irruptions, and not the normal sway of 'necessary and permanent laws', which defeat the purposes of human γνώμη, and together with γνώμη are the *sole* determinant factors in a series of human events. The normal, ordinary course of Nature attracts no attention and is not felt to need explanation or to be relevant in any way to human action. When he speaks of the future as uncertain, he means not merely that it is unknown, but that it is undetermined, and that human design cannot be sure of completely controlling human events, because other unknown and incalculable agencies may at any moment intervene.

What were the possible alternatives in an age which lacked the true conception of universal causality ? There were two, and only two : Fate and Providence. But both of these were mythical, and associated with superstition. Fate, the older, vaguer, and less personal of the two, was conceived under the aspect of veiled and awful figures : the three Moirai, Ananke, Adrasteia. It was thus that man had his first dim apprehension of that element in the world outside which opposes the will of men and even of gods, thwarts their purpose, and

---

[1] The references will be found in Classen's Introduction to Book I, p. xliv.

beats down their passion. Later ages have at last resolved this inexorable phantom into nothing more—if nothing less—mysterious than the causal sequences of Law. But this solution lay far in the future; Thucydides' contemporaries could conceive it only as a non-human will—a purely mythical entity.

The other alternative was Providence; but any conception of Providence less anthropomorphic than the will of Zeus or the agency of spirits was not possible as yet. The notion of a supreme Mind intervening once, and only once, to bring order into chaos had been reached by Anaxagoras; but this suggestion, so disastrous to the progress of thought, was not developed till Plato took it up. In any case this Mind was merely credited with an initial act of creation; it did not rule the world which it had ordered. Thucydides, moreover, as we saw, had probably considered and rejected Anaxagoras' philosophy. And, after all, the 'Mind' was just as mythical as Fate.

The word 'Chance' suggests to the modern educated intelligence something utterly impersonal; we think at once of the mathematical theory of probability, of the odds at a gambling table, and so on. But we must remember that the current name for 'Chance' in Greek was the name of a mythical Person, Τύχη, a spirit who was actually worshipped by the superstitious, and placated by magical means. The religious spoke of 'the Fortune that comes from the divine', and believed that God's will was manifest in the striking turns of chance, and in spite of appearances was working for the righteous.[1] A less definite belief in Fortune as a divine or spiritual agency was thought worthy of mention by Aristotle.[2] In his own discussion of 'what comes by fortune' or 'spontaneously', Aristotle starts from the very contrast we have noted in Thucydides—the contrast between *purpose* (not Law) and chance. Aristotle, moreover, has no better explanation of Chance than one which involves the *purposes* of

---

[1] v. 104 (We Melians) πιστεύομεν τῇ τύχῃ ἐκ τοῦ θείου μὴ ἐλασσώσεσθαι, ὅτι ὅσιοι πρὸς οὐ δικαίους ἱστάμεθα.

[2] *Phys.* β 4. 196 b 5 εἰσὶ δέ τινες οἷς δοκεῖ εἶναι αἰτία μὲν ἡ Τύχη, ἄδηλος δὲ ἀνθρωπίνῃ διανοίᾳ ὡς θεῖόν τι οὖσα καὶ δαιμονιώτερον.

a mythical person, called Nature. He does not even approach to the conception of causal law, but accounts for 'chance' by the crossing and conflict of these imaginary purposes.[1] Thucydides, who either had never considered or had definitely rejected the notion of purposes in Nature, was even less advanced. He had no explanation to give, and confines himself to the most non-committal name for these invading agencies—'Fortune'.

The recognition of non-human agencies—however undefined—as responsible for observed phenomena is, so far as it goes, a metaphysical belief. It is not a scientific belief, though perfectly consistent with the scientific spirit in the then state of physical knowledge. It is not a religious belief; for Thucydides does not imply that these powers ought to be worshipped or placated. Nothing remains but to call it mythical.

To recur now to the story of Pylos. We noticed that the series of lucky accidents on the Athenian side was paralleled by a series of extraordinary blunders on the Spartan side. In the former series Fortune is prominent to the exclusion of foresight (γνώμη); in the latter we see successive failures of foresight rather than the intervention of Fortune. These count as pieces of luck from the Athenian standpoint; but from the Spartans' they are simply errors of judgement. This point is clearly made in the subsequent speech of the Spartan envoys, who are careful to remark: 'We have not come to this from want of power, nor yet from the pride that comes when power is unduly increased; but *without any change in our position, we failed in judgement*—a point in which the position of all men is alike.'[2] Thus the whole narrative of the occupation illustrates the contrast of fortune and foresight. Fortune, not foresight, has exalted the Athenians; want of foresight, not of fortune, has depressed the Spartans.

It was in this light that Thucydides saw a series of events

[1] *de An.* 434 a 31 ἕνεκά του πάντα ὑπάρχει τὰ φύσει, ἢ συμπτώματα ἔσται τῶν ἕνεκά του.

[2] iv. 18. 2. A translation of this speech will be found on p. 111.

which began with a striking accident, the storm. The element of real luck was sufficient to suggest a belief that Fortune was active to a mind predisposed by superstition or some other cause to look for her agency just here. Thucydides was not superstitious; and he was both careful and acute. The belief accounts for the peculiarities of the narrative; but we have further to account for his having the belief *at just this moment in his story* so strongly upon him as to miss the clues in his informant's report. There must have been something which positively predisposed him to see Fortune at work. We shall explain in the next chapter what this something was.

Here we need only add that the psychological phenomenon we are supposing to have occurred in his mind is closely analogous to what might occur in a Christian historian, narrating from incomplete oral information a critical incident in Church history, which *began with a miracle.* Looking from the outset for the divine purpose, he might easily fail to bring his mind to bear critically on the indications which showed that the whole series of events could be explained as the effect of purely natural causes; for we know from daily experience that a belief in occasional interferences on the part of Providence can co-exist in the same educated mind with a conception of natural causality immeasurably clearer than any that Thucydides could have possessed.

# CHAPTER VII

## THE MOST VIOLENT OF THE CITIZENS

In this chapter we propose to take up the narrative where we left it after the occupation of Pylos. We have reached the point where Cleon comes into the story. We shall mark the circumstances of his entrance, and bring together the other episodes in which Thucydides allows him to appear before us. The hypothesis of 'malignity' would not account for the peculiarities we noted in the earlier narrative where Cleon was not concerned; but it is not finally disposed of as an explanation of the story of Sphacteria, where Cleon is very much concerned. And malignity against Athens as a whole still stands as a theory alternative to the view we expressed in the last chapter. The occupation of Pylos was not an exploit of Cleon's; but it was an exploit of the Athenians. To represent it as a stroke of mere luck might be a means of detracting (at the expense, by the way, of Demosthenes' reputation) from the glory of Athens. These imputations, so damaging to Thucydides' character, so improbable as they seem to us, are still not disproved. We resume the narrative, then, giving as before an abbreviated summary, designed to preserve the points which seem relevant to our problem. That problem is to discover, if we can, something in Thucydides' thoughts about these transactions which will explain how he can have been, as we suggested, positively predisposed to see the work of Fortune in the early part of them. We shall find an influence at work in his mind, the nature of which it will be fairer not to characterize until we have laid the relevant facts before the reader's judgement.

The news came to Lacedaemon that the Peloponnesian fleet

was sunk or captured, and that four hundred and twenty
Spartan citizens with their attendant helots were cut off
on the island, under close watch from the Athenian ships
cruising perpetually round it.[1] The magistrates were sent
to the scene of action, that no time might be lost. They
found that a rescue was impossible. Even if no attack were
made, starvation would speedily reduce the garrison of a
desert island, strewn with rocks and overgrown through
most of its extent with forest. They obtained a truce from
the enemy, and sent envoys to Athens with overtures of
peace.

The envoys addressed the Athenian assembly to the following effect:[2]

'Men of Athens, the Lacedaemonians have sent us to treat
about our men on the island, and to persuade you to such
terms as may at once be advantageous to you and, so far as
the case allows, save our honour in this reverse. If we speak
at some length, this will be no breach of our national custom.
For though it is not our way to use many words when a few
will suffice, we can use more when there is an opportunity
to effect what is wanted, by setting forth some matters that
are pertinent. You must not take them in an unfriendly
way, or as if we were schooling your dullness; but think of
us as putting you in mind of what you know already to be
good counsel.

'You have the opportunity of disposing well of the good
fortune which now is with you, keeping the advantage you
have won, and gaining as well respect and high fame. You
may escape what happens to men when they obtain some
good which is out of the ordinary: *they are always coveting
more in hope, because their present good fortune likewise was
unexpected.*[3] But those who have oftenest come in for the
ups and downs have good reason to be above all mistrustful
of their successes. Your city, no less than ours, may very

---

[1] iv. 14. 5 ff

[2] iv. 17 ff. The first half of the speech is translated verbatim.

[3] iv. 17. 4 αἰεὶ γὰρ τοῦ πλέονος ἐλπίδι ὀρέγονται διὰ τὸ καὶ τὰ παρόντα ἀδοκήτως
εὐτυχῆσαι.

well have learnt this by experience. You may read the
lesson again by looking closely at our present misfortunes,
when we who have the highest repute among the Hellenes
come before you and here make requests which formerly we
thought ourselves more in the position to grant. But note
that we have not come to this from want of power nor yet
from the pride that comes when power is unduly increased ;
but, without any change in our position, we failed in judgement (γνώμη)—a point in which the position of all men is
alike. Therefore you too have no reason to think, because
your city is now strong in itself and in its new acquisitions,
that the hand of Fortune (τὸ τῆς Τύχης) also will always be
on your side. Wise men find safety in setting down their
gains to uncertainty—it is they who will meet misfortunes
too with sober foresight—and know that war does not wait
upon a man's choice of this or that enterprise to take in hand,
but goes as the chances (αἱ τύχαι), here or there, may lead.
Such men are least of all likely to trip ; and not being elated
by confidence that their footing in the struggle is sure, they
will be most disposed to end it in the hour of their good
fortune. And this is how you, Athenians, would do well to
deal with us, to prevent its being thought at some future day,
if ever you should reject us and fall into one of the many
possible disasters, that your advantage now, when all has
gone well with you, was due to fortune (τύχη) ; whereas you
may, if you choose, leave to later times a reputation for
strength combined with prudence, beyond the reach of
risk.'

The envoys go on still further to dwell on the prudence
of reasonable terms as the best security for a lasting peace,
and to recommend again the moderate use of unexpected
victory. An adversary who will only be exasperated by
violence (βιασθείς) and overbearing extortion will feel in
honour the obligation laid upon him by conciliatory sacrifices.
'If you decide for peace, you have the opportunity of becoming firm friends with the Lacedaemonians, upon their
own invitation, and by way of concession instead of violence
(βιασαμένοις).'

The narrative continues. 'The Lacedaemonians said all this
with the idea that the Athenians had formerly been desirous
to make terms and had only been prevented by their own
opposition, but that now peace was offered they would
welcome it and restore the prisoners. But the Athenians
thought that, now they held the men on the island, it was
always in their power to make terms whenever they chose
and they *coveted something more*.[1] They were urged on
above all by Cleon, the son of Cleainetos, who was the popular
leader in those days and stood highest in the confidence of
the multitude. He persuaded them to answer that first of
all the men on the island must surrender themselves and their
arms and be conveyed to Athens; when that was done, the
Lacedaemonians were to restore Nisaea, Pegae, Troezen, and
Achaea. On these conditions they could recover their men and
make a peace of such duration as both parties should approve.
The places mentioned had not been taken in war, but had
been surrendered under the former treaty by the Athenians
in a time of reverse. Then it had been Athens that was
suing for terms.[2]

'The envoys made no reply, beyond requesting the appointment of a commission to hear both sides and quietly come to
any understanding they could about details. Cleon fell upon
this proposal with all his vehemence.[3] He had always known,
he said, that they had no fair intentions, and now it was
clear. They would not say a word before the people, but

---

[1] iv. 21. 2 τοῦ δε πλέονος ὠρέγοντο. Compare the envoys' use of this phrase
above (p. 111, note 3).

[2] The places had been evacuated when a 'thirty years' peace' was concluded at the end of the earlier Peloponnesian war, in which Athens had
at first been brilliantly successful and later lost all, or nearly all, she had
gained. In the course of the present war they had never been in Athenian
hands, and the demand for their 'restoration' (ἀποδόντας) was impudent as
well as extortionate. We have already explained why Cleon stood out for
the two Megarian ports; but we must remember that this demand was to
Thucydides as inexplicable as Pericles' obstinacy about the Megarian decrees.
The demand for Achaea was also part of the western policy. That for
Troezen may have been a blind.

[3] iv. 22. 2 Κλέων δὲ ἐνταῦθα δὴ πολὺς ἐνέκειτο. The particle δή hints that
such a reasonable proposal was just the thing to unchain all his violence.

wanted to be closeted with a select few. No! if they had
any honest meaning, let them declare it to all! But the
Lacedaemonians saw that even if they were disposed to make
some concessions in their distress, it was impossible to speak
before a multitude, for fear lest, if their proposals failed, they
should be misrepresented to their allies. They saw too that
the Athenians were not going to do as they were invited on
reasonable conditions. So they went home unsuccessful.'

We shall return later to the sentences in which Cleon first
appears upon the scene in this episode. He is introduced as
as if we had never heard of him.[1] In point of fact he has
come before us once already—though only once—namely, in
the debate at which the assembly revoked its first ferocious
order for a general massacre of innocent and guilty in the revolted city of Mytilene. The opponent of that generous impulse
of remorse, the insistent advocate of cruelty and revenge, was
Cleon. As soon as the change of feeling became known, ' the
assembly was immediately summoned and various opinions
were put forward. Cleon, the son of Cleainetos, who had
carried the previous proposal to put the Mytileneans to death,
came forward again to speak. He was at all times the most
violent of the citizens,[2] and just now stood by far the highest
in the confidence of the people.' Then follows the speech,
which, for characterization, is a masterpiece. There is not
a touch of the gross or cringing flatterer ; it is not the Cleon
of Aristophanes. He breaks out at once in violent denuncia-
tion of the sovereign people. A democracy is incapable of
empire. They are fooled by the fine speeches of hireling
orators ; they weakly vacillate before appeals to pity and the
generosity of strength. They are ready to forfeit the legitimate
satisfaction of revenge, and thereby to hasten the dissolution
of their power, whose only bonds are force and fear. The

---

[1] The hypothesis of interpolation here from iii. 36. 6 may be dismissed.
The phrase here is similar, but differs in that Cleon is here correctly called
δημαγωγός (i.e. προστάτης τοῦ δήμου). He had become so since the Mytilenean
affair, by the death of Lysicles.

[2] iii. 36. 6 βιαιότατος τῶν πολιτῶν.

allies need a bloody example to teach them submission. Otherwise, let the Athenians resign their empire and stop at home to play at their arm-chair morality! Every sentence rings with the tone of insolent violence, the strength which treads down pity and 'in its haste for vengeance upon others thinks fit to abrogate those common laws of humanity wherein had lain its own hope of mercy in the hour of defeat'.[1]

After this one appearance, which leaves an indelible impression of unrestrained force and cruelty, Cleon drops out of the story till the present passage. The counsellor of violent revenge is now the counsellor of grasping extortion. 'The Athenians *coveted more*'; and the man above all who urges them on is Cleon.[2] It is he who persuades them to formulate an extravagant demand which amounts to breaking off the negotiations. As in the case of the Mytilenean decree, the Athenians are offered a chance for reconsideration; the envoys propose a commission to go quietly into the details and come to a reasonable understanding. Again, as in the former case, Cleon intervenes, and 'falls upon the proposal with all his vehemence' in slanderous accusation. The parallel is striking; but here it ends. The Mytilenean decision was revoked in spite of him, and Athens was just, and only just, saved from an awful act of insolent cruelty; but this time Cleon prevails. 'Confident in the hope of their strength,'[3] certain of being able to make terms when they choose, the assembly dismisses the ambassadors to return home empty-handed. Cleon has had his way: we shall see whither it will lead him.

It would take too long to follow the subsequent story in detail: we will rapidly resume it.[4]

Winter was coming on, and the Spartans on the island

---

[1] iii. 84. 3 (not referring to Cleon).

[2] iv. 21. 2 τοῦ δὲ πλέονος ὠρέγοντο. μάλιστα δὲ αὐτοὺς ἐνῆγε Κλέων. τοῦ πλέονος ὀρέγεσθαι is the verb corresponding to the noun πλεονεξία, 'covetous desire to get the better.'

[3] v. 14. 1 ἔχοντες τὴν ἐλπίδα τῆς ῥώμης πιστήν (referring to this occasion).

[4] iv. 26 ff.

were still uncaptured; they were kept alive by venturous blockade-running. The stormy season would soon make it difficult to provision the Athenian fleet. The Athenians at home began to repent of their refusal to make terms,[1] and dark looks were turned on Cleon. Repentance was no more to his mind now than it had been in the Mytilenean affair; for, personally committed to the rejection of peace, he had gone too far to retreat without blasting his career. The dramatic story of his challenge to the generals is well known. 'He came forward and said he was not afraid of the Lacedae-monians.' He would sail himself with only a small force of light-armed auxiliaries,[2] and with these and the soldiers already at Pylos in twenty days he would either bring the Lacedaemonians home alive or kill them on the spot. He chose Demosthenes, already on the scene of action, for his colleague. 'Laughter seized the Athenians at his wild words;[3] but they were welcome to moderate men who reflected that they would gain one or other of two goods: either they would be rid of Cleon, which they would have greatly preferred, or if they were disappointed, he would put the Lacedae-monians in their hands.'

Cleon's stroke was brilliantly successful; but all the credit, in Thucydides' narrative, falls not to him, but to Demosthenes, who again receives the timely aid of Fortune.[4] Demosthenes, we are told, had already, before Cleon left Athens, planned an attack upon Sphacteria,[5] and he was encouraged by a fire which burnt the woods on the island and so exposed the enemy. The fire had been 'unintentionally' kindled by an Athenian soldier, one of a party who had landed on the shore to cook their midday meal. 'A wind sprang up and the greater part of the woods were burnt before they knew what

---

[1] iv. 27. 2.

[2] 28. 4. It has been observed that the choice of light-armed troops is put as if it were a further piece of rashness. The sequel proved that it was prudent.

[3] iv. 28. 5 κουφολογίᾳ.

[4] Plut. *Nic.* viii speaks of Cleon on this occasion as τύχῃ χρησάμενος ἀγαθῇ καὶ στρατηγήσας ἄριστα μετὰ Δημοσθένους.

[5] 29. 2.

was happening.'[1] But for this lucky accident, the attack
upon so strong a body of the best fighting-men in Greece,
sheltered by thick undergrowth, would have been almost a
forlorn hope. Really, the gales might be in league with
Athens! The storm which first drove the fleet into Pylos
is seconded by the wind which sweeps the forest fire over
Sphacteria. When the troops landed for the attack, 'the
dispositions were made by Demosthenes who had originally
planned the assault.'[2] The Spartans were driven slowly
to their last stand, and the two hundred and ninety-two who
were left alive surrendered.

'So the promise of Cleon, *mad as it was,* resulted in
success: for he brought the men within twenty days, just as
he had undertaken.'[3]

Much ink has been expended on the phrase: 'mad as it
was.' How can Thucydides call the promise mad, at the
very moment when he is recording its fulfilment? The best
comment is a sentence from Herodotus, where Artabanus is
warning Xerxes against rash haste in taking up so great an
enterprise as the conquest of Greece. 'I know not,' he says,
'aught in the world that so profits a man as taking good
counsel with himself; for even if things fall out against one's
hopes, still one has counselled well, though fortune has made
the counsel of none effect: *whereas if a man counsels ill
and luck follows, he has gotten a windfall, but his counsel is
none the less silly.*'[4]

What use will Cleon make of his windfall? Surely, now,
the Athenians will tempt fortune no further. They resolve
to keep the captives in chains 'till some agreement shall
be reached'. Meanwhile the Messenians from Naupactos
are established at Pylos, from whence they make descents;
deserting helots begin to come in and join them. This was

[1] 30. 2 ἐμπρήσαντός τινος κατὰ μικρὸν τῆς ὕλης ἄκοντος καὶ ἀπὸ τούτου
πνεύματος ἐπιγενομένου τὸ πολὺ αὐτῆς ἔλαθε κατακαυθέν.

[2] 32. 4. Thucydides seems to emphasize the skill of Demosthenes, as if
he were half aware that the Pylos narrative hardly did him justice.

[3] iv. 39. 3 καὶ τοῦ Κλέωνος καίπερ μανιώδης οὖσα ἡ ὑπόσχεσις ἀπέβη.

[4] Hdt. vii. 10 (δ') Rawlinson's trans.

the only danger which could touch the Lacedaemonians at home, and they sent a second embassy for peace. Here is another opening for moderation in victory. But no! 'The Athenians were *coveting greater things*'[1]—again that ominous phrase—'and though the Spartans sent again and again, they kept on dismissing the envoys unsuccessful. Thus ended the affair of Pylos.'

We lose sight of Cleon till the scene of war is shifted to Chalcidice. The combatants had actually concluded a truce with provisions for the discussion of a permanent peace; but the negotiations broke down through Brasidas' refusal to surrender Skione, which had revolted from Athens just two days after the truce had been declared. The Athenians in a rage carried a resolution for the destruction of Skione and the massacre of its inhabitants.[2] Another act of force and fury—once more the entrance-cue for 'the most violent of the citizens'. 'They were induced to carry the decree by the advice of Cleon.' This, however, is but a passing glimpse. The last scene opens at the beginning of Book V.

Cleon himself sails with an expedition to Chalcidice, where he is to meet with more than his match. Brasidas, ensconced in Amphipolis, lays a trap into which Cleon is driven by the impatience of his own men and the rashness of his disposition. 'He behaved as he had done at Pylos, where his good luck had given him confidence in his own wisdom.[3] He never so much as expected that any one would come out to fight him. . . . He imagined he could go and come, without a battle, whenever he chose. . . . He even thought he had made a mistake in coming without siege-engines; for, had he brought them, he could have taken the place in its undefended state.' Brasidas knew how to turn to advantage the contempt of an enemy. A sudden sally from the town; and the Athenians' disorderly retreat breaks into a rout. 'The Athenian right made a

---

[1] iv. 41. 3 μειζόνων τε ὠρέγοντο.

[2] iv. 122. 6.

[3] v. 7. 3 ἐχρήσατο τῷ τρόπῳ ᾧπερ καὶ ἐς τὴν Πύλον εὐτυχήσας ἐπίστευσέ τι φρονεῖν.

better stand, and though Cleon, who indeed had never thought of holding his ground, fled immediately and was overtaken by a Myrkinian targeteer and slain, the rest rallied on the crest of the hill and repulsed Clearidas two or three times, and they did not give in until the Myrkinian and Chalcidian horse and the targeteers hemmed them round and broke them with a shower of darts.' [1] Thus contemptuously is Cleon's end recorded: the victor of Sphacteria is spurned out of the history in a parenthesis. Mad elation and self-confidence, born of unexpected luck, have brought him to the ignominious death of a coward.

The first of these incidents which calls for remark is the speech of the Spartan envoys in the abortive negotiations for peace which came between the occupation of Pylos and the capture of Sphacteria. This speech, half of which we translated, is a curious document. We remember that Thucydides in the introduction to the History [2] remarked with regret on the difficulty of remembering or learning by report the exact words used by statesmen and envoys. The speeches set down represent, he told us, 'what seemed to me to be just what would have been necessary for each speaker to say on the occasion, and I have kept as closely as possible to the general sense of the actual words.' In the present instance it is obvious that in a way the 'general sense' of the envoys' plea has been preserved. They must have formulated the Spartans' request for peace, asked for the release of the prisoners, and hinted—they could do no more till they had some certainty of success—that the 'friendship of Sparta', the only *quid pro quo* openly named, would turn out to cover some more tangible return. From our knowledge of Laconian eloquence and from examples of it elsewhere in Thucydides,[3] we should expect

[1] v. 10. 9.

[2] i. 22.

[3] The following are the other speeches made by Spartans in the first part of the history: (1) Archidamus advises delay in going to war, i. 80-5 (strictly to the point ; short eulogy of Spartan institutions, 84); (2) Sthenelaidas, i. 86 (extremely curt) ; (3) Archidamus to Peloponnesian generals, ii. 11 (short and businesslike); (4) Archidamus to Plataeans, ii. 72 (a few

further a few crisp, dry aphorisms about luck: 'To-day to
me, to-morrow to thee.' The situation itself, as we are later
told, precluded any definite statement about the only question
of practical business : what substantial equivalent the Spartans had to offer in exchange for the prisoners. In such
circumstances, the whole case might be put in three minutes;
we do not expect a homily, five-sixths of which are devoted
to a general disquisition on the theme of moderation in
prosperity. Nothing could be less 'laconic' than the speech
Thucydides has given us. Further, he was quite aware of
this, and knew that his readers would remark it. The exordium
apologizes for what may seem a departure from national
custom : 'It is not our way to use many words when few
will suffice'; but the justification offered : 'we can use
more when there is an opportunity to effect what is wanted
by setting forth some matters that are pertinent,' sounds
vague and indeed (to be candid) all but meaningless in the
mouths of the speakers. We suspect that the matters to be
set forth are more to the point in explaining what Thucydides
has in his mind than in influencing the Athenians to abandon
the fruits of victory. There is obviously some connexion
between the sacrifice of dramatic probability here and the
sacrifice of historic probability in the Pylos episode. In the
handling of 'what was done' Thucydides has presented the
action as undesigned and fortuitous. In the speech we have
a dissertation on luck in war and moderation in unlooked-for
success.

The Lacedaemonians, we shall be told, are 'moralizing'.
A sudden reversal of fortune was in itself a phenomenon
peculiarly interesting to the Greek mind, and the theme of
moderation in prosperity was the standing moral which they
drew from such occurrences—a most venerable commonplace.

---

sentences); (5) Brasidas at Acanthus, iv. 85 (length apologized for by
Thucydides : 'for a Lacedaemonian, he was not an incapable speaker,'
84. 2) ; (6) Brasidas to his men, iv. 126 (short and pointed); (7) Brasidas to
his men, v. 9 (similar to the last). None of them presents a parallel to that
of the envoys on this occasion.

That, of course, is true; but it does not explain the problem
of the Pylos narrative. If that were all, we should have to
suppose that Thucydides distorted his facts there for the
purpose of moralizing—a supposition we have proved incredible.

Let us say, then, that Thucydides is using the device of
speech-writing to convey his own opinion that Athens ought
to have made peace after Sphacteria, and that Cleon's
exorbitant demands were a mistake in policy. This certainly
was Thucydides' opinion; but again it gives no answer to our
problem. The policy was just as bad, whether the occupation
of Pylos was casual or carefully designed in every detail.

It is evident that the moral of the speech was, to Thucydides' view, illustrated by the subsequent career of Cleon.
He behaved at Amphipolis ' as he had done at Pylos, where
his good luck had given him confidence in his own wisdom '.
' He never so much as expected that any one would come out
to fight him ', and so on. We are to understand that Cleon's
head was turned by the success of his ' mad ' undertaking.
Elated and over-confident, he rushes into a still more difficult
enterprise. That is how we put it in our histories; but the
Greeks used a somewhat different language, and put a somewhat different construction on such a sequence of events as
this. They interpreted it according to a certain philosophy
of human nature which it will concern us to take account of.

If we turn back to the episode in which Cleon makes his
first appearance in the History, we find this philosophy set
forth in remarkable terms by Diodotus in the Mytilenean
debate. Diodotus is replying to the great speech of Cleon
which we referred to above; he explains how futile is
Cleon's policy of inflicting exemplary punishment on revolted
allies. The question of the purpose and true nature of
punitive justice was much in the air at this time, and the
speech of Diodotus is Thucydides' contribution to the controversy. The passage is so interesting, and so important for
our purpose, that we will give it in full.

' In the cities of Greece the death penalty has been affixed
to many offences actually less than this; yet still, intoxicated

by their hopes, men take the risk.[1] No man ever, before embarking on a dangerous course, passed sentence on himself that he would not succeed in his design; and no city entering on revolt ever set about doing so with the conviction that her resources—whether her own or obtained from her allies— were inadequate. All men are born to error in public, as in private, conduct; and there is no law that will hinder them; for mankind has exhausted the whole catalogue of penalties, continually adding fresh ones, to find some means of lessening the wrongs they suffer from evil-doers. Probably in early ages the punishments affixed to the worst offences were milder; but as transgressions went on, in time they seldom stopped short of death; yet still, even so, there are transgressors.

'Either then some greater terror than death must be discovered, or at any rate death is no deterrent. No; poverty inspires daring by the stress of necessity; the licence of prosperity inspires covetous ambition by insolence and pride; and the other conditions of human life, as each is possessed by some irremediable and mastering power, by passion lead men on to perilous issues.

'Desire and Hope are never wanting—the one leading the way, the other busy in attendance. Desire devising the attempt, and Hope flattering with suggestions of the riches in Fortune's store, very often lead to ruin, and, invisible as they are, prevail over the dangers that are seen.

'And besides these Fortune contributes no less to intoxication; for sometimes she presents herself unexpectedly at a man's side and leads him forward to face danger at a disadvantage; and cities even more than individuals, in proportion as their stake is the greatest of all—freedom or empire— and each, when all are with him, unthinkingly rates himself the higher.[2]

---

[1] iii. 45. 1 τῇ ἐλπίδι ἐπαιρόμενοι κινδυνεύουσι.

[2] iii. 45. 4 ἀλλ' ἡ μὲν πενία ἀνάγκῃ τὴν τόλμαν παρέχουσα, ἡ δὲ ἐξουσία ὕβρει τὴν πλεονεξίαν καὶ φρονήματι, αἱ δ' ἄλλαι ξυντυχίαι ὀργῇ τῶν ἀνθρώπων ὡς ἑκάστη τις κατέχεται ὑπ' ἀνηκέστου τινὸς κρείσσονος ἐξάγουσιν ἐς τοὺς κινδύνους.

ἥ τε Ἐλπὶς καὶ ὁ Ἔρως ἐπὶ παντί, ὁ μὲν ἡγούμενος, ἡ δ' ἐφεπομένη, καὶ ὁ μὲν

'In a word, it is impossible—and only a simpleton would
suppose the contrary—that human nature, when it is passion-
ately bent upon some act, should be averted from its purpose
by force of laws or any other terror.'

We shall have something to say later of the extraordinary
and highly poetical language in which this theory of human
nature is set forth; here we shall note the main features of
the theory itself, the far-reaching significance of which will
become apparent in the sequel. We observe that human
nature is subject to two sorts of influences, which correspond
to the two general names γνώμη (in the widest sense) and Τύχη.
(1) There are, first, the man's own vices of *character*—'daring,
covetousness, pride' and the other 'irremediable and mastering
powers' which 'possess' him. (2) These vices, in the second
place, are 'supplied' or inspired by the external circumstances
of his *condition* (ξυντυχία)—especially by the two extreme
conditions of grinding poverty and licentious prosperity.

Next, in these conditions man is peculiarly liable to
*temptation*, which comes to him in two ways. (1) One of
two violent *passions* may seize on him. Hope is busy in
attendance flattering him with suggestions of the wealth in
Fortune's store; unrestrained Desire leads him on to lay
plans for yet further gain. (2) *Fortune*, herself, intervenes to
complete his intoxication. Appearing at his side unexpectedly,
she encourages him by giving success which, though he has
not designed it, he is apt to credit to his own ability. So he
comes to overrate his strength, and face dangers which are
beyond it.

In this scheme the two factors, human character and

---

τὴν ἐπιβουλὴν ἐκφροντίζων, ἡ δὲ τὴν εὐπορίαν τῆς Τύχης ὑποτιθεῖσα, πλεῖστα βλά-
πτουσι, καὶ ὄντα ἀφανῆ κρείσσω ἐστὶ τῶν ὁρωμένων δεινῶν.

καὶ ἡ Τύχη ἐπ' αὐτοῖς οὐδὲν ἔλασσον ξυμβάλλεται ἐς τὸ ἐπαίρειν· ἀδοκήτως γὰρ
ἔστιν ὅτε παρισταμένη καὶ ἐκ τῶν ὑποδεεστέρων κινδυνεύειν τινὰ προάγει· καὶ οὐχ
ἧσσον τὰς πόλεις, ὅσῳ περὶ τῶν μεγίστων τε, ἐλευθερίας ἢ ἄλλων ἀρχῆς, καὶ μετὰ
πάντων ἕκαστος ἀλογίστως ἐπὶ πλέον τι αὐτὸν ἐδόξασεν. The meaning of the last
clause seems to be that intoxication is infectious : each man in a crowd is
more carried away than he would be if he were alone. For the construction
αὐτὸν ἐδόξασεν compare Plato, *Philebus*, 48 E.

external Fortune, appear twice over, in different aspects. First, we are thinking of comparatively permanent conditions, such as extreme poverty or wealth, and of the comparatively permanent vices which gain upon a man slowly in such circumstances. Second, we have the sudden access, at critical moments, of temptation under the two forms of a violent passion, Hope or Desire, and of Fortune appearing in unexpected successes. These besetting agencies take advantage of the faults of character already produced by Prosperity and Penury, and they bring about a condition of blind intoxication, the eclipse of rational foresight. When this state is reached the man is marked for his doom; neither the force of laws nor any other terror will ' avert' his fatal course.

The point which now concerns us is that the train of thought in these few sentences of Diodotus' speech contains the motive and the moral of *the whole of Cleon's career as Thucydides has chosen to present it*. We know, from other sources, that Cleon was prominent in politics before the war broke out. After Pericles' death he soon became the leading Athenian statesman and remained so to the end of his life. During all this time he appears to have led the policy of the war-party, and in a history of the war we should expect to hear of him constantly. But out of all his public actions Thucydides has selected three, and only three,[1] to put before us. These are the Mytilenean debate; the capture of Sphacteria and the negotiations preceding it; his last campaign at Amphipolis. On the first of these occasions Thucydides puts in his mouth a speech which is evidently meant to reveal the character of the 'most violent of the citizens'; one of the vices of prosperity, ruthless 'insolence' ($\H{v}\beta\rho\iota\varsigma$), might be taken as its keynote. On the second occasion, at Sphacteria, we see him at a moment when Fortune, the temptress, unexpectedly stands at his side. His promise was 'mad' for he was intoxicated with ambitious passion, and he had just betrayed another vice of prosperity, 'covetousness' ($\pi\lambda\epsilon\text{ov}\epsilon\xi\acute{\iota}a$). Thucy-

---

[1] Except the glimpse at iv. 122. 6 where Cleon advocates the massacre of the Skioneans. This repeats and renews the impression of the Mytilenean debate.

dides reiterates in the envoys' un-laconic speech just that part of his theory of human nature which is relevant—the danger of covetousness in the flush of success. In the third and last episode, at Amphipolis, Thucydides in his own person points out that his train of *causes* has led to its inevitable end. Infatuate pride ($\phi\rho\acute{o}\nu\eta\mu\alpha$), the third vice of prosperity, brings ruin.

The three episodes, put together, form the complete outline of a *drama,* conforming to a well-known type which we shall study in the next chapter. The first act reveals the hero's character; the second contains the crisis; the third, the catastrophe. But though complete in outline, the drama is obviously defective in other respects. The reason is that, while the plot is tragic, Cleon is not a tragic figure. It is true that at his first appearance, in the Mytilenean speech, he does attain tragic proportions, for the character is treated with perfect seriousness and expressed with astonishing force. But to allow Cleon to remain on this level would have been fatal to Thucydides' larger design, which we shall study later; it would never do to let him become the hero of this part of the war. Besides, Thucydides could not conceal his contempt, and probably saw no reason to conceal it. On both these grounds he does not allow Cleon a second full-length speech. Modern historians complain that Thucydides ought to have given his reply to the Spartan envoys before Sphacteria; that he has missed an obvious opportunity of stating the policy of the war-party; and that there is some unfairness in not doing so. But artistic considerations were decisive. A long speech from Cleon at this point, if it even approached the force and impressiveness of the Mytilenean speech, would have established him as a hero, or a villain on the heroic scale; he would have bulked much too largely for a minor character. Hence Cleon's little personal drama, though its plot is kept complete, is deliberately spoilt;—'laughter seized the Athenians at his wild words.' From that moment he is degraded from the tragic rank; and his story runs out pitiably to its contemptible close—in a parenthesis.

What immediately concerns us now is the difference that

this dramatizing of Cleon must make to our view of Thucydides' treatment of him. It is evident that the historian saw him not purely, or even primarily, as an historic person, but as a type of character. His career is seen through the medium of a preconceived theory of human nature, and only that part of the career is presented which conforms to the theory and illustrates a certain part of it. The principle of this selection has no place in historic method; it has no place in Thucydides' original design of a detailed journal of the war. The Mytilenean episode, for instance, shows us Cleon at a moment when his action had *no* effect on the course of the war, since his advice was rejected. The principle is artistic, idealizing, dramatic. Thucydides has stripped away all the accidents and particulars of the historic individual; he has even stripped away his personality, leaving only an abstract, generalized type. Now, we do not deny that Thucydides both hated and despised the man Cleon; or that these feelings operated as a psychological cause to facilitate the erection of their object into an impersonation of insolent Violence and Covetousness. But when this result was effected, the attitude of feeling must have undergone a simultaneous change. To idealize is an act of imaginative creation, and the creator cannot feel towards the creature as one man feels towards another. He is a spectator, not an actor in the drama revealed to his larger vision. We need talk no longer of ' a personal grudge against an able, but coarse, noisy, ill-bred, audacious man'; for none of these epithets, except ' able', quite fits the impression we get from the Mytilenean speech. Nor is it even a man, a complete concrete personality, that is there presented; it is rather a symbol, an idea. The personality is contemned and thrust out, and with its banishment personal antipathy gives place to a noble indignation against Violence itself—αὐτὸ τὸ βίαιον, as Plato might call it. We have left the plane of pedestrian history for the 'more serious and philosophic' plane of poetry.

We have here reached a broad distinction of type between

Thucydides' work and history as it was written in the nineteenth century. The latter can be described generally as *realistic*, if we stretch this term to cover both the scientific (and sometimes dull) school and their graphic (and sometimes inaccurate) rivals. The scientific principle is realistic in the sense that it tends to regard any ascertainable fact as worth ascertaining, and even as neither more nor less valuable than any other. The graphic principle is realistic in that it attempts to visualize the past, and is as careful to tell us that Robespierre was sea-green as it is to tell us that he was incorruptible. The realism which has grown upon the novel and the drama has taught us that to see a man's exterior is halfway to understanding his character. Hence the graphic school delight in personal, biographical touches; and in delineating an age they find a broadside or a folk-song more illuminating than the contents of a minister's dispatch-box.

Now Thucydides belongs to neither of these schools; or rather he tried to be scientific and hoped to be dull, but he failed. As his work goes on the principle that governs his selection and his presentation of events is less and less scientific. He originally meant to choose the facts which would be useful in the vulgar practical sense; he projected a descriptive textbook in strategy. But he ended by choosing those which were useful for a very different end—a lesson in morality; and he comes, as we shall see, to treat events out of all proportion to their significance as moments in a war between Athens and Sparta. The graphic method he keeps strictly for events, not for persons. The fortification of Pylos, for instance, is vividly pictured in a single sentence describing the mudlarks. Imagination, with this sharply defined glimpse of the thing seen to work from, can fill in all the rest. But the characters are never treated graphically; he does not tell us that Cleon was a tanner with a voice like Kykloboros, or that Pericles was called 'squill-head' from the shape of his skull. He tells us that the former was the 'most violent', the latter the 'most powerful' of the citizens. The characters throughout are idealized to a very high degree of abstraction —a method which is not practised by either school of moderns.

Our attention in the next chapter will be directed to a closer analysis of this idealistic treatment. We shall study the method still as exemplified in the story of Cleon; but, as we have said, Cleon is not the hero of the history as a whole, or even of this part of it; the cycle of his fortunes is only an epicycle on a larger orbit. But orbit and epicycle exhibit the same type of curve. We have to trace this curve in both and also to study the relation of the smaller body to the greater. Cleon, in other words, has two aspects: he is quasi-hero of his own little tragi-comedy and also a minor character in the tragedy of Athens.

# CHAPTER VIII

## MYTHISTORIA AND THE DRAMA

THE epithet 'dramatic' has often been applied to Thucydides' work; but usually nothing more is meant than that he allows his persons to speak for themselves, and presents their character with vividness.[1] The dramatization which we have pointed out in the treatment of Cleon is a very different thing; it is a principle of construction which, wherever it operates, determines the selection of incidents to be recorded, and the proportions and perspective assigned them. In this chapter we shall attempt to describe and analyse the type of drama that we have to do with, and to trace the literary influence under which Thucydides worked.

We ought first, perhaps, to meet a possible objection. It may be urged that Thucydides in his preface expressly excludes anything of the nature of poetical construction from his literal record of what was said and what was done. He criticizes the methods of poets and story-writers, and warns us that, at the cost of making his story 'somewhat unattractive', he intends to exclude 'the mythical' (τὸ μυθῶδες). He cannot, therefore, it might be inferred, have done what we have thought we found him doing. But we would ask for a careful examination of the passage in question. What was in Thucydides' thoughts when he wrote it, and above all, what precisely did he mean to exclude when he banished 'the mythical'?

The words occur towards the end of the introduction,[2]

---

[1] This seems to be all that Plutarch means: ὁ Θουκυδίδης ἀεὶ τῷ λόγῳ πρὸς ταύτην ἁμιλλᾶται τὴν ἐνάργειαν, οἷον θεατὴν ποιῆσαι τὸν ἀκροατήν, de Glor. Ath. 3.
[2] i. 1-23.

which is designed to establish Thucydides' belief that the
Peloponnesian war was the most memorable of all that had
ever been in Greece. The possible rivals, he points out, are
the Trojan war and the Persian invasion. For the first of
these events the only literary evidence we have is that of
the epic poets, and chiefly of Homer, whose record cannot
be checked by direct observation, while much of his theme
through the lapse of time has passed, or 'won over', into
the region of the mythical and incredible.[1] The only tests
we have are certain indications in the existing condition of
Greece which seem inconsistent with the past state of things
as represented by the literary authorities. With these indications we must be content; and they suffice to show that the
epic poets embellished their tale by exaggeration.[2] The
story-writers, again, on whom we depend for the history of
the Persian wars, were not bent upon accurate statement of
truth;—witness the carelessness of Herodotus about points
of detail. Their object was rather to make their recitations
attractive and amusing to their audience; and if we discount
their evidence accordingly, we shall find, going by ascertained
facts alone, that the Peloponnesian war was the greatest
ever seen.

Thucydides next passes abruptly to the formulation of his
own method; he intends to record what was said and what
was done as accurately and literally as possible. The result,
he then remarks, will probably be somewhat unattractive to
an audience at a recitation, because the facts recorded will
have nothing 'mythical' about them;[3] he will be content,
however, if they are judged useful by people who wish to
know the plain truth of what happened.

The phrase 'winning over into the mythical' is illuminating.
It suggests the transformation which begins to steal over all
events from the moment of their occurrence, unless they are

---

[1] i. 21 τὰ πολλὰ ὑπὸ χρόνου αὐτῶν ἀπίστως ἐπὶ τὸ μυθῶδες ἐκνενικηκότα.

[2] i. 21 ὡς ποιηταὶ ὑμνήκασι περὶ αὐτῶν ἐπὶ τὸ μεῖζον κοσμοῦντες. Cf. i. 10. 3
τῇ Ὁμήρου ποιήσει, εἴ τι χρὴ κἀνταῦθα πιστεύειν, ἣν εἰκὸς ἐπὶ τὸ μεῖζον μὲν
ποιητὴν ὄντα κοσμῆσαι.

[3] i. 22. 4 καὶ ἐς μὲν ἀκρόασιν ἴσως τὸ μὴ μυθῶδες αὐτῶν ἀτερπέστερον φανεῖται ...

arrested and pinned down in writing by an alert and trained observer. Even then some selection cannot be avoided—a selection, moreover, determined by irrelevant psychological factors, by the accidents of interest and attention. Moment by moment the whole fabric of events dissolves in ruins and melts into the past; and all that survives of the thing done passes into the custody of a shifting, capricious, imperfect, human memory. Nor is the mutilated fragment allowed to rest there, as on a shelf in a museum; imagination seizes on it and builds it with other fragments into some ideal construction, which may have a plan and outline laid out long before this fresh bit of material came to the craftsman's hand to be worked into it, as the drums of fallen columns are built into the rampart of an Acropolis. Add to this the cumulative effects of oral tradition. One ideal edifice falls into ruin; pieces of it, conglomerates of those ill-assorted and haphazard fragments, are carried to another site and worked into a structure of, perhaps, a quite different model. Thus fact shifts into legend, and legend into myth. The facts *work loose*; they are detached from their roots in time and space and shaped into a story. The story is moulded and remoulded by imagination, by passion and prejudice, by religious preconception or aesthetic instinct, by the delight in the marvellous, by the itch for a moral, by the love of a good story; and the thing becomes a legend. A few irreducible facts will remain; no more, perhaps, than the names of persons and places—Arthur,[1] Caerleon, Camelot; but even these may at last drop out or be turned by a poet into symbols. ' By Arthur,' said Tennyson, ' I always meant the soul, and by the Round Table the passions and capacities of man.' The history has now all but won over into the mythical. Change the names, and every trace of literal fact will have vanished; the story will have escaped from time into eternity.

When we study this process, we seem to make out two phases of it, which, for the criticism of Thucydides, it is necessary to distinguish. The more important and pervasive

---

[1] We assume that Arthur was historic; but he may have been Arcturus for all we know.

of the two is the moulding of fact into types of myth contributed by traditional habits of thought. This process
of *infiguration* (if we may coin the word) may be carried
to any degree. Sometimes the facts happen to fit the mould,
and require hardly any modification ; mere unconscious
selection is enough. In other cases they have to be stretched
a little here, and patted down there, and given a twist before
they will fit. In extreme instances, where a piece is missing,
it is supplied by mythological inference from the interrupted
portions which call for completion ; and here we reach the
other phase of the process, namely *invention*. This is no
longer a matter of imparting a form to raw material ; it
is the creation of fresh material when the supply of fact
is not sufficient to fill the mould. It leads further to the
embroidery of fabulous anecdote, which not only has no
basis in fact, but is a superfluous addition, related to fact
as illustrations in a book are related to the text.

The process, in both its phases, can be illustrated from
the version preserved by Thucydides [1] of the legend of
Harmodius and Aristogeiton, the tyrant-slayers. Harmodius'
sister, whom the tyrant insults, makes her first appearance
in this account. She is superfluous, since the murderers
had already a sufficient private motive arising out of the
love-quarrel. That is not in itself an argument against
her historical character, for superfluous people sometimes
do exist; but other circumstances make it not improbable
that she owes her existence to the mythical type which
normally appears in legend when tyrants have to be slain.
The two brothers, or lovers, and the injured sister, or wife—
the relationships vary—are the standing *dramatis personae*
on such occasions. Collatinus, Brutus, and Lucretia are
another example from legend ; while the purely mythical
type which shapes such legends is seen in the Dioscuri
and Helen.[2] The suggestion is that Harmodius and Aris-

[1] vi. 54 ff.

[2] Even aspirants to tyranny have to be killed on this pattern. Thus one
version of Alcibiades' death was that the *brothers* of a woman with whom he
was spending the night set fire to the house and cut him down as he leapt
out through the flames. Plut. *vit. Alcib.* fin.

togeiton were identified with the Heavenly Twins. If
there is any truth in the story of how Peisistratus was
conducted back to Athens by a woman dressed as Athena
and accepted by the citizens as the goddess in person,[1] it
is not surprising that the next generation of Athenians
should have recognized the Dioscuri in Harmodius and his
friend. Given that identification, the injured sister is felt
to be a desirable, if not indispensable, accessory; she is
filled in by inference, and she becomes a candidate for
the place of ' basket-bearer ' in the Panathenaic procession,
at which the murder took place. Thus, the legend of
Harmodius illustrates both the phases of the process we
described : first, it is moulded on the mythical type of the
Heavenly Twins, and then invention supplies the missing
third figure.[2]

Mythical types of this sort can be discovered and classified
only after a wide survey of comparative Mythistoria; for we
all take our own habits of thought for granted, and we cannot
perceive their bias except by contrast. The Greek who knew
only Greek legend could not possibly disengage the substance
from the form; all he could do was to prune away the fabulous
and supernatural overgrowths, and cut down poetry into
prose. It is thus that Thucydides treats myths like the story
of Tereus, Procne, and Philomela [3]; he rationalizes them,
thinking that he has reduced them to history when he has
removed unattested and improbable accretions, such as the
transformation of Tereus into a hoopoe. But history cannot be made by this process (which is still in use); all
that we get is, not the original facts, but a mutilated legend ;
and this may very well be so mutilated that it is no longer
possible to distinguish the informing element of fiction, which
was discernible till we effaced the clues.

The phenomenon that especially concerns us now is some-

---

[1] Herod. i. 60.

[2] On this subject see Mücke, *Vom Euphrat zum Tiber* (1899), who points out
other examples of the mythical type.

[3] ii. 29.

thing much wider than the mythical infiguration of a single incident here or there, such as the legend of the Tyrant-slayers. It is the moulding of a long series of events into a plan determined by an *art form*. When we set the *Persians* of Aeschylus beside the history of Herodotus, we see at once that the tragedian in dramatizing the events of Xerxes' invasion, some of which he had personally witnessed, has also worked them into a theological scheme, preconceived and contributed by his own mind. Further we remark that Herodotus, although he is operating in a different medium and writing a saga about the glory of Athens, uses the same theological train of thought as a groundwork, and falls in with the dramatic conception of Aeschylus. This is a case of the infiguration of a whole train of events by a form which is mythical, in so far as it involves a theological theory of sinful pride punished by jealous divinity, and is also an art form, by which the action is shaped on dramatic principles of construction, involving such features as climax, reversal, catastrophe. The theory and the form together provide the setting of the whole story—the element which makes it a work of art. This element is so structural that it cannot be removed without the whole fabric falling to pieces, and at the same time so latent and pervasive, as not to be perceptible until the entire work is reviewed in its large outline. Even then it can be detected only by a critic who is on his guard and has not the same scheme inwrought into the substance of his own mind; for if he is himself disposed to see the events in conformity with the scheme, then the story will answer his expectation and look to him perfectly natural.

When Thucydides speaks of 'the mythical', it seems probable from the context that he is thinking chiefly of *inventive* 'embellishment'. The accretions of fabulous anecdote are comparatively easy to detect; they often bring in the supernatural in the forms of vulgar superstition, and being for this reason improbable, they require better evidence than is forthcoming. Also, poets tend to *magnify* their theme for purposes of panegyric, flattering to their audience;

they will, for instance, represent Agamemnon's expedition
as much larger than it probably was.   It is on these grounds
that Thucydides objects to the evidence of Ionian Epos and
Herodotean story-telling.[1]   He warns us against the faults
which struck his notice ; and he was on his guard against
them, even more than against the popular superstition and
dogmatic philosophy of the day, which he tacitly repudiates.
But there was one thing against which he does not warn us,
precisely because it was the framework of his own thought,
not one among the objects of reflection,—a scheme contributed,
like the Kantian categories of space and time, by the mind
itself to whatever was presented from outside.   Thucydides,
like Descartes, thought he had stripped himself bare of every
preconception ; but, as happened also with Descartes, his
work shows that there was after all a residuum wrought
into the substance of his mind and ineradicable because
unperceived.   This residuum was his philosophy of human
nature, as it is set forth in the speech of Diodotus,—a theory
of the passions and of their working which carried with it
a principle of dramatic construction presently to be described.
That he was not forearmed against this, he himself shows
when, in attacking Herodotus, he accuses him of trivial errors
of fact, and does not bring the one sweeping and valid in-
dictment which is perfectly relevant to his own point about
the embellishment of the Persian War.   The dramatic construction of Herodotus' work, which stares a modern reader
in the face, apparently escaped the observation of his severest
ancient critic.

Another proof can be drawn from Thucydides' own account
of a series of events which he evidently believed to be
historical, the closing incidents, namely, of Pausanias' career.[2]
He shows us the Spartan king intriguing with the Persian,

---

[1] Cf. Plut. *malig. Herod.* 3 (855 D) αἱ γὰρ ἐκβολαὶ καὶ παρατροπαὶ τῆς ἱστορίας
μάλιστα τοῖς μύθοις δίδονται καὶ ταῖς ἀρχαιολογίαις, ἔτι δὲ πρὸς τοὺς ἐπαίνους.  This
refers to digressions (παρενθῆκαι), which are regarded as legitimate, when
used for the purposes named.

[2] i. 128 ff.

and 'bent upon the empire of Hellas'. Pausanias commits certain treacherous acts; boasts of his power to the Great King; 'intends, if the king please, to marry his daughter'; is so 'uplifted' by the king's answer that he can no longer live like ordinary men;[1] behaves like an oriental; cannot keep silence about his larger designs; makes himself difficult of access, and displays a harsh temper. We know all these symptoms well enough, and we foresee the end. Pausanias is recalled, but the evidence against him is insufficient. He writes a letter betraying his designs and ending with an order for the execution of the bearer. The messenger, whose suspicions are aroused, opens the letter and shows it to the authorities at Sparta. The ephors arrange that they shall be concealed behind a partition and overhear a conversation between the king and his treacherous messenger, who contrives to draw from Pausanias a full and damning avowal. The end follows in the Brazen House.

This is not the sort of thing that Thucydides objects to as 'mythical'; it is not 'fabulous', not the embroidery of mere poetical invention; and so he reports it all in perfect good faith. What does not strike him, and what does strike us, is that the story is a drama, framed on familiar lines, and ready to be transferred to the stage without the alteration of a detail. The earlier part is a complete presentation of the 'insolent' type of character. The climax is reached by a perfect example of 'Recoil' ($\pi\epsilon\rho\iota\pi\epsilon\tau\epsilon\iota\alpha$), where the hero gives the fatal letter to the messenger, and thus by his own action precipitates the catastrophe. The last scene is staged by means of a theatrical property now so cheapened by use as to be barely respectable—a screen![2] The manner of the hero's death involved sacrilege, and was believed to bring a curse upon his executioners. Could we have better proof

---

[1] Thuc. i. 130 πολλῷ τότε μᾶλλον ἦρτο καὶ οὐκέτι ἐδύνατο ἐν τῷ καθεστῶτι τρόπῳ βιοτεύειν.

[2] It is possible that in this scene we can just trace a dramatic motive, which is all but rationalized away,—the idea, namely, that Pausanias cannot fall till he has *committed himself by his own act*, to which act he must be tempted by the traitor. This feature of Aeschylean drama will be discussed in the next chapter.

that Thucydides was not on his guard against dramatic construction, and was predisposed to see in the working of events a train of 'causes' which tragedy had made familiar?

When we are alive to the dramatic setting, we can infer with some certainty the stages through which the Thucydidean story of Pausanias has passed. The original stratum of fact must have been that Pausanias somehow misconducted himself, was recalled, and put to death in circumstances which were capable of being used by superstition and policy against the ephors. These facts worked loose into a legend, shaped by imagination on the model of preconceived morality and views of human nature. The mould is supplied by drama; and meanwhile fabulous invention is busy in many minds, embroidering the tale with illustrative anecdotes.[1] Thucydides brushes away these extravagant and unattested accretions, and reduces the legend again to what seemed to him a natural series of events. It is only we who can perceive that what he has left is the dramatized legend, not the historical facts out of which it was worked up. It is not wildly paradoxical to think that the historian who accepted the legend of Pausanias might frame on the same pattern the legend of Cleon. Not that Thucydides invented anything; all that was needed was to select, half unconsciously, those parts of his life which of themselves composed the pattern.[2]

We must now come to closer quarters with the epithet 'dramatic'. It is worth noting, at the outset, that in the mere matter of external form, the history seems to show the influence of tragedy,—a fact which need not surprise us, if we remember that Thucydides had no model for historical writing. The brief abstract of the annalist was a scaffold, not a building; and Thucydides was an architect, not a carpenter. Chroniclers and story-writers like Herodotus had

---

[1] Some of these anecdotes, preserved by Herodotus, will come up for discussion later.

[2] Another instance is Thucydides' narrative of Themistocles' latter days. This is rationalized Saga-history, influenced by drama.

chosen the lax form of epic, congenial to ramblers; but whatever the history was to be, it was not to be like Herodotus, and it was to draw no inspiration from the tradition of Ionian Epos. So Thucydides turned to drama— the only other developed form of literature then existing which could furnish a hint for the new type to be created. The severe outline and scrupulous limitations of this form satisfied his instinct for self-suppression. The epic poet stands before his audience and tells his own tale; but the dramatist never appears at all: the 'thing done' (δρᾶμα) works itself out before the spectators' eyes; the thing said comes straight from the lips of the actors.

Best of all, to Thucydides' thinking, if we, of after times, could ourselves have watched every battle as it was won and lost, and ourselves have heard every speech of envoy and statesman; we should then have known all, and much more than all, this history was designed to tell. But as this cannot be, we are to have the next thing to it; we shall sit as in a theatre, where the historian will erect his mimic stage and hold the mirror up to Nature. Himself will play the part of 'messenger' and narrate 'what was actually done' with just so much of vividness as the extent of his own information warrants. For the rest, the actors shall tell their own tale, as near as may be, in the very words they used, 'as I heard them myself, or as others reported them.'

Speeches are much more prominent in Thucydides' history than they are in that of Herodotus. The change seems partly due to the later historian's preference for setting forth motives in the form of 'pretexts', instead of giving his own opinion; but it is also due to his being an Athenian. Plato similarly chose to cast his speculations in the dramatic form of dialogue, allowing various points of view to be expressed by typical representatives, without committing himself to any of them. Even oratory at Athens was dramatically conceived; the speech-writer did not appear as advocate in court; he wrote speeches in character to be delivered by his clients. It has often been remarked that the debates in Thucydides resemble in some points of technique the debates in a Euripidean play.

There is moreover in one respect an intellectual kinship
between Thucydides and the dramatist who was contempora-
neously moulding the form of tragedy to the strange uses of
realism, and working away from Aeschylus as Thucydides
had to work away from Herodotus. The two men are of very
different temperaments ; but in both we seem to find the same
sombre spirit of renunciation, the same conscious resolve
nowhere to overstep the actual, but to present the naked
thoughts and actions of humanity, just as they saw them.
No matter how crude the light, how harsh the outline, so that
the thing done and the thing said shall stand out as they
were, in isolated sharpness, though

> Mist is under and mist above, . . .
> And we drift on legends for ever.[1]

These considerations, however, touch only the question of
external form : they show why so much that we should state
directly is stated indirectly by Thucydides, in speeches. The
choice of this form is consistent with a complete absence of
*plot* or of dramatic construction : otherwise Thucydides could
not have chosen it at starting ; for at that moment the plot
lay in the unknown future. We mention the point only
because evidently it was somewhat easier for an historian
who consciously borrowed the outward form of tragedy, to
take unconsciously the further step, and fall in with its
inward form and principle of design. It is this which we
now wish to define more closely. The type of drama we
have detected in the history is not the Euripidean type ;
it will be found, on examination, to show an analogy with
the older form existing in the tragedies of Aeschylus.

The resemblances are reducible to two main points. The
first is an analogy of technical construction, seen in the use
and correlation of different parts of the work. The second
is a community of psychological conceptions : a mode of
presenting character, and also a theory of the passions which
has a place not only in psychology, but in ethics. We shall
begin by studying the structure ; but we may bear in mind

[1] Eurip. *Hippol.* 191 ff.   Mr. Gilbert Murray's translation.

that this structure is closely involved with the psychological theory.

An art form, such as the Aeschylean drama, shapes itself as a sort of crust over certain beliefs which harden into that outline. When this has happened, the beliefs themselves—the content of the mould—may gradually be modified and transmuted in many ways. Finally, they may melt and almost fade away, leaving the type, which is preserved as a traditional form of art. This survival of an element of technical construction may be illustrated by the instance of 'reversal' (περιπέτεια). A 'reversal of fortune' is the cardinal point of primitive tragedy; and it originally means an overthrow caused by an *external* supernatural agency—Fate or an angry god. When the belief in such agencies fades, 'reversal' remains as a feature in drama; but the change of situation is now caused by the hero's own act. The notion of 'recoil' comes in: that is to say, the fatal action itself produces results just the opposite of those intended—a perfectly natural occurrence. In this way a piece of technique outlasts the belief which gave rise to it.

The Aeschylean drama appears to us to have gone through a process of this kind. The structure, as we find it, seems to imply an original content of beliefs in some respects more primitive than those explicitly held by Aeschylus himself, but surviving in his mind with sufficient strength to influence his work. Similarly, as we hope to show, in transmission from Aeschylus to Thucydides, the dramatic type has again outlasted much of the belief which informed it in the Aeschylean stage. It is the artistic structure which is permanent; the content changes with the advance of thought. Hence, if we point to Aeschylean technique in Thucydides, we are not necessarily attributing to him the creed of Aeschylus.

We must first attempt to describe the structure of Aeschylean tragedy.[1] In order to understand it we must try to

---

[1] The description which follows is based on an analysis of the impression made on the writer by an Aeschylean tragedy. It is of course not sus-

imagine a yet more primitive stage in the development of the drama than any represented in extant Greek literature, a stage which the earliest of Aeschylus' plays has already left some way behind. A glance at the development of modern drama may help us.

Certain features which survived in Greek tragedy suggest that we should look back to a type somewhat resembling the mediaeval mystery and some of the earliest modern dramas, such as *Everyman*, which are like the mystery in being religious performances and in the element of allegorical abstraction. Their effect, due in part to each of these features, may be described as *symbolic*. *Everyman* is a sermon made visible. To watch it is like watching the pastime called 'living chess', in which the pieces are men and women, but the man who is dressed like a bishop is nothing more than a chessman who happens to be automatic. He has not the episcopal character; his dress is a disguise with nothing behind it; his words, if he spoke, would be the speech of a parrot. And so it is with *Everyman*. The persons are not persons at all, but *personae*, masks, symbols, the vehicles of abstract ideas. They do not exist, and could not be conceived as existing, in real space and time. They have no human characters, no inward motives, no life of their own. Everyman, as his name is meant to show, is in fact not *a* man, but Man, the universal.

The main development of modern drama shows, in one of its aspects, the process by which this symbolic method gives way to the realistic. The process consists in the gradual filling in of the human being behind the mask, till the humanity is sufficiently concrete and vital to burst the shell and step forth in solid flesh and blood. The symbol comes to contain a type of character; the type is particularized into a unique individual. The creature now has an independent status and behaviour of its own. Every gesture and every word must be such as would be used by an

ceptible of demonstration ; the only test is the reader's own impression. The description is not exhaustive, but is designed only to bring out a neglected aspect.

ordinary human being with the given character in the given situation. Once created, the personality is an original centre; it cannot be made to do what we please or to utter our thoughts. In some such terms as these a modern novelist or playwright will speak of his characters; and it is thus that they appear to us.

Now we can observe a certain intermediate stage in which these two methods, the symbolic and the realistic, are balanced in antagonism, so as to produce a curious effect of tension and incoherency. A good instance is Marlowe's *Faustus*. Faustus himself occupies the central plane; he is a living man, but still imprisoned in a symbolical type. The intrusion of humanity has gone far enough to disturb the abstract effect, and it reacts on some of the persons in the play who ought to be purely symbolic. Lucifer, it is true, is kept apart and remains non-human; but Mephistophilis oscillates in our imagination between the ideal and reality, with a distressing result. Again, on a lower level than Faustus there is yet another grade of persons, in contrast with whom he shows up as heroic and ideal. These are the vintner, the horse-courser, and other pieces of common clay picked out of a London alley; they belong to a different world, and we feel that they could no more communicate with the tragic characters than men can talk with angels.[1] Thus there are in this one play four sets or orders of persons: (1) the purely abstract and *symbolic,* such as Lucifer, who only appears on an upper stage at certain moments, and takes no part in the action; (2) the *intermediate,* for instance Mephistophilis, who ought to be symbolic, but treads the lower stage, a cowled enigma,[2] horrible because at moments he ceases to be symbolic without becoming human; (3) the

---

[1] We hope it is true that Marlowe did not write the comic scenes; but we are only concerned with the effect of the play as it stands.

[2] In the Elizabethan Stage Society's representation Mephistophilis is cowled and *his face is never seen.* The effect is indescribably horrible. At certain moments in Greek Tragedy the mask must have produced a somewhat similar effect, though the familiarity of the convention would make it much less in degree. The longing to see the actor's face, when his words are enigmatic, is almost enough to drive a modern spectator insane.

*heroic* or tragic: Faustus, who is an ideal half realized, hanging together on its own plane; (4) the *real*: common mortals who would attract no attention in Fleet Street.

The Greek drama, although in the detail of historical development it started at a different point from the modern, and followed another course, seems, nevertheless, to pass through a phase analogous to that which we have just described. The original substance of the drama was the choral lyric; the actors (as they afterwards became) began as an excrescence. At a certain stage the actors are assimilated to the chorus and move in the same atmosphere. Thus in the earliest play of Aeschylus, the *Suppliants*, we find that the chorus of Danaids are actually the heroines of the action, which centres round them, so that they are not merely on the same plane with the actors, but themselves a complex actor, and the effect is simple, coherent, and uniform. In the *Prometheus*, again, the chorus belong to the same ideal world as the Titan hero, a world in which abstract symbols like Mastery and Violence can move without showing as unreal against the other persons.[1] The whole drama is on the symbolic plane, the life in it being due to anthropomorphic imagination, not to the intrusion of realism.

But in the latest plays of Aeschylus, the beginning of a change is clearly marked: the actors are becoming human, while the lyric is rising above them, or else remains suspended in a rarer atmosphere from which they are sinking. This is a natural stage in the passage from pure symbolism to realism. The advance shows itself externally in the *drifting apart* of the lyrical element from the dialogue,— a separation which, of course, widens in the later tragedians, till the choral ode, though still an indispensable and very beautiful feature, becomes in point of construction little more than an interlude, which relieves the concentrated intensity of the action. This change is commonly taken as a phenomenon which needs no explanation; but really it is caused

[1] Contrast the utter unreality of Iris and Lyssa in the *Hercules Furens*. They are tolerable only when regarded as dream-phantoms.

inevitably by the *coming to life* of the persons in the drama. In proportion as these become more real, the lyric becomes more ideal and further removed from the action.

In the stage observable in Aeschylus' latest plays, the choral part is still *dramatic*, and of equal importance with the dialogue. The two elements are evenly balanced; but at the same time they have begun to occupy different worlds, so that we are sensible of the transition from one to the other. The result is a curious duplication of the drama which now has two aspects, the one universal and timeless, the other particular and temporal.

The nature of this phenomenon will, we hope, become clear, if we take as an illustration the *Agamemnon*. In this play, the visible presentation shows how the conqueror of Troy came home and was murdered by the queen. The events that go forward on the stage are *particular* events, located at a point of legendary time [1] and of real space. The characters are certain individuals, legendary or historic—there is to Aeschylus no difference here—who lived at that moment and trod that spot of earth. But in the choral odes the action is lifted out of time and place on to the plane of the universal. When the stage is clear and the visible presentation is for the time suspended, then, above and beyond the transient spectacle of a few suffering mortals caught, just there and then, in the net of crime, loom up in majestic distance and awful outline the truths established, more unchangeably than the mountains, in the eternal counsels of Zeus. The pulse of momentary passion dies down; the clash and conflict of human wills, which just now had held us in breathless concentration, sink and dwindle to the scale of a puppet-show; while the enduring song of Destiny unrolls the theme of blood-haunted Insolence lured by insistent Temptation into the toils of Doom. As

---

[1] By legendary time we mean the time occupied by events which have worked so loose from real time that you can only date them within a century or so, and do not think of dating them at all, till challenged. They are near the stage in which the only date is ' once-upon-a-time ', the verge of mythical time which has no dates at all.

though on a higher stage, uncurtained in the choral part, another company of actors concurrently plays out a more majestic and symbolic drama. On this invisible scene walk the figures of Hybris and Peitho, of Nemesis and Ate—not the bloodless abstractions of later allegory, but still clothed in the glowing lineaments of supernatural reality. The curtain lifts for a timeless moment on the spectacle of human life in an aspect known to the all-seeing eyes of Zeus; and when it drops again, we turn back to the mortal tragedy of Agamemnon and Clytemnestra, enlightened, purified, uplifted, calm.[1]

Thus we find in Aeschylus something analogous to the hierarchy of persons we noted in *Faustus*; although, for various reasons, there is not the same crude effect of incoherency and tension. The supernatural characters— Zeus, supreme above all, and the demonic figures [2] of Hybris, Nemesis, Ate, and the rest, are not *seen*, as Lucifer is seen on the upper stage of the Elizabethan theatre, but remain in the spiritual world to which lyrical emotion exalts the inward eye—the world where metaphor (as we call it) is the very stuff of reality, where Cassandra quickens and breathes, and whence she strays among mortal men like a fallen spirit, sweet-voiced, mad, and broken-winged. Hence the effect is far more awful and solemn than the actual apparition of Lucifer; and when Apollo and Athene and the spirits of vengeance take human shape in the *Eumenides*, a spell is broken, a veil rent, an impression shattered, for which not the most splendid symphony of poetical language can atone.

Here, however, we would confine our attention to the *Agamemnon*. At the lower end of the scale we find a further advance of realism in some minor characters, the watchman and the herald; the nurse in the *Choephori* is of the same order. These are allowed some wonderful touches of common humanity, below the heroic level; for they are not directly

---

[1] The metaphor of the invisible upper stage which the writer has used in describing his impression will be shown later to have justification in ancient pictorial art.

[2] This expression will be justified later.

concerned in the central action, and a little irrelevant naturalism does no harm, if it is not carried far. But they are only just below the heroic standard, and are certainly not the sort of people you would have met in a walk to the Piraeus.

Thus, the two planes in the *Agamemnon* are divided by an interval less wide and less abrupt than the divisions in *Faustus*. In psychological conception also the union is very close, since the heroic characters are still so abstract and symbolic that they are barely distinguishable from the pure abstractions of the lyrical world. Agamemnon, for instance, is simply Hybris typified in a legendary person. He is a hero flown with 'insolence' (the pride and elation of victory), and that is all that can be said of him. He is not, like a character in Ibsen, a complete human being with a complex personality,—a centre from which relations radiate to innumerable points of contact in a universe of indifferent fact. He has not a continuous history: nothing has ever happened to him except the conquest of Troy and the sacrifice of Iphigenia; nothing ever could happen to him except Pride's fall and the stroke of the axe. As we see him, he is not a man, but a single state of mind, which has never been preceded by other states of mind (except one, at the sacrifice in Aulis), but is isolated, without context, margin, or atmosphere. Every word he says, in so far as he speaks for himself and not for the poet, comes straight out of that state of mind and expresses some phase of it. He has a definite relation to Cassandra, a definite relation to Clytemnestra; but no relation to anything else. If he can be said to have a *character* at all, it consists solely of certain defects which make him liable to Insolence; if he has any *circumstances*, they are only those which prompt him to his besetting passion.

Now it is in some such way as this that Thucydides presents his principal characters. Cleon is a good instance. He is allowed no individuality, no past history, no atmosphere, no irrelevant relations. He enters the story abruptly from nowhere.  A single phrase fixes his type, as though on a play-bill: 'Cleon, the most violent of the citizens and first in the people's confidence'; that is all we know of him. There follows a speech in which the type reveals itself in a state of mind,—Violence in its several phases.  Then he vanishes, to reappear, before Sphacteria, as Violence with one of its aspects ('covetousness') emphasized, and a sudden passion of ambitious self-confidence (ἐλπίς) added thereto. Finally, we see him wrecked by this passion at Amphipolis. Pericles is introduced in the same way, with a single epithet: 'Pericles, the son of Xanthippos, a man at that time first among the Athenians, and *most powerful* (δυνατώτατος) in action and in speech.'[1]  His characteristic quality is wise foresight (γνώμη—the opening word of his first speech [2]); and he stands also, in the Funeral Oration, for the glory (τιμή) of Athens.  Alcibiades we shall study later.  In every case the principal characters are nearly as far removed from realism, nearly as abstract and impersonal as the heroic characters in Aeschylus.  Thucydides, in fact, learnt his psychology from the drama, just as we moderns (whether historians or not) learn ours, not by direct observation, but from the drama and the novel.

But we can carry the analogy further; it extends to minor points of Aeschylean technical construction, which follow naturally upon the drifting apart of lyric and dialogue.  In the *Agamemnon* we note that the separation of the two planes has gone far enough to make it impossible for the members of the chorus to interfere with the action at its crisis.  The elders, when they hear the death-cry, cannot enter the palace; not because the door is locked, nor yet because they are feeble old men.  Rather they are old men because an impassable barrier of convention is forming between chorus and actors, and their age gives colour to their powerlessness.  The need of a separate stage for the actors, though tradition may cling to the old orchestra, is already felt.  The poet is half aware of the imaginative

---

[1] Thuc. i. 139.  [2] Thuc. i. 140.

separation, and he bridges it by links of two kinds—formal links of technical device, and internal connexions of a psychological sort, which will occupy us in the next chapter.

The formal links are provided by what is called 'tragic irony'. The dialogue is so contrived that, instructed by the lyric, we can catch in it allusions to grander themes than any of which the speakers are conscious, and follow the action with eyes opened to a universal significance, hidden from the agents themselves. Tragic irony, however, is not a deliberately invented artifice; it arises of itself in the advance from the purely symbolic stage of drama. In that earliest stage the whole dialogue might be called 'ironical', in the sense that it is the poet's message to the audience, not the expression of the persons' characters, for they have none. But it becomes ironical in the strict sense only when the persons begin to have elementary characters and minds, and so to be conscious of one meaning of their words, which is not the whole meaning or the most important. The effect is now no longer merely symbolic, but *hypnotic*; the speaker on the stage is like a somnambulist—alive, but controlled and occupied by an external personality, the playwright.

Tragic irony is used by Aeschylus with great freedom; because his persons are still so near to the symbolic, they have so little character and psychology of their own, that they do not mind serving as mouthpieces. Here and there we find instances of perfect irony, where the speaker's words bear both constructions equally well, and are at once the natural expression of the appropriate state of mind and also a message from the poet to the spectator, applying one of the lyrical themes. This is the only sort of irony admitted by Sophocles, whose characters have become so human that they will not speak merely for another. In Aeschylus, however, there are whole speeches which are hypnotic, and hardly in character at all. The effect is so unfamiliar to readers schooled in realism that it is often missed.

The first two speeches of Clytemnestra, for instance, seem to be of this kind; notably, the beacon speech. If we try to interpret this as a realistic revelation of Clytemnestra's character and thoughts, we shall not find that it helps us to much insight, because its main function has nothing to do with her character. The poet is speaking through her, and the thoughts are his. The early part of the play, down to the entrance of Agamemnon, is an overture, in which Aeschylus musters and marshals the abstract themes which are to be the framework of the trilogy. One of them is expressed in the beacon speech; and it is this. The fire of Idaean Zeus has fallen upon Troy, 'neither before its season nor striking as an idle glancing shaft beyond the stars'; but that *same* fire, the symbol of Justice, speeds now to 'strike the roof of the Atreidae'. From mountain top it leaps and hastens across the sea to mountain top; and like the torch passed from hand to hand in the race, it is itself a runner and the only one which 'running first and last reaches the goal'.[1] This description of the symbolic fire conducted along the beacon chain is given to Clytemnestra because it can be given to no one else, not because it is the best means of illustrating her psychology. The speech, by the way, also exhibits another artifice employed to link the two planes—the allusive verbal echo between dialogue and lyric. The symbol of the fire, in a slightly varied form, recurs at the beginning of the next chorus, and the keyword (σκήπτειν) is reiterated to mark the correspondence.

Now the speeches in Thucydides can be roughly classed under four heads. There are, first, a few realistic speeches by minor characters; for instance, the short, sharp utterance of the Spartan ephor,[2] which has the trick of the laconic

---

[1] The notion that it is the *same* fire which passes from beacon to beacon is subtly conveyed throughout. Note especially the words: πέμπειν and its derivatives, repeated many times (' conduct', ' send on its way'); πορευτοῦ λαμπάδος 299; φῶς μολόν 305; σθένουσα λαμπὰς ὑπερθοροῦσα 308, and so on. Towards the end comes thrice the ominous word σκήπτειν: ἔσκηψεν 314; ἔσκηψεν 320; κἄπειτ' Ἀτρειδῶν ἐς τόδε σκήπτει στέγος | φάος τόδ' οὐκ ἄπαππον Ἰδαίου πυρός 322; echoed in the following chorus: ὅπως ἂν | μήτε πρὸ καιροῦ μήθ' ὑπὲρ ἄστρων | βέλος ἡλίθιον σ κ ή ψ ε ι ε ν. | Διός πλαγὰν ἔχουσιν εἰπεῖν, κ.τ.λ.

[2] Thuc. i. 86 (Sthenelaïdas).

practical man. Next, there are idealistic speeches, designed as direct expressions of character or of national ideals; the Funeral Oration will serve as an example. These shade off, through a class in which sketches of national character are introduced indirectly, with some strain upon dramatic probability,[1] into a class where irony is openly employed in the tragic manner. Cleon's Mytilenean speech, for instance, is nearly all of the character-revealing sort, but it contains a passage about the evil results of exceptional prosperity which is without any true application to the position of Lesbos or to the history of the revolt. It runs as follows[2]:

' Conceiving a reckless confidence in the future, and hopes that outran their strength though they fell short of their desires, they went to war; and they thought fit to prefer might to right, for where they thought they saw a chance of success, they set upon us when we were doing them no wrong. It is always so: when exceptional prosperity comes sudden and unexpected to a city, it turns to insolence: and, in general, good fortune is safer for mankind when it answers to calculation than when it surpasses expectation, and one might almost say that men find it easier to drive away adversity than to preserve prosperity. We were wrong from the first. We ought never to have put the Mytileneans above the rest by exceptional treatment; then their insolence would not have come to this height. It is a general rule that human nature despises flattery, and respects unyielding strength.'

These words are patently inapplicable to the revolted island, whose exceptional position was notoriously a survival of the status originally enjoyed by every one of the allies, but now forfeited by all but a few; to speak of it as a sudden access of prosperity is simply meaningless. We are driven to see in the passage a use of tragic irony; Thucydides puts into Cleon's mouth the very moral which his own career is to illustrate. The device is unskilfully em-

---

[1] e. g. the Corinthians' sketch of the Athenian character, i. 70.
[2] iii. 39. 3.

ployed, since dramatic probability is too completely sacrificed. Sophocles would not have passed these sentences, which on the speaker's lips have not even a plausible meaning; but Aeschylus would have passed them, and after all Thucydides was only an amateur tragedian.

A fourth use of speeches is illustrated by the Spartan envoys' homily before Sphacteria. This is still further removed from realism, and resembles the beacon speech, which is but one degree below the lyric plane. The historian, reluctant to break silence in his own person, sets forth the theme and framework of his drama in the form of a solemn warning. He has already described the Athenians at Pylos as ' wishing to follow up their present good fortune to the furthest point '.[1] This is a dangerous frame of mind, against which Themistocles had warned the Athenians after Salamis, when they wished to press forward and destroy the Persians' bridges over the Hellespont.[2] 'I have often,' says Themistocles, ' myself witnessed occasions, and I have heard of many from others, where men who had been conquered by an enemy, having been driven quite to desperation, have renewed the fight and retrieved their former disasters. We have now had the great good luck (εὕρημα εὑρήκαμεν) to save both ourselves and all Greece by the repulse of this vast cloud of men; let us then be content and not press them too hard, now that they have begun to fly. Be sure that we have not done this by our own might. It is the work of gods and heroes, who were jealous that one man should be king at once of Europe and Asia. . . . At present all is well with us—let us then abide in Greece, and look to ourselves and to our families.'

The warning of the Spartan envoys is conceived in the same spirit; but it is unheeded and unanswered. No answer, indeed, was possible; the speech is not an argument, but a prophecy. A reply from Cleon, a statement of the war party's policy, such as modern critics desiderate, would be as inappropriate as a reply from Clytemnestra to the Second

---

[1] iv. 14. 3 βουλόμενοι τῇ παρούσῃ τύχῃ ὡς ἐπὶ πλεῖστον ἐπεξελθεῖν.
[2] Herod. viii. 109 Rawlinson trans.

Chorus in the *Agamemnon*. The stage is clear while this prophecy, addressed not to the actors but to the spectators, passes unheard by those who, could they have heard it, might have been saved.

One further point of formal resemblance between Aeschylus and Thucydides is the allusive echoing of significant phrases, which sustain the moral motive dominant in the plot. We have seen an instance of this device in the repetition of the words ' coveting more ' (πλέονος ὀρέγεσθαι), which reappear at critical moments after the use of them in the envoys' speech ; and we shall note other examples later. This completes the analogy with Aeschylean form, so far as concerns external peculiarities.

Before returning to Thucydides' narrative, however, we have yet to analyse a somewhat complex feature of Aeschylean psychology, which is connected with the *internal* relations between the two phases of the drama—the universal, or supernatural, and the particular, or human. We shall then be in a position to consider whether some traces of this psychology are not to be seen in Thucydides' treatment of certain characters. The topic will need a chapter to itself.

# CHAPTER IX

In the last two chapters we have studied the little drama of Cleon's exaltation and fall, and noted some analogies of treatment which point to Aeschylean influence. Thucydides, however, is not primarily interested in Cleon, nor does he allow him to hold the stage. Cleon's personal drama works itself out on its own lines, but the thread of it crops up only at those points where it crosses the woof of a larger web and contributes a dark stain to its pattern. It is with the tracing of this pattern that we shall henceforth be occupied ; and though it spreads backward and forward some way beyond the limits of Cleon's story, it will be convenient to start from the point we have reached. The treatment of the Pylos incident is still not completely explained, for that episode is not a part of Cleon's story, but belongs to the larger plot and marks a critical stage in its development. The heroine, we need hardly say, is Athens herself, whose character is set in the focus of so many lights, and whose tragic destiny takes a larger sweep, ' in proportion as her stake is the greatest of all—freedom or empire.' Athens, we shall come to see, has a character of her own and a psychological history, passing through well-marked phases, which are determined partly by this character, and partly by the intervention of external or internal forces. One of these forces is embodied in Cleon; and in order to make out how the mode of its operation is conceived, we must again look for assistance from Aeschylus.

From the standpoint of form, we have attempted to describe the duplication of the drama discernible in the *Agamemnon*. There are, as it were, two parallel trains of action: the human action visibly presented on the stage, and an abstract, universal counterpart of it, revealed in the lyric. The persons on this abstract plane are what we commonly (and somewhat misleadingly) call *personifications*, such as Hybris, Peitho, Nemesis, Ate. They are universals, not particular concrete instances, like this or that legendary man or woman in whom they are embodied. We might change the instances and leave the abstract plot unaffected ; Hybris runs the same course, whether it be impersonated in Agamemnon or in Xerxes.

And, further, that course is *inevitable*; its law is written unalterably, whatever be the power that legislates—Destiny, or Justice, or the Will of Zeus. We see it illustrated in the tale of Troy or in the tale of Thebes: Sin leads through Sin to punishment. The taint steals down the lineage of a house once smitten with God's curse; sorrow is heaped on sorrow; till the last light is smothered in the dust of death.[1] In this abstract procession the first figure is linked to the last with iron bands.

But if that be so, wherein lies the guilt of the human agents in any particular case ? Are not the unseen powers responsible ($\alpha\dot{\iota}\tau\iota\alpha\iota$), and may not the sinner cast his burden on Necessity ? Thus we reach the problem of free will on the lower, human plane,—a moral problem, corresponding to the artistic problem which arises when the two elements in the drama begin to drift apart. The characters must not seem to be the blind puppets of superhuman powers; the dice of God must not be too heavily loaded. If, when seen from above, Guilt appears to gravitate by unalterable necessity to its punishment; seen from the level, the guilty man must choose the act that precipitates his unknown fate. Is there not here a contradiction fatal at once to the moral doctrine and to the aesthetic effect ?

The solution, if there be one, must be psychological; we require a theory of human motives which will allow of our conceiving them, simultaneously, both as supernatural causes coming from without, and also as integral parts in the working

[1] Soph. *Ant.* 593.

of the agent's mind. Modern psychology is, of course, not equal to the task of this reconciliation. If we conceive of every mental state as completely determined in a continuous series by preceding states and by natural environment, the problem of free will arises in relation to causal law and lies wholly within the normal sphere, the intervention of supernatural causes being left out of account.

Aeschylus, however, was not hampered by determinism; and he was helped by some psychological conceptions, surviving from the mythical order of thought, which have so completely dropped out of our scheme of things that it is easy for us to misinterpret, or to overlook, them in the ancient writers. They are, nevertheless, essential to Aeschylus' scheme, and we shall find the after-working of them in Thucydides. We hope to carry the analysis as far as it can safely go ; but it must be remembered that we are dealing with a poet and theologian, not with a psychologist, and moving in a region of thought where one phase melts into another at no rigidly definable point.

The problem arises at every link in the chain of terrible deeds. Agamemnon, Clytemnestra, Orestes, commit, each of them, an act which is both the execution of divine justice and also a sin. Modern ethics will of course admit that an action may be both right and wrong. It will be externally right if it produces more good than any possible alternative ; but the same action may be also internally wrong, if the agent intends to do harm and only does good by accident. Thus a Christian will hold that Judas' betrayal of his Master was one of the causes of the Redemption ; but Judas will be damned for it to the nethermost circle. Aeschylus, however, had not reached this modern way of conceiving a right action done from a wrong motive ; the psychology involved is less distinct and partly mythical.

At the beginning of the *Agamemnon*, the balance of right and wrong stands as follows. Agamemnon has committed two of these ambiguous acts. The sacrifice of Iphigeneia was enjoined by the chartered representative of Heaven, Calchas,

the seer; yet it was a deed of horror, for it was an offence
against nature, symbolized by Artemis, the patroness of young
creatures. So too the conquest of Troy was the stroke of
Zeus; but the same avenging fire will fall on the house
of the conqueror, who has brought the innocent with the
guilty to suffering which only the guilty had deserved. Paris
may have merited death; but what of Cassandra?

In regard to the second of the two acts the conqueror
of Troy has goné beyond his divine mandate; the excess
and spirit of his vengeance have carried to his account with
Justice an adverse balance. What concerns us is the psychological process by which this has occurred; and to understand
it we must refer to Clytemnestra's second speech,[1] where,
as in the former speech about the beacons, she is setting
forth, not her own character, but an indispensable moment
in Aeschylus' moral theme.

As if endowed with second sight, she bodes the indiscri-
minate slaughter of young and old among the Trojans in the
captured city. The conquerors, released from the weary discipline of a siege, and the nights of restless watching under
the cold dews, rove uncontrolled through Troy and lodge
themselves at hazard in her plundered palaces. The sentence
ends with a magnificent stroke of irony[2]: 'The unlucky
wretches will sleep all night long and keep no watch!'
The words sound sympathetic until we catch the second
meaning which lies under them. A man is 'unlucky'
(δυσδαίμων) when an evil spirit is haunting near him; his
peril is the greater if he is not on the watch (ἀφύλακτος).
And the name of the spirit follows almost immediately: *Eros*,
the spirit of lust after forbidden rapine, may fall upon the

---

[1] *Agam.* 330 ff.

[2] *Agam.* 348 · τῶν ὑπαιθρίων πάγων
δρόσων τ' ἀπαλλαγέντες ὡς δυσδαίμονες
ἀφύλακτον εὐδήσουσι πᾶσαν εὐφρόνην.

It is questionable how these lines should be punctuated and construed;
but any interpretation preserves the ironic ambiguity. The correction ὡς δ'
εὐδαίμονες ('and how blest! will sleep' &c.) merely makes εὐδαίμων the ironical
equivalent of δυσδαίμων.

host, unsentinelled against this invisible assailant.[1] And when Clytemnestra ends by saying that she utters these bodings '*as a woman*'[2] (or 'as a wife'), we know that she is thinking of Chryseïs and the poet is thinking of Cassandra.

The Greeks believed that in the hour of sudden triumph, when 'Fortune', as Diodotus says, 'presents herself unexpectedly at a man's side,' the conqueror is in a perilous condition; for in the flush and tumult of his feelings reason is clouded and caution laid asleep. Then comes Temptation, and it is especially with the manner in which it comes that we are now concerned; since it is at this point that we are apt to miss the psychological conceptions, unfamiliar to us, which govern Aeschylus' design and will reappear, in somewhat altered form, in Thucydides.

Internally, temptation takes the form of a violent passion, uncontrollable if its victim is unguarded and secure. The conquerors of Troy are beset by Eros, the spirit of rapine; but this passion is not conceived as a natural state of mind determined by a previous state—the effect of a normal cause; it is a spirit (δαίμων) which haunts, swoops down, and takes possession of the soul, when reason slumbers and keeps no watch. Eros is constantly spoken of by the Greeks as a disease (νόσος); but that word had not the associations merely of a wasting and painful bodily corruption. Disease was caused by invading spirits, those malignant *Keres* of whom Age and Death are the chief, and who seize as much upon the soul as upon the body. Abnormal states of mind —the intoxication of wine, religious enthusiasm, nympholepsy, poetic inspiration, an army's panic fear, the raving of the

---

[1] Ἔρως δὲ μή τις πρότερον ἐμπίπτῃ στρατῷ
πορθεῖν ἃ μὴ χρὴ κέρδεσιν νικωμένους.

Eros, as the *lust of blood*, is alluded to in Agamemnon's first speech where he compares the Trojan horse to a ravening lion that has leapt over the city's wall and is glutted with the royal blood that it has licked. *Agam.* 818

ὑπερθορὼν δὲ πύργον ὠμηστὴς λέων
ἄδην ἔλειξεν αἵματος τυραννικοῦ . .

Cf. 1479 Ἔρως αἱματολοιχός ; *Sept.* 679 ὠμοδακὴς Ἵμερος.

[2] 360 τοιαῦτά τοι γυναικὸς ἐξ ἐμοῦ κλύεις.

prophet, the madness of the lover—all these were phenomena of the same order, all instances of spiritual occupation. This to the Greeks was a very familiar idea. The entering of a god or spirit into a man's body, so that he becomes ἔνθεος, was the central doctrine of the orgiastic cults. Official religion recognized it in the oracular possession of the Pythian priestess. Medical practice recommended the wild music of the Corybant's timbrel and drum as a purge to exorcize the fiends of madness.[1] Plato, in his study of Peitho and Eros (the *Phaedrus*), avails himself in all earnestness of the idea of indwelling divinity as the most natural mode of conceiving the relation between the all-pervading Form of Beauty and the world which it penetrates and informs with its splendour. His 'participation' (μέθεξις) is first conceived as a mystical relation, the participation of the mortal in the immortal, long before it withers up and becomes a logical relation of subject to predicate; the neoplatonist only restores its original significance. Even in Aristotle the theory of tragedy looks back to the belief that the passions, which art is to purge, are spirits of madness to be exorcized by wild music and the frantic rhythm of the dance. They are, in Diodotus' words, 'irremediable and mastering powers', which 'possess' the various conditions of human life, and lead men on into danger[2].

In theological theory the violent passions are conceived as forms of delusion sent by God upon the sinner to drive him to his punishment. This aspect of them we shall study later at some length; here it remains to note that the idea of spiritual possession provides the psychological link we needed

---

[1] Arist. *Vesp.* 119. See the evidence collected in Susemihl and Hicks, *Politics of Aristotle* i–v. p. 644 (note on κάθαρσις).

[2] Thuc. iii. 45 αἱ ἄλλαι ξυντυχίαι ὀργῇ τῶν ἀνθρώπων ὡς ἑκάστη τις κατέχεται ὑπ' ἀνηκέστου τινὸς κρείσσονος ἐξάγουσιν ἐς τοὺς κινδύνους. κατέχεσθαι is of course regularly used of spiritual occupation of all kinds. ἀνηκέστου recalls Aesch. *Agam.* 384 βιᾶται δ' ἁ τάλαινα Πειθώ, | πρόβουλου παῖς ἄφερτος Ἄτας· | ἄκος δὲ πᾶν μάταιον. κρείσσων is associated with the 'daemons', who were called 'the stronger ones', οἱ κρείσσονες, Plato, *Euthyd.* 291 A μή τις τῶν κρειττόνων παρὼν αὐτὰ ἐφθέγξατο; Aelian, *V. H.* iv. 17 Pythagoras called the noise in his ears φωνὴ τῶν κρειττόνων.

between the abstract and symbolic series in which Hybris, Koros, Eros, hold a place, and the level of human drama, where these passions become literally *embodied* in individual men and women. Eros, for instance, is in its higher aspect a supernatural 'cause', an agency from God, ministering to the divine purpose. But when Eros takes possession of me, it is also *my* passion, an internal spring of action; and I become responsible (αἴτιος) for the results that come of it.

A character in Aeschylus, as we remarked above, should be thought of, at any given moment, as a single state of mind, with no background or margin of individual personality. It has neither a past nor a future, except a few other states which come in a settled order, but are (as it were) a *discontinuous* series, with gaps of any length between the terms. The masked and muffled figures posed on the stage contain no more concrete humanity than this. Agamemnon, as we see him, is Insolence, possessed at the moment by Eros, who is the inward tempter sent to blind him and drive him to his fall. This Eros is outwardly symbolized, not indeed in Cassandra, but in Agamemnon's relation towards her—a one-sided relation which (as it were) falls short of her, leaving her white spirit wounded but unstained.

Now let us turn to Clytemnestra; for in her we shall see Temptation besetting the king in its other, external, shape. The earlier scenes, down to the entrance of Agamemnon, are an overture, of which the keynote is *Waiting*;—the note which is struck in the opening words of the sentinel, tired of his yearlong watch upon the constellations, as they rise and set in the slow procession of the seasons. We watch the mustering of solemn storm-clouds, and feel the increasing tension of expectancy before the first blinding flash. Clytemnestra is an enigma; her words are spoken from the lips, and reveal nothing. She is like a compressed spring, a nameless undetermined force, charged, and awaiting the touch that will release it. Then, in the scene with Agamemnon, she becomes animate in a peculiar way: a spirit has entered her, and the name of it is Temptation or Delusion, Peitho or Apatê [1].

Dr. Headlam [2] has interpreted this famous scene, in which the proud and masterful princess, at the death-grip now with the opposing principle of Agamemnon's lordship, lures and flatters him to the committal act of pride, which calls down his doom. Temptation in the inward form of passion has already mastered him; now, from outside, as incarnate in another person, she spreads the final snare.[3] Clytemnestra too is ministerial; she is sent by God to draw him to the meeting ways where a false step is perdition. Another angel of Justice has left the ranks of that invisible company and taken shape in this woman.

Clytemnestra, however, is not, like Hamlet, the *conscious* scourge and minister of Heaven, fulfilling an explicit command. In herself she is the woman with the man's courage and brain, masterful and ambitious [4]; and she stands as a Queen defending her native right of sovereignty against her consort and the veiled captive at his side. As between wife and husband, her account with Agamemnon is exactly balanced : he has sinned, through Eros, against divine Justice and against her ; but her relation with Aegisthus was an equal sin, and she has forfeited her claim.[5] Hence her vengeance on Agamemnon, in so far

---

[1] The effect is prepared for in her previous (third) speech to the herald (587 ff), and symbolically illustrated by the lion-cub simile in the following chorus (717).

[2] *Cambridge Praelections* (1906), p. 126. I owe this tragic conception of Peitho, and the interpretation of the scene, to Dr. Headlam.

[3] *Agam.* 1371 ΚΛ. πολλῶν πάροιθεν καιρίως εἰρημένων
τἀναντί' εἰπεῖν οὐκ ἐπαισχυνθήσομαι.
πῶς γάρ τις ἐχθρὸς ἐχθρὰ πορσύνων, φίλοις
δοκοῦσιν εἶναι, πημονῆς ἀρκύστατ' ἂν
φράξειεν ὕψος κρεῖσσον ἐκπηδήματος ;

Schol. ad loc. ὁ φιλικῶς ὑπερχόμενός τινα καὶ ἀπατῆσαι βουλόμενος εἰς ἄφυκτον φραγμὸν ἐμπλέκει αὐτὸν τῆς Ἀπάτης.

[4] *Agam.* 10 ὧδε γὰρ κρατεῖ γυναικὸς ἀνδρόβουλον ἐλπίζον κέαρ,—a fine example of Aeschylus' power of describing a character in five words.

[5] Clytemnestra is queen in her own right in a country originally matriarchal; Agamemnon is merely her consort. Under a gynaecocratic system the husband-consort's sin would be thought to be as outrageous as the wife's is under the patriarchal system recognized by the foreigner Agamemnon

as it is conjugal, or rather *queenly*, is unjust; much more is
the murder of Cassandra.[1]   With regard to Iphigeneia, her
daughter, she has justice on her side.   Revenge upon this
score had been a long-harboured motive ; and if, at the
moment of the crime, it had been the dominant and real
force in her, the sin would have been much less, and Aegisthus
would not have been involved in her punishment.   From the
scene where she reveals her motives to the chorus [2], we think
it could be shown that the long-cherished, rational design of
just vengeance for Iphigeneia was, *at the moment of the
murder*, eclipsed in her mind by a sudden passion which she
herself describes as 'the lust for blood to lick'.[3]   When she
first appears, standing over her victims, she is drunken with
this passion [4] and with the triumph of vindicated queenship.

> 'There Agamemnon lies,
> My *husband* !' [5]

Then, as she begins to recover her reason, comes the mention

and familiar to us. The situation is symmetrical. It is no question of
mere womanly jealousy; but a conflict of two principles of society. Similarly the sacrifice of Iphigeneia, her daughter and *heir*, was as great an
outrage as Agamemnon would have felt the sacrifice of the son, Orestes,
to be. Clytemnestra would have acquiesced in the latter as Agamemnon
did in the former, but she would regard the murder of the daughter as an
attempt to secure the throne, which on her own death would pass from
Agamemnon to the daughter and the daughter's husband. (See Frazer,
*Adonis, Attis, Osiris*, p. 28.) For the whole question of the conflict of
patriarchy and matriarchy see Miss J. E. Harrison, *Prolegomena to the Study
of Greek Religion*, and Ridgeway, *Cambridge Praelections*, 1906. I am convinced
that this conflict is vaguely but unmistakably present to Aeschylus' mind,
and that the conception of Clytemnestra can only be understood by taking
account of it.

[1] Clytemnestra describes this as εὐνῆς παροψώνημα τῆς ἐμῆς χλιδῆς (l. 1446).
It is something over and above her due, even as she conceives it (ἐκ
περιουσίας, Schol.). See also 1396 where δικαίως . . . ὑπερδίκως μὲν οὖν is, by
tragic irony, an unconscious confession that she has gone beyond justice.
1384 παίω δέ νιν δίς : these are the two blows which Agamemnon's two sins
have merited; but Clytemnestra adds a third, above due measure : καὶ
πεπτωκότι τρίτην ἐπενδίδωμι.                              [2] *Agam.* 1371–1576.

[3] 1478 Ἔρως αἱματολοιχός, the very passion described by Agamemnon (see
above, note on p. 157).

[4] 1427 Χο. . . . ὥσπερ οὖν φονολιβεῖ τύχᾳ φρὴν ἐπιμαίνεται, | λίπος ἐπ' ὀμμάτων
αἵματος εὖ πρέπειν.

[5] 1404 οὗτός ἐστιν Ἀγαμέμνων, ἐμὸς | πόσις.   πόσις has all the maximum

of Iphigeneia, as if this other motive were re-emerging from temporary obscuration. In the next speech it is overpowered again by the passion against Chryseïs and Cassandra, but as the scene proceeds she insists exclusively on Iphigeneia. The dialogue becomes lyrical, and we begin to see the crime as it appears from the higher plane. She who was just before triumphing over her 'husband' now cries out that she is not to be named Agamemnon's wife; the deed is not hers: the ancient bitter fiend has appeared in her shape.[1] But it is not she who first thinks of this supernatural aspect; it is suggested by the chorus, and then she catches at it.[2] When she claims to be an incarnation of the fiend who haunts the race, the chorus answer : 'That thou art guiltless (ἀναίτιος) of this murder, who shall aver? It cannot, cannot be; though perchance the fiend of his sire (Atreus) might be thy helper (συλλήπτωρ).'[3]

Thus Aeschylus indicates that Clytemnestra was indeed a minister of heaven, but not a *conscious* minister at the moment. The righteous and rational motive, connected with Iphigeneia, was for the time superseded by an unrighteous passion—'the lust for blood to lick', which comes upon one and another of the race 'till the old woe be laid to rest'. This passion may come, as she says it does, from the evil fiend of the house;[4] but when it filled her it was *her* passion, and withal unrighteous in excess, and so she is not guiltless.

Clytemnestra, then, is possessed in two ways. Her consciousness, at the moment of her act, is merged in, and identified

---

emphasis of position. Cf. (just above, 1400) Χο . . . ἥτις τοιόνδ' ἐπ' ἀνδρὶ κομπάζεις λόγον. ΚΛ. πειρᾶσθέ μου γυναικὸς ὡς ἀφράσμονος.

[1] 1497      ΚΛ. αὐχεῖς εἶναι τόδε τοὔργον ἐμόν;

                μηδ' ἐπιλεχθῇς

       'Αγαμεμνονίαν εἶναί μ' ἄλοχον, κτλ.

[2] 1468 Χο. δαῖμον, ὃς ἐμπίτνεις, κτλ. 1475 ΚΛ. νῦν δ' ὤρθωσας στόματος γνώμην, | τὸν τριπάχυντον | δαίμονα γέννης τόνδε κικλήσκων.

[3] 1506. Cf. *Choeph.* 909 ΚΛ. ἡ Μοῖρα τούτων, ὦ τέκνον, παραιτία, partly responsible, not wholly ; a collateral, supernatural cause, which becomes natural when it takes possession of the agent. Contrast the complete disclaiming of responsibility in *Iliad*, Τ, 86 : ἐγὼ δ' οὐκ αἴτιός εἰμι, | ἀλλὰ Ζεὺς καὶ Μοῖρα καὶ ἠεροφοῖτις 'Ερινύς.

[4] 1477 δαίμονα γέννης . . . | ἐκ τοῦ γὰρ "Ερως αἱματολοιχὸς | νείρῃ τρέφεται, πρὶν καταλῆξαι | τὸ παλαιὸν ἄχος.

with, a violent passion, a manifestation of the hereditary curse or fatal genius of the race. In the earlier temptation scene, she is further an incarnation of Peitho, the spirit of Delusion sent in this external shape to ruin Agamemnon; although, since she is not conscious of this ministerial character till all is over, she cannot cast her responsibility on Fate.[1]

It may help us to glance at a few incidents in 'history' where this latter idea of incarnate Temptation occurs.

Miltiades, the victor of Marathon, died in disgrace; his last expedition against Paros had failed disastrously, and he was tried for his life on the charge of having deceived Athens to satisfy a private revenge. The people let him off with a fine of fifty talents, but he died soon afterwards of a wound received, it was said, while he was at Paros. How he came by the wound was a matter of some obscurity; the current tale is told by Herodotus [2] as follows:—

'Now for so much of the story all the Hellenes agree; but for the sequel we have only the Parians' account that it happened thus. When Miltiades was at his wits' end, a captive woman sought an interview with him. She was a Parian by birth, and her name was Timo, and she was underpriestess of the Lowerworld Divinities. She, coming into Miltiades' presence, advised him, if he set great store upon taking Paros, *to do whatsoever she should suggest to him*.[3] Thereupon, at her suggestion, he made his way to the knoll that is in front

---

[1] Her unconsciousness, of course, makes the great difference between her and Orestes, who was commanded by Apollo. Again, in the *Choephori* (892 ff.), where Orestes is about to murder her, in pleading for life she does not mention Iphigeneia at all to Iphigeneia's brother, but she does refer to Agamemnon's adulteries. This is Aeschylus' way of indicating that her death is deserved, because her queenly vengeance was her real motive *at the moment* of her crime, and it is for that that she is now to be punished. He also indicates it by putting the Iphigeneia chorus at the *beginning* of the *Agamemnon*, the Helen chorus (connected with the *conjugal* relation) next before the Temptation scene.

[2] Herod. vi. 134.

[3] τὰ ἂν αὐτὴ ὑποθῆται, ταῦτα ποιέειν.

of the city and leapt over the enclosure-wall of Demeter
Thesmophoros, not being able to open the doors. And having
leapt over he went towards the Megaron to do such and such
things within it,—either to touch one of the things which it is
not lawful to touch, or to perform some act, whatever it might
be. And he came up to the doors, and immediately a shuddering
horror came over him and he hastened back by the way he
came. And in leaping down from the wall he strained his
thigh; but some say that he struck his knee.

'So Miltiades sailed back home, being in evil case: he
neither brought money to the Athenians nor had he added
Paros to their dominion, though he had blockaded the island
six and twenty days and laid it waste. And when the Parians
learnt that the underpriestess of the Gods, Timo, had guided
Miltiades, desiring to take vengeance for this, they sent men
to inquire of the God at Delphi, as soon as they had rest from
the siege. And they sent them to ask whether they should
Put to death the underpriestess of the Gods, for that she had
shown their enemies how to take their country and had
revealed to Miltiades the sacred things which it is unlawful
for men to know. But the Pythia would not suffer them,
saying that the cause of these things was not Timo, but,
because it was necessary that Miltiades should not make
a good end, *she had presented herself to him to guide him to
his destruction.*' [1]

So long as we confine our attention to 'history' and
neglect the study of mythical types, we cannot perceive
that a story like this is a temptation myth, containing
the very motive we have seen in the *Agamemnon*. When
Destruction (Ate) is about to overtake the sinner, he is
safe till he commits some overt act which will put him in
her power.[2] To 'suggest' (ὑποτίθεσθαι) this act is the function
of Temptation, Peitho or Apatê, who comes incarnate in a
woman, Clytemnestra or Timo. Thucydides would have re-

---

[1] οὐ Τιμοῦν εἶναι τὴν αἰτίην τούτων, ἀλλὰ δέειν γὰρ Μιλτιάδεα τελευτᾶν μὴ εὖ,
φανῆναί οἱ τῶν κακῶν κατηγεμόνα. Stein, followed by Macan, thinks that the
meaning is that a φάσμα, apparition, in Timo's shape, had misled Miltiades.

[2] See W. Headlam, *Cambridge Praelections* (1906), p. 118.

jected this story because the evidence was insufficient—
the very ground on which Herodotus expresses scepticism.
Some modern histories still recite it with about as much
scepticism as Herodotus. We fail to see that it is mythical
because the idea of impersonation is unfamiliar to us, but
Herodotus failed to see it because that idea was *too* familiar
to him.

Let us look now at the story of another conqueror, Pausanias, the victor of Plataea.[1] When the battle is just won,
Peitho comes to him likewise, in the form of a woman. He
is tempted to an act of violence, such as Ajax had committed
when Troy fell, such too as Agamemnon expiated at the hands
of his outraged queen.

'As soon as the Greeks at Plataea had overthrown the
barbarians, a woman came over to them from the enemy.
She was one of the concubines of Pharandates, the son of
Teaspes, a Persian; and when she heard that the Persians
were all slain and that the Greeks had carried the day,
forthwith she adorned herself and her maids with many
golden ornaments and with the bravest of the apparel that
she had brought with her,[2] and alighting from her litter
came forward to the Lacedaemonians, ere the work of slaughter
was well over.' She recognized Pausanias, and, embracing
his knees, said: 'O king of Sparta! save thy suppliant
from the slavery that awaits the captive. Already I am
beholden to thee for one service—the slaughter of these men
who had no regard either for gods or spirits. I am by birth
a Coan, the daughter of Hegetoridas. The Persian seized
me by force ($\beta i \eta$) and kept me under constraint.'

Will Pausanias yield and do the act of violence which this
woman, the innocent vehicle of Temptation, unwittingly suggests by deprecating it? No; this time he eludes the snare.
'Lady,' he answered, 'fear nothing: as a suppliant thou

---

[1] Herod. ix. 76.

[2] We are curiously reminded of Hesiod's description of how Pandora was
decked to tempt man to his bane : ζῶσε δὲ καὶ κόσμησε θεὰ γλαυκῶπις ᾿Αθήνη· |
ἀμφὶ δέ οἱ Χάριτές τε θεαὶ καὶ πότνια Πειθὼ | ὅρμους χρυσείους ἔθεσαν χροΐ, *Erga* 72.

art safe.' We breathe again; but a moment later appears another tempter.[1] Lampon, the soothsayer of Aegina, came in haste to Pausanias with 'a most unholy word'. 'Son of Cleombrotus,' he said earnestly, 'what thou hast already done is passing great and glorious, and God has given it to thee to deliver Greece and lay up for thyself the greatest glory of all the Hellenes whom we know.' The action which Lampon prompts is a deed of cruel vengeance; Pausanias is to do to Mardonius as Xerxes had done to Leonidas, and hang his dead body on a cross; so will he have praise in Sparta and in all Greece. But Pausanias again evades the trap. He rebukes Lampon for his ill counsel: 'First thou liftest me up on high, me and my country and my work; and then thou dost cast me down, bidding me to maltreat a dead man, and saying that if I do this I shall be the more well spoken of.' So Lampon is dismissed; and Pausanias takes further precautions against the lust of rapine in his army.[2]

These incidents can be classed as fabulous anecdotes. Miltiades ended his life under a cloud; therefore he must have been guilty of some impious act; therefore Temptation must have come to him and brought him to ruin. Pausanias, for a while, prospered after his victory; therefore he must have escaped Insolence; but Temptation always comes to a man in such circumstances; so he must have spared a captive woman and resisted a prompting to cruel excess in vengeance. Such is the logic, or mytho-logic, by which ancient history was made.[3]

---

[1] Herod. ix. 78.          [2] Herod. ix. 80.

[3] Tradition was not to be put off with the account of Pausanias' end given by Thucydides (i. 134); he must have been the victim, not only of Hybris, but of Eros. Accordingly a man of Byzantium informs his namesake, Pausanias the traveller, that 'the reason why the intrigues of Pausanias were detected, and why he alone failed to find protection in the sanctuary of the goddess of the Brazen House, was simply that he was sullied with an indelible taint (ἄγος) of blood'. When he was at the Hellespont he lusted after a Byzantine maiden Kleonike. She was brought to him at nightfall, and by upsetting the lamp awakened Pausanias from his sleep.

Let us return now to the story of Pylos and Sphacteria. We are concerned no longer with the minor drama of which Cleon is the hero ; but with the tragedy of Athens, whose character has been studied in the earlier books. She is adventurous, restless, quick, ambitious; if she fails in one attempt, she immediately conceives a new ambition (ἐλπίς) to take its place ; so rapidly does the act follow the decision, that hoping and having are to her the same.[1] A dangerous temperament, this, peculiarly liable to be carried away in the flush of success. 'And Fortune,' says Diodotus, ' contributes to intoxication ; for sometimes she presents herself unexpectedly at a man's side and leads him forward to face danger at a disadvantage ; *and cities even more than individuals, in proportion as their stake is the greatest of all—freedom or empire.*' We have seen this temptation of external circumstance at work in the Pylos episode, and it is enough to make us expect that temptation will appear in another form. For Elpis and Eros also in such a case ' are never wanting—Eros leading the way and devising the attempt, Elpis busy in attendance and *suggesting* the wealth in fortune's store [2]—and invisible as they are, they are stronger than the dangers that are seen '. One of these passions might be expected to come to Athens with flattering and delusive suggestions.

Elpis had not to the Greek the associations which Christianity has given to ' Hope ' ; [3] she is not a virtue, but a dangerous passion. The future is dark and uncer-

Haunted by the terrors of a guilty conscience, the king leapt up and killed the maiden, not knowing who she was. All sorts of purifications he tried in vain, and 'paid the penalty, as was natural, to Kleonike and to the god ' (*Paus.* iii. 17).

[1] i. 70 (Corinthians, characterizing the Athenians) ἦν δ᾽ ἄρα του καὶ πείρᾳ σφαλῶσιν, ἀντελπίσαντες ἄλλα ἐπλήρωσαν τὴν χρείαν· μόνοι γὰρ ἔχουσί τε ὁμοίως καὶ ἐλπίζουσιν ἃ ἂν ἐπινοήσωσι διὰ τὸ ταχεῖαν τὴν ἐπιχείρησιν ποιεῖσθαι ὧν ἂν γνῶσιν. See the whole chapter.

[2] iii. 45 ἡ δὲ (Ἐλπὶς) ἐφεπομένη . . . τὴν εὐπορίαν τῆς Τύχης ὑποτιθεῖσα (the word used of Timo's *suggestion* to Miltiades).

[3] To the Christian the hope of immortal life is a duty ; to the Greek it was ' seeking to become a god ' (ἀθάνατος = θεός)—the worst symptom of infatuate pride, exciting φθόνος.

tain, and although rational foresight (γνώμη) can see a little way into the gloom, Fortune, or Fate, or Providence, is an incalculable factor which at any moment may reverse the purposes and defeat the designs of man. Elpis is the passion which deludes man to count on the future as if he could perfectly control it; and thus she is a phase of infatuate pride, a temptress who besets prosperity[1].

Again and again we find this conception of her in the earlier poets. There is hardly one who has a good word for Elpis. ' Hope and Danger are twins among mankind, spirits of evil both'.[2] ' Hope and alluring Temptation feed us all, straining after the unattainable'.[3] ' Up and down toss the Hopes of men, cleaving the waste foam-drift on a sea of lies. No mortal upon earth has ever found a sure token from God of the thing which is still to be done; but of what shall be all discernment is blinded'.[4] ' Blind Hopes' were the only remedy Prometheus could give to man in place of the foreknowledge of death—' a great boon', say the chorus, with innocent irony.[5] Hope is called ' blind' because she looks to the invisible future; she is ' light' (κούφη) and ' winged', like the flying bird which the child will never catch.[6]

With these associations in mind, we will now take up again Thucydides' narrative,[7] and consider whether certain expres-

---

[1] Compare the following moral from Polybius ii. 4 Αἰτωλοὶ δέ, τῇ παραδόξῳ χρησάμενοι συμφορᾷ, πάντας ἐδίδαξαν μηδέ ποτε βουλεύεσθαι περὶ τοῦ μέλλοντος, ὡς ἤδη γεγονότος, μηδὲ προκατελπίζειν βεβαιουμένους ὑπὲρ ὧν ἀκμὴν ἐνδεχόμενόν ἐστιν ἄλλως γενέσθαι· νέμειν δὲ μερίδα τῷ παραδόξῳ, πανταχῇ μέν, ἀνθρώπους ὄντας, μάλιστα δὲ ἐν τοῖς πολεμικοῖς.

[2] Theognis, 637.

[3] Simon. ap. Stob. 96, 16, p. 529 Ἐλπὶς δὲ πάντας κἀπιπειθείη (a form of Peitho) τρέφει ἄπρηκτον ὁρμαίνοντας.

[4] Pindar, Ol. xii. 5 αἵ γε μὲν ἀνδρῶν πόλλ' ἄνω, τὰ δ' αὖ κάτω ψευδῆ μεταμώνια τάμνοισαι κυλίνδοντ' Ἐλπίδες . . . τῶν δὲ μελλόντων τετύφλωνται φραδαί.

[5] Aesch. Prom. 252.

[6] Aesch. Agam. 404 διώκει παῖς ποτανὸν ὄρνιν. Euripides, Aegeus frag. 11 πτηνὰς διώκεις, ὦ τέκνον, τὰς ἐλπίδας. Solon v. (Gaisf.) 36 χάσκοντες κούφαις Ἐλπίσι τερπόμεθα.

[7] iv. 53 ff.

sions employed in it are, as they are usually taken to be, mere poetical metaphors out of which all literal meaning has faded, or, on the other hand, are intended to suggest the circle of ideas which we have been studying.

The Athenians followed up their success next year by the capture of Cythera, the island which commands the entrance to the Laconian Gulf. The Lacedaemonians were much disheartened by their 'great and unlooked-for disaster'[1] at Sphacteria. They were involved in a war at sea 'and that a war against Athenians, to whom to miss an enterprise was always to fall short of some anticipated achievement; and at the same time so many strokes of Fortune coming together within a short time against all calculation[2] caused them the greatest dismay. They feared lest some new reversal of fortune (περιτύχῃ), like that of Sphacteria, should overtake them '.

In the same summer a conference of the Sicilian states was held at Gela; and Thucydides gives a speech in which Hermocrates of Syracuse appeals for united action against the designs of Athens. Some expressions which occur in it are worth noting. In the opening sentences our attention is caught by a reminiscence of Diodotus' Mytilenean speech. 'No one,' says Hermocrates, 'is driven into war in ignorance of what it means; no one is deterred from it by fear, if he conceives that he will gain some coveted end.'[3] The 'covetous designs' of Athens upon Sicily, he says later,[4] are pardonable; human nature will always seek rule where it finds submission. He touches on the secure blessings of peace in contrast with the hazards of war; and then follows a curious passage about the uncertainty of hopes in the future. 'If there be any one who makes sure that he will effect something (in revenge upon

---

[1] iv. 55. 1 τοῦ ἐν τῇ νήσῳ πάθους ἀνελπίστου καὶ μεγάλου.

[2] iv. 55. 3 τὰ τῆς Τύχης πολλὰ καὶ ἐν ὀλίγῳ ξυμβάντα παρὰ λόγον.

[3] iv. 59 οὔτε φόβῳ, ἢν οἴηταί τι πλέον σχήσειν, ἀποτρέπεται. Cf. iii. 45 (Diodotus) ἁπλῶς τε ἀδύνατον καὶ πολλῆς εὐηθείας ὅστις οἴεται τῆς ἀνθρωπείας φύσεως ὁρμωμένης προθύμως τι πρᾶξαι ἀποτροπήν τινα ἔχειν ἢ νόμων ἰσχύι ἢ ἄλλῳ τῳ δεινῷ.

[4] iv. 61. 5 τοὺς μὲν Ἀθηναίους ταῦτα πλεονεκτεῖν καὶ προνοεῖσθαι πολλὴ ξυγγνώμη.

Athens) by right or by force, let him not take his disappointment to heart.  Let him know that too many before now who have prosecuted revenges against those who wronged them, so far from succeeding, have themselves perished; and *others who with no inconsiderable power have conceived hopes of some coveted gain, instead of grasping it, have in the end lost even what they had.*[1]  *Revenge may be just, and yet not prosper; and strength is not sure because it is full of hope.*  The instability of the future everywhere controls the event;[2] and, though most treacherous, is also most salutary, since mutual fear makes men think twice before they attack one another.'  The speaker disclaims that ambitious folly by which men arrogate as complete a mastery over Fortune, which is beyond their control, as over their own purposes.[3]

Immediately after this speech Thucydides describes the return of the Athenian fleet from Sicily, whither it had proceeded from Sphacteria.  The officers in command had concluded a treaty in conjunction with their allies in the west.  They had been sent, we remember, 'to finish the war in that region',[4] and they did so; but they returned to find Athens in an altered mood.  Two of them, Pythodorus and Sophocles, were banished, and the third, Eurymedon, was fined, on the charge of having been bribed to withdraw 'when they had the chance of subjugating Sicily'.  '*So indignant were the Athenians, in the enjoyment of their present good fortune, at the idea of any check.  They thought they could accomplish anything—what was almost beyond their means as well as what was within them, with any force, no matter whether great or insufficient.  The reason was the good fortune which against all calculation had attended most of their undertakings and now suggested the strength of Hope.'*[5]

---

[1] iv. 62. 3 ἐλπίσαντες ἕτεροι δυνάμει τινὶ πλεονεκτήσειν . . . ἀντὶ τοῦ πλέον ἔχειν προσκαταλιπεῖν τὰ αὑτῶν . . .

[2] Τιμωρία γὰρ οὐκ εὐτυχεῖ δικαίως, ὅτι καὶ ἀδικεῖται· οὐδὲ ἰσχὺς βέβαιον, διότι καὶ εὔελπι. τὸ δὲ ἀστάθμητον τοῦ μέλλοντος ὡς ἐπὶ πλεῖστον κρατεῖ . . .

[3] iv. 64 μηδὲ μωρίᾳ φιλονικῶν ἡγεῖσθαι τῆς τε οἰκείας γνώμης ὁμοίως αὐτοκράτωρ εἶναι καὶ ἧς οὐκ ἄρχω Τύχης.

[4] iii. 115.

[5] iv. 65 οὕτω τῇ [τε] παρούσῃ εὐτυχίᾳ χρώμενοι ἠξίουν σφίσι μηδὲν ἐναντιοῦσθαι,

Cleon was not the only victim of covetous ambition inspired by undesigned good luck. His overweening confidence
at Amphipolis, when he ' never so much as expected that any
one would come out and fight him ', appears as illustrative
of the reckless confidence of the Athenians who ' in the enjoyment of their present good fortune were indignant at the
idea of any check '.

And who conveyed to the Athenians the flattering suggestions of Hope? who was the channel through which
she insinuated her strength? We need only turn back to
the story of the peace negotiations and repeat the sentences
in which Cleon intervenes. ' The Athenians thought that,
now they held the men on the island, *it was always in their
power to make terms whenever they chose, and they coveted
something more.*[1] *They were urged on above all by Cleon,
the son of Cleainetos, who was the popular leader in those
days and stood highest in the confidence of the multitude,
and he persuaded them.*'

To make his meaning unmistakable, Thucydides says later[2]
that Athens refused the offers of peace on this occasion because
she had ' *confidence in the hope of her strength* '. It is not
without design that Cleon, both at his first appearance in
the Mytilenean debate[3] and again at this second, disastrous
intervention, is described as ' first in the people's *confidence* '.
His little, personal catastrophe, could they have foreseen
it, might have warned his trusting followers of the peril
that lurks in ' coveting more ' ; as the speech of the Spartan
envoys, could they have listened, had actually warned them
in those very words.

---

ἀλλὰ καὶ τὰ δυνατὰ ἐν ἴσῳ καὶ τὰ ἀπορώτερα μεγάλῃ τε ὁμοίως καὶ ἐνδεεστέρᾳ
παρασκευῇ κατεργάζεσθαι. αἰτία δὲ ἦν ἡ παρὰ λόγον τῶν πλεόνων εὐπραγία αὐτοῖς·
ὑποτιθεῖσα ἰσχὺν τῆς ἐλπίδος. Cf. i. 138. 2 (of Themistocles tempting Artaxerxes
to undertake the conquest of Greece) τὴν ... τοῦ Ἑλληνικοῦ ἐλπίδα, ἣν ὑπετίθει
(suggested, insinuated) αὐτῷ δουλώσειν.

[1] iv. 21 τοῦ δὲ πλέονος ὠρέγοντο. μάλιστα δὲ αὐτοὺς ἐνῆγε Κλέων ... τῷ
πλήθει πιθανώτατος· καὶ ἔπεισεν ...

[2] v. 14 ἔχοντες τὴν ἐλπίδα τῆς ῥώμης πιστήν.

[3] iii. 36. 6 Κλέων ... ὢν καὶ ἐς τἆλλα βιαιότατος τῶν πολιτῶν τῷ τε δήμῳ
παρὰ πολὺ ἐν τῷ τότε πιθανώτατος.

'And so the promise of Cleon, *mad as it was*, resulted in success.' Yes, mad as it was! The promise was inspired by Ἐλπὶς μαινομένη, the spirit who lured Xerxes to the sack of Athens, when in her train there followed certain other invisible and awful figures,—Hybris, Koros, Dikê.[1]

Thus Cleon stands to Athens as Peitho or Apatê, incarnate in Clytemnestra, Timo, the Coan captive, Lampon, stood to their victims. The passion with which he is identified at the moment is Elpis, combined with 'Covetousness'. His intervention at the Mytilenean crisis was of a similar kind; but Athens was not then elated by undesigned success, and she escaped temptation.

We cannot, of course, *prove* what we have here put forward; it is only the analysis of the impression actually produced on us by Thucydides' story. If the reader does not find that it interprets his own impression, we can do no more; but we will ask him to suspend judgement till we have pointed out how the rest of the drama is worked out by means of the same conceptions. The '*causes*' of the Sicilian expedition, as we have so far seen them, are 'Fortune, attending against all calculation the enterprises of Athens'; 'Covetousness' impersonated in Cleon; Elpis, mad, delusive confidence and ambition, incarnate in the same individual.[2] These are the

---

[1] Herod. viii. 77 (oracle) :

... Ἐλπίδι μαινομένῃ λιπαρὰς πέρσαντες Ἀθήνας·
δῖα Δίκη σβέσσει κρατερὸν Κόρον, Ὕβριος υἱόν,
δεινὸν μαιμώοντα, δοκεῦντ' ἀνὰ πάντα πιθέσθαι.

The sack of Athens and the destruction of the temples were the committal acts to which Xerxes was tempted by Elpis, thus precipitating his own ruin (Ate).

[2] The epithet μανιώδης stuck to Cleon ; see Suidas, s. v. Κλέων. Referring to Thucydides' expression κουφολογία (iv. 36—Cleon's 'wild words' at which the Athenians laughed), Plutarch (*malig. Herod.* 2, p. 855) says that a writer who uses unnecessarily harsh expressions—who should speak, for instance, not of Cleon's κουφολογία, but of his θρασύτης καὶ μανία—οὐκ εὐμενής ἐστιν ἀλλ' οἷον ἀπολαύων τῷ σαφῶς διηγεῖσθαι τοῦ πράγματος. He adds that it is another sign of malignity in a historian if he goes out of his way to drag in the misfortunes and errors of his characters : ὅθεν ὁ Θουκυδίδης οὐδὲ τῶν Κλέωνος ἁμαρτημάτων ἀφθόνων ὄντων ἐποιήσατο σαφῆ τὴν διήγησιν. It is curious that this

first terms in a series of ' causes ' which lead in a determined order to an end that can be predicted. We have now only to follow out its later course.

writer should, even for controversial purposes, pitch upon Thucydides' treatment of Cleon as a case where Thucydides actually departs from his plan of recording τῶν γενομένων τὸ σαφές in order *not* to be 'malignant' against Cleon. Plutarch himself does not shrink from the word μανία (*vit. Nic.* vii).

# CHAPTER X

## THE MELIAN DIALOGUE

THE second half of the History opens with a summary and, for the most part, colourless record of diplomatic negotiations and battles, including a long description of the victory of Mantinea, which restored the Lacedaemonian prestige.[1] Except in one critical incident, which we reserve for the next chapter, the story presents no features that call for discussion. Accordingly we pass on to the end of Book V, where, suddenly, we come upon one of the most extraordinary and interesting passages in the whole work—the Melian Dialogue. It is extraordinary because the expedition to Melos, considered as an episode in military history, was of no importance whatever; if it had never happened, the main result of the Peloponnesian War would have been the same. The interest lies in the dialogue which accompanies the narrative; and here we happen to possess the detailed comments of an ancient critic, Dionysius, who singles out this passage—as well he might—for special remark. His observations are instructive, and we shall take note of them as we proceed.

The narrative begins as follows.[2] 'The Athenians made an expedition against the island of Melos. . . . The Melians are colonists from Lacedaemon, who would not submit to Athens like the other islanders. At first they remained quiet and were on neither side, but later, when the Athenians tried to coerce them by ravaging their land, they had come to open hostilities.[3] The generals of this expedition, Cleo-

---

[1] The Second Part begins at v. 26, and the remainder of Book V covers the years 421–416.

[2] v. 84 ff.

[3] See iii. 91.

medes and Tisias, encamped with their army on Melos ;
and before doing any harm to the country they sent envoys
to negotiate.  Instead of bringing these envoys before the
people, the Melians asked them to explain their errand to
the magistrates and the chief citizens.'

The Athenians sneeringly remark that the magistrates are
evidently afraid of their deluding the people with seductive
arguments; they accept, however, the proposal of a conference,
in which the Melians are to criticize and reply to each
statement as it is made.  The Melians answer that they
have nothing to say against the quiet interchange of explanations ; [1] but, they add, the presence of the army shows
plainly that the Athenians have come, not to argue, but
to judge.  The alternative before themselves is war, if they
make out the justice of their case, and slavery, if they are
convinced by the Athenians.

From this point to the end, the historian changes from
narrative to full dramatic form, prefixing, as in a play, the
names — ' Athenians ', ' Melians ' — to the speeches. [2]  The
Athenians begin the statement of their case as follows. [3]

*Athenians.*   Well, then, we on our side will use no
fine words ; we will not go into a long story, which would
not convince you, to prove either that our empire is justified
by our having overthrown the Persians, [4] or that our present
attack upon you was provoked by any injury on your part.
Nor is it of any use for you to urge that, although Lacedaemonian colonists, you have not fought for Sparta, or to plead
that you have never wronged us.  Let us both keep to
practical matters, and to what we really have in our minds.
We both know that in human reckoning the question of
justice comes up for decision only when the pressure of

---

[1] Note how this situation recalls Athens' refusal, prompted by Cleon, to
discuss terms quietly in a *private* conference with the Spartan envoys before
Sphacteria, iv. 22.

[2] Dion. Hal. *Thucyd.* 37 ἐπὶ μιᾶς δ' ἀποκρίσεως τοῦτο τὸ σχῆμα διατηρήσας τὸ
διηγηματικόν, προσωποποιεῖ τὸν μετὰ ταῦτα διάλογον καὶ δραματικόν.

[3] The speeches are abbreviated.

[4] The standing official justification of the Athenian empire ; cf. vi. 83, &c.

necessity is equal on both sides; in practical matters the stronger exact what they can, and the weak concede what they must.

'Thucydides begins,' says Dionysius, 'by putting together a statement which is unworthy of Athens and inappropriate to the circumstances.' The opening words 'amount to a confession that their hostilities are not justified by any provocation'. The rest comes to this: 'You are right in thinking that you are yielding to coercion; we are not unaware that we are wronging you, and we intend to get the better of your weakness by violence.' '*Such words would be appropriate to an oriental monarch addressing Greeks*[1]; but it would not be like Athenians speaking to the Greeks, whom they had freed from the Persians, to say that while the question of justice is for equals, between the weak and the strong the issue rests with violence.'

The *Melians* reply that, if the Athenians will speak only of expediency and hear nothing of justice, still, even so, it is to their own interest to listen to reason. If ever they fall themselves, the vengeance that overtakes them will be a terrible example to mankind. Then they may repent of having set a precedent of unreasonable severity.

*Athenians.* We do not look forward with dismay to the fall of our empire, if it should ever come. The danger is not from Sparta — ruling states are not harsh to the vanquished—but from our own subjects who may rise and overpower their masters. But you may leave that danger to us. We will now point out that, while we are here in the interest of our own empire, our present words are designed to save your city. We want to add you to our empire with the least trouble, and it is for the interests of us both that you should be preserved.

Dionysius comments: The reference to the clemency of Sparta amounts to saying 'tyrants are not hated by tyrants'.

---

[1] *Thucyd.* 39 βασιλεῦσι γὰρ βαρβάροις ταῦτα πρὸς Ἕλληνας ἥρμοττε λέγειν.

' The words "you may leave that danger to us" would hardly have been used by a wrecker or a pirate, indulging the passion of the moment and regardless of vengeance to come.'

*Melians.* It may be your interest to rule, but how can it be ours to be enslaved?

*Athenians.* Because by submission you will avert the worst of fates; while we shall profit by not destroying you.

*Melians.* But will you not allow us to remain neutral and be friends instead of enemies?

*Athenians.* No, your enmity is not half so mischievous to us as your friendship; to our subjects, your hate is an argument of our power, your friendship of our weakness.

*Melians.* But are your subjects blind to the difference between neutrals and revolted allies?

*Athenians.* Why, both, in their opinion, have no lack of justification; but they think that we are afraid to touch you. Thus, besides adding to our empire, we shall gain in security. As masters of the sea, we cannot afford to let islanders, and weak ones too, escape us.

*Melians.* But does not security lie in the opposite course? For, to leave justice aside, as you direct, and speak only of expediency, will you not turn all who are now neutral into enemies?

*Athenians.* We are not afraid of the mainland peoples, who are free and can take precautions against us at their leisure, but of islanders like you, who are outside our empire, and of those who are already within it and chafing at constraint. They are the most likely in their recklessness to bring themselves and us into a danger which we foresee.

*Melians.* Surely, if you and your subjects will take all this risk, you to keep your empire and they to be rid of it, we who are still free should be cowards to submit to slavery.

*Athenians.* Not if you prudently reflect. There is no question for you of honour, or of avoiding the shame of being defeated by equals. You have to think of saving yourselves, instead of opposing overwhelming strength.

*Melians.* But we know that the chances of war sometimes redress the inequality of numbers. To yield now would extinguish all hope at once; but if we act we have still a hope of standing upright.

*Athenians.* Hope is a consolation in danger, and when men have some other support she may bring them to harm, but not to utter ruin. But when men stake all they have (for she is naturally a spendthrift), in the moment of their fall she is recognized for what she is, and nothing is left them in respect of which they might be on their guard against her, now she is known.[1] You are weak and depend on a single turn of the scale. Do not choose that fate, like so many who, when ordinary human means might still save them, in the hour when all their visible hopes fail them at the pinch, turn to the invisible, to divination and oracles and the like, which ruin men by the hopes which attend them.[2]

' Thucydides,' says Dionysius, ' makes the Athenians reply in a style of labyrinthine contortion, about Hope turning out for evil to mankind. I cannot understand how any one can praise this passage as appropriate in the mouths of Athenian officers : that the hope that is from the gods (ἡ παρὰ τῶν θεῶν ἐλπίς) ruins mankind, and that divination and oracles are no help to those who have chosen a life of piety and righteousness. It was the first and highest praise of Athens that in every matter, and at every season, she followed the gods, and accomplished nothing without divination and oracles.' ' The Athenians' next answer is still more brutal.'

*Melians.* We know, you may be sure, how hard our

---

[1] v. 103 Ἐλπὶς δὲ κινδύνῳ παραμύθιον οὖσα τοὺς μὲν ἀπὸ περιουσίας χρωμένους αὐτῇ, κἂν βλάψῃ, οὐ καθεῖλεν· τοῖς δὲ ἐς ἅπαν τὸ ὑπάρχον ἀναρριπτοῦσι (δάπανος γὰρ φύσει) ἅμα τε γιγνώσκεται σφαλέντων καὶ ἐν ὅτῳ ἔτι φυλάξεταί τις αὐτὴν γνωρισθεῖσαν οὐκ ἐλλείπει. The last clause means that men are so utterly ruined by Elpis that they have no goods left which they could be on their guard against risking in another venture.

[2] ἐπειδὰν πιεζομένους αὐτοὺς ἐπιλίπωσιν αἱ φανεραὶ ἐλπίδες, ἐπὶ τὰς ἀφανεῖς καθίστανται, μαντικήν τε καὶ χρησμοὺς καὶ ὅσα τοιαῦτα μετ᾽ ἐλπίδων λυμαίνεται. Cf. iii. 45. 5 (Diodotus) ἥ τε Ἐλπὶς καὶ ὁ Ἔρως ... ὄντα ἀφανῆ κρείσσω ἐστὶ τῶν ὁρωμένων δεινῶν.

struggle will be against your power and also against Fortune, if she is not impartial. Yet we trust that in respect of fortune that is from Heaven [1] we shall not stand lower than you, because we are pure men standing against the unrighteous. And our weakness will be compensated by the aid of the Lacedaemonians, who are bound in honour to save their kinsmen. Thus our boldness is not utterly unreasonable.

*Athenians.* Oh, as for the favour of the divine, we too do not expect to be left behind. *Our claims and our actions do not go beyond men's common opinions about the divine, or their wishes for themselves. Of divinity we believe, and of humanity we know, that everywhere, by constraint of nature, it rules wherever it can hold the mastery. We did not lay down this law, nor are we the first to observe it; it existed already when we inherited it, and we shall bequeath it to exist for ever.*[2] We observe it now with the knowledge that you or any one else, if you had our power, would do the same. As for the honour of Lacedaemon, we congratulate your innocence, but do not envy your folly. The Spartans are very virtuous among themselves; but towards others, a word is enough to describe their conduct: they are the most notorious instance we know of men who identify the honourable with the pleasant, and the just with the expedient.

We will follow this horrible conversation no further, but only quote the conclusion of Dionysius' commentary, which runs thus: 'It is clear that the historian was not present at this conference, and received no report of it from the Athenians or the Melians who took part in it. From his own statement in the previous book we know that after his command at Amphipolis he was banished and spent in Thrace

---

[1] v. 104 τῇ μὲν τύχῃ ἐκ τοῦ θείου.

[2] v. 105 τῆς μὲν τοίνυν πρὸς τὸ θεῖον (τοῦ θείου, Krüger) εὐμενείας οὐδ' ἡμεῖς οἰόμεθα λελείψεσθαι· οὐδὲν γὰρ ἔξω τῆς ἀνθρωπείας τῶν μὲν ἐς τὸ θεῖον νομίσεως, τῶν δ' ἐς σφᾶς αὐτοὺς βουλήσεως δικαιοῦμεν ἢ πράσσομεν. ἡγούμεθα γὰρ τό τε θεῖον δόξῃ τὸ ἀνθρώπειόν τε σαφῶς διὰ παντὸς ὑπὸ φύσεως ἀναγκαίας, οὗ ἂν κρατῇ, ἄρχειν· καὶ ἡμεῖς οὔτε θέντες τὸν νόμον οὔτε κειμένῳ πρῶτοι χρησάμενοι, ὄντα δὲ παραλαβόντες καὶ ἐσόμενον ἐς αἰεὶ καταλείψοντες χρώμεθα αὐτῷ.

all the rest of the years of war. The dialogue is an invention, and the only question is whether he has made it appropriate to the circumstances and fitting to the characters of the interlocutors, "keeping as closely as possible to the general sense of what was really said," according to his own profession in the proem to the history.

'Now, the Melians' words about freedom, where they appeal to the Athenians not to enslave an Hellenic state which was doing them no wrong, are suitable both to the speakers and to the facts. But is there any such propriety in Athenian officers speaking as these do about justice, not allowing the question to be discussed or mentioned, but *bringing in the law of violence and covetousness*,[1] and declaring that the only rights of the weak consist in the pleasure of the stronger? I cannot think this statement befitting to officers sent on a mission to a foreign state by the city whose laws were fairest of all.

'Again, the Melians were citizens of an insignificant state which had never performed any glorious action. The Athenians, on the contrary, had chosen to abandon their land and their city in the Persian war, rather than submit to a dishonourable summons. I cannot believe that, while the Melians thought more of honour than of safety and were ready to endure the last extremity sooner than be driven to any unseemly action, the Athenians would charge with folly men who were making the very choice they had made themselves in the Persian invasion. No, in my belief, if any one else had ventured to speak like this in the presence of Athenians, he would have grievously offended the men who civilized the world.

'For these reasons I cannot approve this dialogue, as compared with the other which I have contrasted with it in detail. In that other the Lacedaemonian Archidamus makes a just demand to the Plataeans; and the style employed is clear and pure, without any contorted tropes and incoherencies. In the Melian dialogue, the wisest of the Greeks produce the most dishonourable arguments, conveyed

---

[1] Dion. Hal. *Thucyd.* 41 τὸν τῆς βίας καὶ πλεονεξίας νόμον εἰσάγοντες.

in a most unpleasing style. *Unless indeed we are to suppose that the historian, nursing a grudge against the city which had condemned him, has poured upon her all these shames, which were bound to make all men hate her.*[1] For the thoughts and words of representatives, entrusted with high powers to negotiate for their country with foreign states, are always attributed to the whole community which sends them.'

The ancient critic, we notice, is not quite satisfied with the explanation, ' a personal grudge.' He is dissenting from the common verdict which singled out this passage in the history for special praise,[2] and the gist of his judgement is that the dialogue is dramatically a failure, *unless indeed we are to think* that the improbabilities are due to deliberate malice. We believe, however, that as before, in the case of Cleon, a personal grudge is not the whole, or the main, account of the matter; and we think that the admirers of this passage were better judges than Dionysius of its artistic quality.

We have already remarked that, as an incident in the Peloponnesian war, the Melian expedition was a trivial affair; the population of a small island was wiped out, and that was the end of it. The significance of the event is only moral, and it is meant to be studied from that side. Our first question is: Why has Thucydides abandoned his practice of writing public speeches, and preferred the dramatic form of conversation?

The proposal for a private discussion is made by the Melians and accepted by the Athenian officers with a sneer. ' Well then,' say the latter, ' let us have no fine words about justice on either side, but keep to practical matters, and say what we really have in our minds.' What the Athenians have in their minds is then disclosed in all its horrible deformity. The cynical avowal of unprovoked aggression; ' the law of violence and covetousness '; the admission that what they fear is not the victory of Sparta but the vengeance

---

[1] Εἰ μὴ ἄρα μνησικακῶν ὁ συγγραφεὺς τῇ πόλει διὰ τὴν καταδίκην, ταῦτα τὰ ὀνείδη κατεσκέδασεν αὐτῆς, ἐξ ὧν ἅπαντες μισήσειν αὐτὴν ἔμελλον.

[2] Ch. 37 init.

of their own oppressed subjects ;—all this culminates in the
blasphemous insult to heaven. 'Of divinity we believe, and
of humanity we know that everywhere, under constraint of
nature, it rules wherever it can hold the mastery. We did
not make this law, nor are we the first to observe it. It
existed already when we inherited it; we shall bequeath it to
exist for ever.' Words to make the blood of any Greek run
cold, even without the ghastly reminiscence of Antigone's
appeal to the over-ruling Law of God :

> Not of to-day nor yesterday, it lives
> For ever, and none knows from whence it dawned.

But there is another reminiscence, no less significant.
When Xerxes calls together the Persian nobles to lay before them his design of conquering Greece, the speech put
in his mouth by Herodotus [1] opens thus : 'Persians, I shall
not lay down a new law among you which I myself have
introduced, but I shall observe one that I have received
from them that were before me. For, as I learn from older
men, we have never reposed ourselves since we took the
supremacy from the Medes . . . but God thus leads us on,[2]
and we, following this guidance in many enterprises, are
much advantaged.'

Dionysius, as himself a Greek, feels that the language
which Thucydides assigns to the Athenians is 'fit only
for an oriental monarch', and that no Greek could have
used it ;—except, we will add, on one condition : *that the
speaker be mad*. And, in fact, as we read the dialogue,
the impression deepens that the Athenian spokesman is out
of his right mind. We can, moreover, put a name to the
special form of his madness, which shows the peculiar
symptoms of a state classed, perhaps rightly, by the Greeks
as pathological. The two notes of it are Insolence ($ὕβρις$)
and Blindness ($ἄτη$, in the subjective sense). 'Insolence' is
a weak translation of the Greek term, which covered two
types of insane exaltation, distinguishable, but closely allied.
One is exuberant, sanguine, triumphant, fed by alluring

---

[1] Herod. vii. 8.

[2] Θεός τε οὕτω ἄγει. Cf. Soph. *Ant.* (loc. cit. infra, p. 184) θεὸς ἄγει πρὸς ἄταν.

Hope, leaping to clasp hands with unconquerable Desire. The other is cold-drawn, masked, cruel, cynical, defiant of the gods, self-assured of its own worldly wisdom. The former type we shall meet with presently; the latter is portrayed with finished art in the dialogue which leads up to the Melian massacre. Both are blind,—blind to the doom towards which the one speeds exultingly, blind to the vengeance which the other impiously denies.

This effect of blindness comes out curiously in an utterance of the Athenians later in the dialogue:[1] 'Surely you are not going to turn to that sense of '*honour*' which ruins so many when *dishonour* and danger stare them in the face! Many whose eyes were still open to the end whither they were borne have been drawn on, under the powerful spell of a mere name, by this so-called '*honour*', until, victims of a phrase, they have voluntarily fallen upon irremediable calamities and sunk by their folly to a deeper depth of *dishonour* than fortune would have inflicted.' Observe how in this sentence αἰσχύνη is used both in the moral sense of 'honour', and to mean merely the disgrace of being beaten. The speaker is not conscious of any change of meaning; he has lost all sense of the difference between honour and success, dishonour and defeat. He is already smitten with the blindness by which insolent cruelty brings vengeance on itself.

'Reverence, daughter of Forethought, crowns mankind with goodness and with joys. But over them steals a dim mist of unconsciousness and turns aside the straight path of action, away from right-mindedness.'[2]

Thucydides' first reason for choosing the dialogue form is that this pathological state of mind cannot be directly

---

[1] v. 111. 3 οὐ γὰρ δὴ ἐπί γε τὴν ἐν τοῖς αἰσχροῖς καὶ προύπτοις κινδύνοις πλεῖστα διαφθείρουσαν ἀνθρώπους αἰσχύνην τρέψεσθε. πολλοῖς γὰρ προορωμένοις ἔτι ἐς οἷα φέρονται τὸ αἰσχρὸν καλούμενον ὀνόματος ἐπαγωγοῦ δυνάμει ἐπεσπάσατο ἡσσηθεῖσι τοῦ ῥήματος ἔργῳ ξυμφοραῖς ἀνηκέστοις ἑκόντας περιπεσεῖν, καὶ αἰσχύνην αἰσχίω μετ' ἀνοίας ἢ τύχῃ προσλαβεῖν.

[2] Pindar, *Ol.* vii. 43 ; cf. l. 89.

unfolded in a public speech designed to convince a large audience. Another motive which may have influenced him is that this form is better suited to dramatic irony. The reader who has followed us so far will not have missed the passage, which excites Dionysius' astonishment, where Thucydides 'in a style of labyrinthine contortion makes the Athenian speak of Hope as turning out for evil to mankind'. Again we find Elpis spoken of as a personal agency. 'Hope is a consolation in danger, and when men have something else to depend on she may bring them to harm, but not to utter ruin. But when men stake all they have (for she is naturally a spendthrift), in the moment of their fall she is recognized for what she is, and nothing is left them in respect of which they might be on their guard against her now she is known.' This sentence is almost paraphrased from a chorus in the *Antigone*, where Sophocles sets forth the theological theory of Delusion sent by God upon a doomed sinner in the form of passionate Ambition.

'For that far-roving Hope, though many men have comfort of her, to many is a Delusion that wings the dreams of Desire; and he whom she haunts knows nothing till he burn his foot against hot fire. For with wisdom hath one given forth the famous saying that, soon or late, evil seems good to him whose mind God draws to ruin: and from the blindness of that ruin his acts are free no more than for a moment's span.' [1]

---

[1] Soph. *Antigone* 616:—

'Α γὰρ δὴ πολύπλαγκτος 'Ελπὶς
πολλοῖς μὲν ὄνασις ἀνδρῶν,
πολλοῖς δ' Ἀπάτα κουφονόων ἐρώτων·
εἰδότι δ' οὐδὲν ἕρπει,
πρὶν πυρὶ θερμῷ πόδα τις προσαύσῃ. σοφίᾳ γὰρ ἔκ του
κλεινὸν ἔπος πέφανται,
τὸ κακὸν δοκεῖν ποτ' ἐσθλὸν
τῷδ' ἔμμεν ὅτῳ φρένας
θεὸς ἄγει πρὸς ἄταν·
πράσσει δ' ὀλίγιστον χρόνον ἐκτὸς ἄτας.

The last line means that he will soon commit the fatal act, to which blindness (ἄτη) makes him liable, which Elpis-Apatê prompts, and which precipitates Ruin ('Ατη).

The Athenians, on the eve of the Sicilian expedition, are good counsellors to warn the Melians against spendthrift Hope! The irony is repeated at the close of the conference. The Melians had ended with a renewed declaration of trust in ' the fortune from the divine which hitherto has preserved them' and in the help of Lacedaemon. The Athenians reply : ' Well, we must say that this decision of yours makes us think you altogether singular in the way you count upon the future as clearer than what is under your eyes, and contemplate things unseen as already being realized in your fond wishes. The more completely you have staked all on the Lacedaemonians and Fortune and Hopes, the more utter will be your ruin.' [1]

The speaker is unconscious that even now Hope is busy in attendance at Athens, with her flattering suggestion of the wealth in Fortune's store. In the impious exaltation of strength he is unaware of the haunting Spirit of Delusion at his side, who will be known for what she is only in the moment of Athens' fall. The ' dim mist of unconsciousness' has stolen down upon him; he is smitten with madness— blind.

The thoughts and words of representatives, as Dionysius says, are always attributed to the whole community which entrusts them with their mission. Thucydides intends us to feel, with no opening for mistake, that Athens was mad when she committed this act of unprovoked, insolent cruelty, comparable with the act which Cleon had formerly advised and of which she had repented just in time. There was no repentance now. ' The siege was pressed hard, there was treachery among the citizens themselves, and Melos surrendered at discretion. The Athenians thereupon put to death all the adult males whom they caught, and sold into slavery the children and the women. Later, they colonized the island themselves, sending thither five hundred settlers.'

---

[1] v. 113 ἀλλ' οὖν μόνοι γε ἀπὸ τούτων τῶν βουλευμάτων, ὡς ἡμῖν δοκεῖτε, τὰ μὲν μέλλοντα τῶν ὁρωμένων σαφέστερα κρίνετε, τὰ δὲ ἀφανῆ τῷ βούλεσθαι ὡς γιγνόμενα ἤδη θεᾶσθε, καὶ Λακεδαιμονίοις καὶ Τύχῃ καὶ Ἐλπίσι πλεῖστον δὴ παραβεβλημένοι καὶ πιστεύσαντες πλεῖστον καὶ σφαλήσεσθε.

In the older histories it was the custom at this point to censure Thucydides for recording the massacre with no expression of disapproval!

Whose doing was this? Thucydides has not told us who played on this occasion the part which Cleon played in the massacre of Mytilene; but Plutarch informs us.[1] It was Alcibiades. The biographer tells how his public munificence, his illustrious birth, his eloquence, his bodily strength and beauty, disposed the Athenians to indulge his lawlessness and give it the mildest names—of boyish frolic and ambition. Once he shut up the painter Agatharchos in his own house till his portrait was finished, and then gave him the house for his fee. He beat Taureas, in a fit of pique, because he had been his successful rival in providing a chorus. He selected a woman from among the Melian prisoners, and reared the child he had by her. '*Even this the Athenians would have called kindhearted; only that he had been chiefly responsible, by supporting the decree, for the massacre of all the adult male inhabitants of Melos.*'

A dark passage this, which Thucydides, for whatever reason, has omitted. Had the stern historian a touch of weakness which disposed him, not, like his countrymen, to use mild names, but to draw a veil over some part of the brilliant picture? Or—a likelier supposition—is he reserving Alcibiades for a different and more characteristic effect? Cold-blooded cruelty was not the dominant trait in that mutable disposition; he kindly reared the child of his Melian captive, whose father, brothers, husband, perhaps, had perished by the decree which he supported. He may have remembered the compassion of Ajax for his Trojan captive, Tecmessa, and for their infant child Eurysakes, 'whelp of a lioness forlorn,'[2] from whom Alcibiades' family traced their descent[3]; for his own father, Cleinias, had died in battle, and left him to the guardianship of his kinsman, Pericles, as Ajax left Eurysakes to Teucer.

[1] Plut. *Alc.* xvi.

[2] Soph. *Ajax* 545-653 ; 986 ὡς κενῆς σκύμνον λεαίνης.

[3] Plato, *Alcib. I.* 121 A, Alcibiades says, καὶ γὰρ τὸ ἡμέτερον (γένος ἀναφέρεται), ὦ Σώκρατες, εἰς Εὐρυσάκη.

Here, perhaps, we may see another motive for the choice of the dialogue form. One alternative would have been to report the debate in the Athenian assembly, at which the decree of massacre was moved; but a speech from Alcibiades in support of it would have been too close and obvious a parallel to Cleon's Mytilenean speech. Alcibiades is not to appear like a second Cleon; for it was not he, but Athens, that was mad and blinded with the thirst of gain and the thirst of blood. So the historian saw her; so also did Euripides. The prologue to the *Trojan Women*,[1] first performed in the interval between the massacre of Melos and the Sicilian expedition, ends thus:—

> How are ye blind,
> Ye treaders down of cities, ye that cast
> Temples to desolation, and lay waste
> Tombs, the untrodden sanctuaries where lie
> The ancient dead; yourselves so soon to die !

[1] Eur. *Troades*, 95, Mr. Gilbert Murray's version. See also Mr. Murray's Introduction to his translation of the play.

# CHAPTER XI

## ˙ THE LION'S WHELP

THERE are in European history perhaps a dozen born
heroes whom posterity will never reduce to common proportions. They turn the soberest heads in their own generation, infecting the most prosaic observers with poetry; and
when the incorruptible evidence of monument and archive
is wanting, they are put beyond the reach of criticism.
We must submit to be dazzled as their contemporaries were;
only let us realize that we *are* dazzled, and not take the
romantic creatures for more solid stuff than they are, or
ever have been.

When Socrates, at Agathon's banquet, has finished his
encomium of Eros with the innermost revelation of Beauty,
a sudden knocking is heard at the gate of the courtyard,
a noise of revellers, and a flute-girl's voice. A moment
later, drunken, and crowned with a thick wreath of ivy
and violets, Alcibiades stands in the doorway like an apparition. Agathon's company were already flushed with wine;
but the sight of Alcibiades was a more potent intoxication.
The value of their evidence before the court of History will
lie just in the witness they bear to the most important
fact about Alcibiades—the fact that no one could resist
him. The spell of physical beauty was a thing that made
the wisest of that company feel like a fawn trembling in
the clutches of a lion.[1] Another of them, Aristophanes,
handles his Pheidippides tenderly in the *Clouds*. We must
be content with the portrait left us from the days when
two neighbours could not meet in the streets of Athens

---

[1] Socrates in Plato, *Charm.* 155 D.

without passing the news of Alcibiades' latest frolic; but we may bear in mind that they were not bent on collecting the sort of evidence we like to use in our judicious estimates of character.

Plutarch's life of Alcibiades is a vivid and harmonious composition, because Plutarch saw the personality with an artist's intuition of its total effect, and knew that a good anecdote is more illuminating than a volume of criticism. His principal authorities for the early part of his hero's career were Plato and Thucydides. That Plato, who idealized the whole world of things, idealized the persons in his dialogues, we have always perceived; so we fall back on the historian and try to patch up a real Alcibiades, by taking the substance (as we call it) of his narrative for a framework. It may be, however, that the substance is not separable, in this case either, from the form. Even Thucydides' treatment of the character, as we shall now try to show, is already dramatic and 'mythical'.

To avoid breaking the thread, we took the Melian episode out of its chronological order. We must now go back to the early chapters of Book V where the Second Part of Thucydides' history begins, and follow his narrative of the incident in which Alcibiades' type is fixed.

The two great enemies of peace had fallen at Amphipolis, and both sides were weary of the war and disheartened. The Athenians, beaten at Delium and again in the North, 'no longer possessed that confidence in the hope of their strength which had made them reject the earlier proposals of peace, when good fortune was with them and they expected to triumph. They repented of having lost the fair opportunity of reconciliation after Pylos'.[1] The Spartans too were disappointed. Their annual invasions had not weakened Athens as they had hoped; the disaster of Sphacteria was unprecedented in the annals of Lacedaemon; and the occupation of Pylos and Cythera was a constant menace,

---

[1] v. 14 οὐκ ἔχοντες τὴν ἐλπίδα τῆς ῥώμης πιστὴν ἔτι, ᾗπερ οὐ προσεδέχοντο πρότερον τὰς σπονδάς, δοκοῦντες τῇ παρούσῃ εὐτυχίᾳ καθυπέρτεροι γενήσεσθαι.

for at any moment a general revolt of the serfs might spread like a conflagration. Their kinsmen, captured on the island, were still in durance at Athens, the earlier negotiations for their recovery having failed, while Athens, in the flowing tide of success,[1] had refused fair terms. But now the troublers of Greece, Cleon and Brasidas, were lying quiet in Thracian soil; and their successors in influence —Nikias at Athens, and King Pleistoanax, lately restored from exile, at Sparta—both made for peace.

Nikias is described for us in terms which are designed to set his character in pointed contrast to Cleon's. He too had been favoured by Fortune, but he had escaped the delusions of Hope.[2] More than for any of his contemporaries, the tide of success[3] had flowed steadily for Nikias; but his only ambition was, 'while he was still unscathed and held in repute, to preserve his good fortune to the end. For the moment he desired to have rest from toil himself and to give rest to his countrymen, and for the time to come to leave behind the name of a man who in all his life had never brought disaster on his city. He thought this end could best be achieved by taking no risks and trusting himself as little as possible to Fortune; and that risks were best avoided by peace'. A sober and reverent man, who thanked the gods for blessing him with success in arms and an unstained reputation; well fitted to give his name to the peace with which the first part of Thucydides' history concludes; infinitely pathetic, as an unwilling leader of the wild chase for empire in the western seas.

We need not follow the intricate disputes and diplomatic manœuvres which worked up the latent ill-feeling on both sides to the pitch of exasperation. In the spring of 420 the war-party at Athens came in at the elections. Nikias was not returned to the office of General; but in his place appears for the first time another, very different, figure,

---

[1] v. 15. 2 εὖ φερόμενοι.
[2] οὐ συνηπατήθη ταῖς ἐλπίσι τῶν πολιτῶν, Plut. Nic. et Crassi comp. iv.
[3] v. 16. 1 εὖ φερόμενος.

whose fortunes were to be strangely and fatally linked with his.

'Foremost among those who desired an immediate renewal of war was Alcibiades, the son of Cleinias, a man who was still of an age that would in any other city have been thought youthful, but influential on account of his illustrious ancestry. He really thought that the Argive alliance was the better policy, but he took that side, against Sparta, because his pride and ambition were piqued. The Lacedaemonians had negotiated the peace through Nikias and Laches, neglecting him on account of his youth and showing no respect for their old connexion with his family, which his grandfather had renounced, but he had set his heart on renewing by his own attentions to the captives from Sphacteria. He thought that on all hands he was being put in the background'.[1]

We noticed in the case of Cleon the care with which Thucydides selects the occasion for the entrance of a principal character; the present instance shows an equal skill. Alcibiades' first recorded exploit in public life was a dishonourable trick played upon an embassy from Sparta. Thucydides chose that this should be so, for reasons which we shall not be long in perceiving. The story of the episode is treated in considerable detail, so as to fix the impression; reduced to the barest summary, it was as follows.

By means of a pledge of co-operation, given at a secret interview, Alcibiades persuaded [2] the ambassadors to contradict before the Assembly a statement they had previously made to the Council; then he turned upon them and denounced them for playing fast and loose. The people lost all patience with them, and so Alcibiades won both his points: he threw Athens into the arms of Argos, and avenged on the Spartans his own wounded pride. He would teach them not to neglect him as too young to be reckoned with, not to disregard the overtures he had made them, courting a renewal of his family connexion by flattering attentions to the prisoners.

[1] v. 43.

[2] v. 45 πείθει πίστιν δούς. Plut. Nic. x. ὁ Ἀλκιβιάδης ... περιῆλθεν αὐτοὺς δι' ἀπάτης καὶ ὅρκων ὡς πάντα συμπράξων. . . .

'The trick which deluded the Lacedaemonians also completely deluded Nikias.'[1] Still urging his pathetic formula,[2] 'Now that your prosperity is on a firm footing, it is best to preserve your good fortune to the end,' Nikias got himself sent on a fool's errand to Sparta. His negotiations miscarried, and immediately, 'in a fit of passion,' Athens concluded the alliance with Argos.[3]

'The statecraft of Alcibiades,' writes Plutarch,[4] 'was treacherous and false. The worst charge against him is a malicious trick (ἀπάτη) by which, as Thucydides tells, he deluded the Spartan envoys and put an end to the peace. Yet this policy, though it plunged Athens again in war, made her strong and terrible, for Alcibiades secured the alliance with Mantinea and Argos'.

Strong and terrible and treacherous, the young lion would have his country to be like himself. 'His disposition was full of shifts and inconsistencies.[5] There were many violent passions in his nature; but strongest of all was ambition and the desire to be first, as may be seen in the anecdotes of his childhood. Once, when he was gripped in a wrestling-match, to save himself from being thrown, he wrenched the clasped hands of his antagonist up to his mouth and made as if to bite them through. The other relaxed his grip and cried, "Do you bite like a woman, Alcibiades?" "No," he answered, "I bite like a lion."'[6]

---

[1] v. 46 ὁ Νικίας, καίπερ τῶν Λακεδαιμονιῶν αὐτῶν ἠπατημένων καὶ αὐτὸς ἐξηπατημένος. . . . Plutarch, Alc. p. 198 τὸν δὲ Νικίαν ἔκπληξις εἶχε καὶ κατήφεια τῶν ἀνδρῶν τῆς μεταβολῆς, ἀγνοοῦντα τὴν ἀπάτην καὶ τὸν δόλον.

[2] v. 46 σφίσι μὲν γὰρ εὖ ἑστώτων τῶν πραγμάτων ὡς ἐπὶ πλεῖστον ἄριστον εἶναι διασώσασθαι τὴν εὐπραγίαν.

[3] v. 46. 5 ἀναχωρήσαντός τε αὐτοῦ ὡς ἤκουσαν οἱ Ἀθηναῖοι οὐδὲν ἐκ τῆς Λακεδαίμονος πεπραγμένον, εὐθὺς δι᾽ ὀργῆς εἶχον, καὶ νομίζοντες ἀδικεῖσθαι . . . ἐποιήσαντο σπονδάς . . . .

[4] Plutarch, Alc. et Cor. comp. 2. 233 μάλιστα δὲ κατηγοροῦσιν αὐτοῦ κακοήθειαν καὶ ἀπάτην. . . .

[5] Cf. Plutarch, Alc. xxiii, for another aspect of his versatility: ἦν γάρ, ὥς φασι, μία δεινότης αὕτη τῶν πολλῶν ἐν αὐτῷ καὶ μηχανὴ θήρας ἀνθρώπων, συνεξομοιοῦσθαι καὶ συνομοπαθεῖν τοῖς ἐπιτηδεύμασι καὶ ταῖς διαίταις, ὀξυτέρας τρεπομένῳ τροπὰς τοῦ χαμαιλέοντος.

[6] Plut. Alc. ii.

And as the lion's whelp the doting multitude would hail
him. 'Though men of repute,' says Plutarch,[1] 'regarded with
abhorrence and indignant fear his reckless defiance of all
law, as a wildness that savoured of despotism, the feeling
of the people towards him is best described in Aristophanes'
line:

> They hunger for him, and hate him, and must have him.

Aristophanes touches it still more closely in the parable:

> Best not to rear a lion in a city;
> But if you rear him, wait upon his moods.'

Both quotations are from the last scene of the *Frogs*,[2] where
the couplet about the lion is put in the mouth of Aeschylus,
in reply to a demand for his advice to Athens about Alcibiades. Coming from Aeschylus, the words must allude—no
Athenian could miss the reference—to the famous simile in
the third chorus of the *Agamemnon*:[3]

> A young babe Lion, still at breast,
>   Was home once by a Herdsman borne,
> Housed beneath roof among the rest
>   And reared there; in his early morn
> And first of age, all gentle, mild,
>   Youth's darling, the delight of Eld;
> And ofttimes, like a nursling child,
>   In arms with happy love was held,
> While the weak flesh, demure and bland,
> With fawning wooed the fostering hand.
>
> But age grown ripe, his humour showed
>   The born touch that his parents had;
> Thank-offering when his nurture owed,
>   A banquet, ere the master bade,

---

[1] *Alc.* xvi.

[2] Ar. *Frogs*, 1425 ff. The first line ποθεῖ μέν, ἐχθαίρει δέ, βούλεται δ' ἔχειν is
spoken by Dionysus in reply to Euripides' question, how Athens feels
towards Alcibiades, who was now for the second time in exile. The MSS.
preserve two alternative forms of Aeschylus' reply:—

> ΑΙΣ. οὐ χρὴ λέοντος σκύμνον ἐν πόλει τρέφειν.
>
>     μάλιστα μὲν λέοντα μὴ 'ν πόλει τρέφειν,
>
>     ἢν δ' ἐκτραφῇ τις, τοῖς τρόποις ὑπηρετεῖν.

The last two lines are those which appear in Plutarch loc. cit. (except that
Plutarch has ἐκτρέφῃ).

[3] Hermann (Opusc. ii. 332 cit. Rogers ad loc.) remarked that these lines
were probably adumbrated from the parable in this chorus.

> With such wild slaughter he prepared,
> It sluiced the dwelling foul with gore,
> While helpless, all aghast, they stared
> Upon that bloody mischief sore :—
> Divine Will there had found him room,
> Housed, to be Priest of slaughtering Doom.[1]

When we find Aeschylus in the *Frogs* referring to these stanzas, they seem to read as an awful prophecy. Treacherous and strong and terrible, the young creature, whose brilliant beauty and wild ways made him the idol and cynosure of the gaping citizens, has already given, in his first public exploit, an earnest of his quality ; he turns upon the Spartans, whose friendship he had courted, as a lion-cub bites the hand it has licked. Such is the impression which Thucydides has conveyed by his choice of this incident to sound the relevant note in Alcibiades' variable character. We cannot doubt that the effect is intentional : Alcibiades comes before us as an incarnation of Apatê. Thus one of a well-known train of mythical figures treads the invisible stage, and a second is soon to follow. Hybris, the cruel spirit of madness, which fell on the Athenian people just before the Sicilian expedition —her entrance we have marked in the Melian dialogue.

Both figures take us back to the other great expeditions for conquest across the seas.

The design here reproduced is from the body of an Apulian *krater*,[2] which dates from about the middle or end of the

---

[1] Aeschylus, *Agam.* 717, Dr. Headlam's version, *Cambridge Praelections*, 1906, p. 120. Dr. Headlam comments : ' Here, expressly, Helen ' (symbolized by the young lion) ' is the instrument of Ate ; and the point is enforced by a technical device widely practised in the choral lyric.' Referring to the lines, φαιδρωπὸς ποτὶ χεῖρα σαί|νων τε γαστρὸς ἀνάγκαις, corresponding to ἐκ θεοῦ δ' ἱερεύς τις Ἄ|τας δόμοις προσεθρέφθη, Dr. Headlam continues : ' The stress of the last sentence, which of course would be accentuated in the singing, falls upon the word Ἄτας : now in the previous strophe the word in the corresponding position of emphasis is σαίνων. Attention is thereby called to a correspondence in idea ; the Lion-cub or Helen is acting like the ἀπάτη of Ἄτη, which we remember in the *Persae* φιλόφρων παρασαίνει.'

[2] Naples Museum, Heydemann, *Cat.* 3253 ; *Mon. Ined. d. Inst. Arch.* ix (1873), Tav. l, li ; *Annali* (1873), p. 22 ff. ; *Wiener Vorlegeblätter*, vii. 6 a ; Baumeister, *Denkmäler*, Taf. vi, Fig. 449, p. 408. My attention was drawn to this vase by Miss Jane E. Harrison.

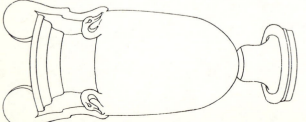

fourth century B.C. The representation falls, as usual, into three tiers. Midway in the second tier and occupying the centre of the whole composition, Darius (inscribed) is seated on a splendid throne. Behind him stands one of his guards with sword drawn ready for execution—ready advisedly, for the old man in the pointed cap and travelling boots, who stands in front of the king with uplifted warning finger, has come on a perilous journey. He is standing on the fatal golden plinth. Aelian tells us that 'if any one desired to give counsel to the Persian King on very secret and dubious matters, he must do so standing on a plinth of gold; if he was held to have given good advice, he took the plinth away with him as a reward; but he was scourged all the same, because he had gainsaid the King'[1]. We are reminded of the warning of Artabanus[2]; the whole scene signifies that to Darius, as to Xerxes, warning was given, only to be disregarded.

The lowest tier contains a group designed to emphasize the wealth and splendour of the King who is going to his doom. The treasurer, holding his account-book, is receiving the tribute.[3] One tributary pours his gold out on the table, another brings three golden cups, three more prostrate themselves in the oriental manner, abhorred of the Greek.

In the uppermost tier is high Olympus, marked by two golden stars; and here is played out the abstract, mythical counterpart of the human drama. To the right, Asia (inscribed) is seated on the altar basis of her national goddess, Aphrodite Ourania—her who at Athens, as Pausanias[4] tells us, was represented in ancient herm-shape, the 'Eldest of the Fates'. In front of Asia, beckoning her to ruin, is

---

[1] Aelian, *V. H.* 12. 62. Attention was first called to this passage by Prof. Brunn in his discussion of the vase, *Sitzungsb. d. Bayer. Akad.* 1881, ii. 107.

[2] Herod. vii. 10.

[3] The account-book is inscribed : Τάλαντα Η ; and on the table is a row of eight figures which are the initials of Μύριοι, Χίλιοι, Ἑκατόν, Δέκα, Πέντε, Ὀβολός, Ἡμιοβόλιον, Τεταρτημόριον. Böckh, *Arch. Zeit.* 1857, p. 59.

[4] Paus. i. 19. 2 ταύτης γὰρ σχῆμα μὲν τετράγωνον κατὰ ταὐτὰ τοῖς Ἑρμαῖς. τὸ δὲ ἐπίγραμμα σημαίνει τὴν οὐρανίαν Ἀφροδίτην τῶν καλουμένων Μοιρῶν εἶναι πρεσβυτάτην.

Apatê (ΑΠΑ[ΤΗ]), her own incarnate passion, yet at the same
time the minister of Zeus, who himself sits serene with
thunderbolt and sceptre. Dress and action of Apatê are alike
significant. She wears the conventional costume of an Erinys
—short *chiton* with a beast's skin over it, and high hunter's
boots; she even has snakes in her hair. Her gesture shows
that she is about to perform the ritual act proper to the
declaration of war—the act of throwing a burning torch
between the combatants.[1] Victory is for Greece; Nike,
standing at the knee of Zeus, points to Hellas, on whom
Athena lays a protecting hand. And since Marathon was
fought on the sacred day of Artemis and Apollo,[2] they too
are present—Apollo with his Delian swan, Artemis mounted
on her stag.[3]

The class of vases to which this *krater* belongs are the
only class which we know to have been influenced by
tragedy; and the arrangement of the design, with its upper
and lower tiers, may recall the description we gave of the
Aeschylean drama.[4] It illustrates in spatial form the double
effect we spoke of—the unseen supernatural action developed
in a parallel series with the human action on the stage. The
link between the two is Apatê, one of those ministering
daemons, ' between mortal and immortal,' who are described
by Diotima in the *Symposium* as ' interpreting and con-
veying, to and fro, to the gods what comes from men, and

---

[1] Schol. ad Eurip. *Phoen.* 1377 πρὸ γὰρ τῆς εὑρέσεως τῆς σάλπιγγος ἐν ταῖς
μάχαις καὶ τοῖς μονομαχοῦσιν ἐν μέσῳ τις λαμπάδα καιομένην ἔρριπτε, σημεῖον τοῦ
κατάρξασθαι τῆς μάχης.

[2] Plut. *de Glor. Ath.* vii. The festival was really in honour of Artemis and
Enyalios; the presence of Apollo is complimentary.

[3] Although scenes of daily life on vases are innumerable, scenes from
*legend* or ' history ' are very few in number. Arkesilas of Cyrene appears,
weighing his silphium; Croesus upon his funeral pyre; Harmodius and
Aristogeiton slaying Hipparchus; Sappho, with Eros, or the Muses, and
once with Alcaeus; the Persians, on the Darius vase. To appear on a vase-
painting was equivalent to a sort of pagan canonization. For a complete
list of historical subjects of vase-paintings see H. B. Walters, *Hist. of Anc.
Pottery*, ii. 149.

[4] This description, by the way, was written before the writer had seen the
design.

to men what comes from the gods'.[1] Porphyry, where he enlarges on the daemonology of this part of the *Symposium*, preserves in a philosophic form some very ancient doctrines of mythology. Speaking of the evil daemons he says : ' All unrestrained lust and hope of wealth and of glory comes through these, and most of all, *delusion*.' [2] That sentence will serve as a commentary on the Apulian vase, on the *Persians* of Aeschylus, or on the last three books of Herodotus.

For Apatê played her part also in the infatuation of Xerxes.[3] When we know the mythical motives of the Persian legend we can almost predict the incidents in the seventh Book of Herodotus. We can confidently predict the *types* of those incidents : for example, we know beforehand that the king will be deluded and outwitted on the eve of his expedition. Turn up the place, and there it is. The Aleuadae of Thessaly, we are told, sent an invitation with promises of help.[4] Xerxes thought they spoke in the name of their whole people ; [5] but really the Thessalians had no part in the intrigues of the Aleuadae.[6] The Pisistratids, again, through the agency of Onomacritus, plied Xerxes with forged oracles, suppressing those which foretold disaster to the Persian arms. ' So at last Xerxes gave way and decided to make an expedition against Greece.' [7]

Now, we do not deny that these incidents may be historical, not 'fabulous' ; but it is well to realize that Herodotus'

---

[1] Plato, *Symp.* 202 E πᾶν τὸ δαιμόνιον μεταξύ ἐστι θεοῦ τε καὶ θνητοῦ . . . ἑρμηνεῦον καὶ διαπορθμεῦον θεοῖς τὰ παρ' ἀνθρώπων καὶ ἀνθρώποις τὰ παρὰ θεῶν.

[2] Porph. *de Abst.* ii. 42 πᾶσα γὰρ ἀκολασία καὶ πλούτων ἐλπὶς καὶ δόξης διὰ τούτων, καὶ μάλιστα ἡ ἀπάτη.

[3] Aesch. *Persae* 94 ff. δολόμητιν δ' Ἀπάταν θεοῦ τίς ἀνὴρ θνατὸς ἀλύξει ; . . . φιλόφρων γὰρ σαίνουσα τὸ πρῶτον παράγει βρότον εἰς ἀρκύστατα.

[4] Herod. vii. 6.            [5] Id. vii. 130.

[6] Id. vii. 172.

[7] Herod. vii. 6 fin. Alcibiades similarly deluded Athens, Plut. *Nic.* xiii καίτοι λέγεται πολλὰ καὶ παρὰ τῶν ἱερέων ἐναντιοῦσθαι πρὸς τὴν στρατείαν· ἀλλ' ἑτέρους ἔχων μάντεις ὁ Ἀλκιβιάδης ἐκ δή τινων λογίων προύφερε παλαιῶν μέγα κλέος τῶν Ἀθηναίων ἀπὸ Σικελίας ἔσεσθαι. καὶ θεοπρόποι τινὲς αὐτῷ παρ' Ἄμμωνος ἀφίκοντο χρησμὸν κομίζοντες, ὡς λήψονται Συρακουσίους ἅπαντας Ἀθηναῖοι· τὰ δ' ἐναντία φοβούμενοι δυσφημεῖν ἔκρυπτον.

motive for putting them in is that they illustrate one regular
link in a chain of mythical ideas. The sequence is so well
established that, if the historical facts had been missing,
fabulous imagination would have supplied their place. In
the same way we do not deny that every detail of Alcibiades'
trick upon the Spartan envoys may be historical. But we do
point out that Thucydides has made it specially prominent,
partly by treating it at considerable length, and partly by telling
us nothing of any other incident in Alcibiades' early career ;
and we seem to have grounds for inferring that, in doing so,
he was in some degree influenced—however unconsciously—
by the same motives as Herodotus. We have already seen
such influence at work in the case of the Melian incident.
There, the disproportion between the military significance of
the events and their 'mythical' import is more striking; and
there again, the treatment seems of a piece with the long tale
of acts of unprovoked cruelty and insolence which Herodotus,
or those who imagined the legend, attribute to Xerxes.

When we reach the narrative of the Sicilian expedition in
Book VI, we are not surprised to encounter another incident
in which the motive of Apatê is clear. To that narrative we
pass straight from the sentence which, at the close of Book V,
records the massacre at Melos. 'They killed all the adult
males whom they caught, and sold their women and children
as slaves, and they colonized the place themselves, sending
later five hundred settlers. And in the course of the same
winter the Athenians began to desire to sail again with a larger
armament than that of Laches and Eurymedon to Sicily, to
conquer it if they could. Most of them knew nothing of the
great size of the island and the numbers of its inhabitants,
barbarian and Greek; and they did not know they were
undertaking a war not much less arduous than the war with
the Peloponnesians.'[1] Then follow five chapters which recite
the long muster-roll of Sicilian states, 'the great power against
which the Athenians were bent on making war, with fair
professions of a desire to succour their kinsmen and newly-

[1] See above, p. 49, note.

acquired allies, though the most genuine account of the matter
was that they were eager to add the whole island to their
empire.'[1]

They were urgently invited by an embassy from Egesta,
a city which had a petty quarrel with its neighbour, Selinus.
Selinus was helped by Syracuse, and the Egestaeans appealed
for succour to their allies at Athens, promising to provide all
the money that was wanted for the war. The assembly
yielded and sent an embassy to find out if the temple
treasures, of which the Egestaeans talked so much, existed,
and to report on the state of the war with Selinus.[2] The
envoys returned in the spring with some citizens of Egesta
who brought sixty talents of uncoined silver, a month's
pay for as many ships which they hoped to obtain from
Athens. The assembly was told many 'false and alluring'
tales, especially about the treasures at Egesta.[3] Their envoys
had been cheated by an ingenious trick : the Egestaeans had
shown them the temple of Aphrodite at Eryx full of bowls and
flagons and censers, which, being silver, made a show out of
proportion to their worth, and entertained the ship's crew everywhere with gold and silver plate borrowed from all the neighbouring towns, Phoenician and Hellenic. The seamen's eyes
were dazzled, and back at home their tongues ran on the bound-
less riches they had seen. Thus they 'had been *deluded* themselves and now persuaded their countrymen'.[4] The trick was
not to be discovered till too late ; for the present, Delusion keeps
the Athenians' eyes dazzled with the sheen of flaunting, golden

---

[1] vi. 6. 1 τοσαῦτα ἔθνη Ἑλλήνων καὶ βαρβάρων Σικελίαν ᾤκει, καὶ ἐπὶ τοσήνδε
οὖσαν αὐτὴν οἱ Ἀθηναῖοι στρατεύειν ὥρμηντο, ἐφιέμενοι μὲν τῇ ἀληθεστάτῃ προφάσει
τῆς πάσης ἄρξαι, βοηθεῖν δὲ ἅμα εὐπρεπῶς βουλόμενοι τοῖς ἑαυτῶν ξυγγενέσι καὶ τοῖς
προσγεγενημένοις ξυμμάχοις, μάλιστα δὲ αὐτοὺς ἐξώρμησαν Ἐγεσταίων πρέσβεις. . . .
With the turn of the sentence cf. iv. 21. 2 (Cleon's intervention before
Sphacteria, above, p. 113), . . . τοῦ δὲ πλέονος ὠρέγοντο, μάλιστα δὲ αὐτοὺς ἐνῆγε
Κλέων. . . .

[2] vi. 6.

[3] vi. 8. 2 καὶ οἱ Ἀθηναῖοι ἐκκλησίαν ποιήσαντες καὶ ἀκούσαντες τῶν τε Ἐγεσταίων
καὶ τῶν σφετέρων πρέσβεων τά τε ἄλλα ἐπαγωγὰ καὶ οὐκ ἀληθῆ καὶ περὶ τῶν
χρημάτων ὡς εἴη ἑτοῖμα ἔν τε τοῖς ἱεροῖς πολλὰ καὶ ἐν τῷ κοινῷ, ἐψηφίσαντο ναῦς
ἑξήκοντα πέμπειν. . . .

[4] vi. 46 αὐτοί τε ἀπατηθέντες καὶ τοὺς ἄλλους πείσαντες.

Wealth. They voted that sixty ships should sail under the command of Alcibiades, Nikias, and Lamachus.

'How else,' says Peitho-Clytemnestra, 'how else pitch the toils of Harm to a height beyond o'erleaping? ...

> I wreathed around him like a fishing-net,
> Swathing in a blind maze,—deadly *wealth* of robe!'[1]

Had Aphrodite, in her precinct at Eryx, a chapel for her attendant spirit, Persuasion?

---

[1] Aesch. *Agam.* 1381, Dr. Headlam's version (*Cambridge Praelections*, 1906, p. 135)  ἄπειρον ἀμφίβληστρον, ὥσπερ ἰχθύων,
περιστιχίζω, πλοῦτον εἵματος κακόν.

Schol. ad loc. τὸ δὲ ' ὕψος κρεῖσσον ἐκπηδήματος ' τοῦτο σημαίνειν βούλεται, ὅτι ὁ φιλικῶς ὑπερχόμενός τινα καὶ ἀπατῆσαι βουλόμενος εἰς ἄφυκτον φραγμὸν ἐμπλέκει αὐτὸν τῆς Ἀπάτης.

# CHAPTER XII

## EROS TYRANNUS

THE Melian Dialogue, as we have already seen, suggested to an ancient critic the parallel between the imperial people and the Eastern monarch. Thucydides, by perpetual coincidences of thought and phrase, and by the turn and colour of all this part of his narrative, has with evident design emphasized this parallel, and so turned against Athens the tremendous moral which his countrymen delighted to read in the *Persians* of Aeschylus and the History of Herodotus. Looking back upon the development of the Empire in the previous fifty years, he saw, as we noted in our study of the first Book, the defection of Athens from the old, glorious ideal of the union of Hellas against the outer darkness of barbarism. The downward process led to this mad war of conquest between Greek and Greek. Athens, tempted by Fortune, deluded by Hope, and blinded by covetous Insolence, was attempting an enterprise comparable with that which it was her boast to have repulsed and broken at Salamis. In the debate upon the expedition we shall hear Nikias reiterate the warnings addressed in vain by Artabanus to the infatuate monarch, and Alcibiades echo the eager tones of Mardonius, who, 'ever desirous of some new enterprise and wishing himself to be regent of Hellas, persuaded Xerxes.' [1]

'Nikias, appointed against his will, saw that Athens was ill-advised and on a flimsy and fair-seeming pretext was bent on a great enterprise, desiring the whole of Sicily.' He attempted to 'avert' their purpose,[2] with little hope of success,

[1] Herod. vii. 6 νεωτέρων ἔργων ἐπιθυμητὴς ἐὼν καὶ θέλων αὐτὸς τῆς Ἑλλάδος ὕπαρχος εἶναι . . . ἀνέπεισε Ξέρξην.

[2] Thuc. vi. 8. 4 ἀποτρέψαι, 'avert,' has religious associations. It recalls the story of Artabanus who is threatened by the vision (Herod. vii. 17) in these

for he saw that the people were not in a mood to hear reason. 'I have never,' he said, 'out of ambition spoken contrary to what I thought, nor will I now; but I will tell you what in my judgement is best. If I exhorted you to preserve what you have, instead of risking things present for the sake of things future and uncertain,[1] my words would be powerless against a temper like yours. Yet I must show you that your haste is ill-timed and that the object for which you are so eager is not easy to grasp.' The position of Athens at home is by no means secure. 'We ought to think of this and not run into danger while the state is far from the desired haven, or grasp at a new empire before we have secured the old. Even if we conquer, we could hardly rule so many cities at such a distance. It is madness for men to attack a land which, if they prevail, they cannot hold, while failure would not leave them where they were before the attempt. ... Because your first fears of Lacedaemon have not been realized and you have unexpectedly got the better of them, now you despise them and desire Sicily. You ought not to be elated at the chance mishaps of an enemy; conquer them in skill before you are confident.'[2]

'If there is one who, in delight at his appointment, urges you to sail, looking only to his own interest; especially one who is too young as yet to hold a command, and wants to

---

terms, 'Thou shalt not escape scatheless, either now or in the time to come, for seeking to *avert* that which must happen' (ἀποτράπων τὸ χρεὸν γενέσθαι). Cassandra's fate was partly a punishment for her attempts to avert by warnings the vengeance of God. No one would listen. Cf. Herod. ix. 16 ὅ τι δεῖ γενέσθαι ἐκ τοῦ θεοῦ, ἀμήχανον ἀποτρέψαι ἀνθρώπῳ· οὐδὲ γὰρ πιστὰ λέγουσι ἐθέλει πείθεσθαι οὐδείς. The word is still reminiscent of a belief that Ruin is an evil spirit to be charmed away by rites of magical 'aversion'.

[1] vi. 9. 3 περὶ τῶν ἀφανῶν καὶ μελλόντων κινδυνεύειν, echoing the Athenians' last words in the Melian dialogue (above, p. 185), τὰ μὲν μέλλοντα τῶν ὁρωμένων σαφέστερα κρίνετε, τὰ δὲ ἀφανῆ τῷ βούλεσθαι ὡς γιγνόμενα ἤδη θεᾶσθε, κτλ.

[2] vi. 11. 5 διὰ τὸ παρὰ γνώμην αὐτῶν πρὸς ἃ ἐφοβεῖσθε τὸ πρῶτον περιγεγενῆσθαι, καταφρονήσαντες ἤδη καὶ Σικελίας ἐφίεσθε. χρὴ δὲ μὴ πρὸς τὰς τύχας τῶν ἐναντίων ἐπαίρεσθαι, ἀλλὰ τὰς διανοίας κρατήσαντας θαρσεῖν. Compare the passage (iv. 65. 4) quoted above, p. 170, which connects the desire for Sicily with the fortune of Pylos, and ends : αἰτία δ' ἦν ἡ παρὰ λόγον τῶν πλεόνων εὐπραγία αὐτοῖς ὑποτιθεῖσα ἰσχὺν τῆς ἐλπίδος.

be admired for his stud of horses and to make something
by his position to maintain him in his extravagance, do not
indulge him with the opportunity to display his personal
brilliance at Athens' risk. Remember that such men, as
well as spending their private substance, do public harm.
This is a great enterprise and not one which a mere youth
can plan and rashly undertake.[1]

'There, beside the man of whom I speak, I see now men
of this kind whom he has summoned to his support, and I am
afraid. I appeal against them to you elder citizens; if any
of you has one such sitting beside him, let him not be ashamed
or fear to seem a coward if he does not vote for war. Do
not, like them, fall sick of *a fatal passion for what is beyond
your reach*.[2] Bethink you that desire gains few successes,
and forethought many.[3] For your country's sake, now on
the brink of the greatest danger she has known, hold up your
hands to vote against them. There is no fault to find with
the boundaries which the Sicilians now observe in this
direction—the Ionian Gulf on the coast voyage, and the
Sicilian Ocean by the open sea. Confirm these limits by
your vote, and leave Sicily to manage her own affairs'. . . .

'President, if you believe that the welfare of Athens is
entrusted to you and you wish to be a good citizen, put the
question over again and lay the proposal once more before
the Athenians. If you hesitate to put a question already
once decided, remember that with so many witnesses present
there can be no question of breaking the law, and that you
would be the physician of the state when her thoughts are
sick. He proves himself a good magistrate who does all he
can to help his country, or to the best of his will at least does
her no harm.'

The speech is charged with allusions to themes which are

---

[1] Compare the effect of this personal reference to Alcibiades with Artabanus' concluding address to Mardonius, Herod. vii. 10. § 7.

[2] vi. 13. 1 μηδ' ὅπερ ἂν αὐτοὶ πάθοιεν, δυσέρωτας εἶναι τῶν ἀπόντων.

[3] Thuc. vi. 13 ἐπιθυμίᾳ μὲν ἐλάχιστα κατορθοῦνται, προνοίᾳ δὲ πλεῖστα. Herod.
vii. 10, Artabanus says: ἐπειχθῆναι μὲν πᾶν πρῆγμα τίκτει σφάλματα . . . ἐν δὲ τῷ
ἐπισχεῖν ἔνεστι ἀγαθά.

now familiar to us.  Only one or two call for comment.  The reference to the natural boundary fixed by the Ionian and Sicilian seas is significant in the mouth of the pious Nikias. Some superstitious feeling still lingered about the impiety of crossing the far, inviolable seas.[1]  To pass the pillars of Heracles is to Pindar a symbol of ambition that outruns the limits of divine appointment.  In this way Xerxes had offended: the bridge over the Hellespont and the canal at Athos[2] had led his armament to the deep waters of Artemisium and Salamis.  The sea too had risen, 'not without Heaven's wrath,'[3] on his prototype, Agamemnon, returning, flown with insolence, from the conquest of the East.  In the herald's tremendous description of the storm we hear the rolling thunder of outraged gods, which we heard before in the *Persians*.  It is echoed again by Poseidon himself in the prologue to the *Trojan Women*, which was performed within a month or two of Nikias' speech :[4]

> These mine hands
> Shall stir the waste Aegean; reefs that cross
> The Delian pathways, jag-torn Myconos,
> Scyros and Lemnos, yea, and storm-driven
> Caphêreus with the bones of drownèd men
> Shall glut him.—Go thy ways, and bid the Sire
> Yield to thine hand the arrows of his fire.
> Then wait thine hour, when the last ship shall wind
> Her cable coil for home!

The warnings of Nikias fell, as he anticipated, upon deaf

---

[1] There seems to be some trace of this feeling in the anger of Poseidon at the nautical skill of the Phaeacians, Hom. *Od. θ.* 565 ; *v.* 162.  It remains as a commonplace in Augustan poetry.  Hor. *Od.* i. iii. 21 :—

> Nequidquam deus abscidit
>      prudens Oceano dissociabili
> terras, si tamen impiae
>      non tangenda rates transiliunt uada.

Plut. *Nic.* xii, describing this speech, says that Nikias ἀναστὰς ἀπέτρεπε καὶ διεμαρτύρετο, καὶ τελευτῶν διέβαλε τὸν Ἀλκιβιάδην ἰδίων ἕνεκα κερδῶν καὶ φιλοτιμίας τὴν πόλιν εἰς χαλεπὸν ἐξωθεῖν καὶ διαπόντιον κίνδυνον.

[2] Herodotus (vii. 24) regards the making of the canal as unnecessary, and an exhibition of pride.

[3] Aesch. *Agam.* 654.

[4] Eurip. *Trojan Women* 87.   Mr. Gilbert Murray's version.

ears; for the thought of the city was sick and it was vain to call for a physician. The name of her sickness was Eros, the fatal, passionate lust for what is out of reach. She has caught the infection from the band of spendthrift youths, sitting there in the assembly at the summons of one who outshines them all. He, pleased with the command he is as yet too young to hold, nourishes hopes of new wealth to feed the stream of his extravagance; he is ambitious to display his brilliance at Athens' risk, and he is hot for an enterprise too great for a mere youth to plan. And yet, is not the planning of great schemes the very office of Youth and ever-young Desire? When delusive Hope is busy flattering men with glimpses of the treasure in Fortune's store, then Desire too is never wanting—Eros, who 'leads the way and devises the attempt'.

'Of the beauty of Alcibiades,' says Plutarch, 'one need only say that it blossomed with every season of his life as boy and youth and man, and bloomed upon his body, making him lovely and pleasant to look upon.' [1] And not only in his body; for 'while the rest of his thronging lovers were smitten with the brilliance of his outward beauty, the love of Socrates was a great witness to the boy's excellent and fair nature, which he discerned shining within his beautiful form and flashing through it'. The pure and watchful attachment of this strange friend was returned with as much fidelity as the wayward moods of the younger allowed. 'Despising himself, and wondering at Socrates, whose wisdom delighted him and whose virtue he reverenced, Alcibiades, in Plato's words, was unwittingly possessed of Anteros, who is the counterpart of Eros, so that all were amazed to see him taking his meals with Socrates, and wrestling with him, and sharing his tent, while to the rest of his lovers he was harsh and untameable.' [2] But in other moods he would 'slip away from Socrates and play the truant, surrendering himself to the pleasures with which flatterers allured him'.[3] Then he would become possessed of another Eros than that which the discernment of Socrates divined through the radiant brilliance of his form.

[1] Plut. *Alc.* i.  [2] Ibid. iv.  [3] Ibid. vi.

When Nikias describes Alcibiades and his friends as 'sick of a fatal passion for what is out of reach', he is quoting from Pindar's story of Coronis, who, not content with one lover, 'fell into a passion for what was out of reach, as many do.[1] Of all men the most foolish sort are they who are ashamed of what is homely and fix their eyes on what is afar off, a-chase of bubbles, with Hopes (ἐλπίσιν) unachievable. Such utter blindness (ἀϝάταν) the spirit of fair-robed Coronis caught.' This Eros is near akin to Elpis; and the two are often coupled with Youth and Wealth. 'He that wins some fresh honour in the time of luxurious youth, out of great Hope soars on the wings of prowess, with a dream that rises beyond wealth. But the joy of mortals in a short while ripens to the full, and soon again falls earthward, shaken by adverse doom. Creatures of a day, something or nothing, man is the shadow of a dream. Only, when a gleam from God comes, a shining light rests on men and life is sweet.'[2] So again, in a more obscure passage,[3] Pindar speaks of wealth giving splendid opportunities and inspiring 'a wilder dream'. Its light is a sure beacon, if, but only if, '*he who has it knows what shall be.*' If not, if his hopes are blind, and soar too high towards the unknown future—we know the rest. 'For each one has Hope with him, Hope, that shoots up in a young man's breast. So long as he has the lovely flower of Youth and his heart is light, a mortal has many dreams that cannot be fulfilled.'[4] And Eros brings Madness in his train : 'Appetite, doubled, is Eros; and Eros, doubled, becomes Madness.'[5] 'The Spirits of Madness are swift to overtake the Loves that cannot be attained.'[6]

---

[1] Pind. *Pyth.* iii. 20 ἀλλά τοι ἤρατο τῶν ἀπεόντων· οἷα καὶ πολλοὶ πάθον. Thuc. vi. 13 μηδ' ὅπερ ἂν αὐτοὶ πάθοιεν, δυσέρωτας εἶναι τῶν ἀπόντων; Plut. *Per.* xx πολλοὺς δὲ καὶ Σικελίας ὁ δυσέρως ἐκεῖνος ἤδη καὶ δύσποτμος ἔρως εἶχεν, ὃν ὕστερον ἐξέκαυσαν οἱ περὶ τὸν Ἀλκιβιάδην ῥήτορες.

[2] Pind. *Pyth.* viii. 88.

[3] *Ol.* ii. 58.

[4] Simonides c. (Gaisf.).

[5] Stob. 64. 29 Προδίκου· Ἐπιθυμίαν μὲν διπλασιασθεῖσαν Ἔρωτα εἶναι, Ἔρωτα δὲ διπλασιασθέντα Μανίαν γίγνεσθαι.

[6] Pind. *Nem.* xi. 48 ἀπροσίκτων δ' Ἐρώτων ὀξύτεραι Μανίαι (cf. ὀξεῖ' Ἐρινύς. *Ol.* ii. 45).

Eros is more particularly the passion of the *tyrant*.  Note how Plato [1] describes the genesis of the 'tyrannical man', who is the successor of a 'democratical' parent, or 'man of the people'.

'Imagine then again, said I, that the "democratical" man is now advanced in years and that once more a young son has been brought up, in *his* habits of life.

'Good.

'Imagine further that the old story of his father's experiences is repeated in his case.  He is led away into every sort of lawlessness,[2]—or liberty, as his seducers call it.  His father and the rest of his family come to the assistance of those appetites which belong to his half-way position, while his seducers reinforce them on the other side.  When these wicked sorcerers and tyrant-makers despair of gaining possession of the youth by any other spell, suppose that they contrive to raise in him a spirit of passionate desire (Ἔρωτα), to champion the rabble of those idle appetites which divide among themselves whatever is available.[3]  It will be like a great winged drone ;— unless you can think of a better comparison for the spirit of desire in such men as these ?

'No, he said, I can think of none better.

'This done, the other appetites, humming like bees round the drone, laden with incense and perfumes and garlands and wines and the loose pleasures of convivial luxury, feeding and nursing him to full growth, implant in him a sting of longing that cannot be satisfied (πόθου κέντρον).  From this moment, with madness for his body-guard, this champion of the soul-mob is goaded to frenzy ; and whenever he catches within

---

[1] Plato, *Rep.* 573.

[2] παρανομίαν.  Cf. Plut. *Alc.* xvi οἱ μὲν ἔνδοξοι . . . ἐφοβοῦντο τὴν ὀλιγωρίαν αὐτοῦ καὶ παρανομίαν, ὡς τυραννικά . . . but the Athenian people used τὰ πρᾳότατα τῶν ὀνομάτων for his misdeeds.

[3] The allusion is to the evil which arises in an oligarchical state, when men are allowed to sell all their property and become paupers, while the purchasers become extravagantly rich.  Thus arises a class of drones, analogous to the idle appetites here.  See 552 B.  Eros becomes 'champion' (προστάτης) of the desires, as the aspirant to tyranny champions the proletariate.

himself any thoughts or passions that are of good report and
still sensible of shame, he slays them and casts them out from
himself as unclean, until he is purged of temperance and has
brought in a complement of madness to fill its place.

' A complete description, said he, of how a " tyrannical " a n
comes to be.

' Is not this, then, I said, the reason why " tyrant " is quite an
old appellation of Eros ?

' Probably, he replied.

' Also, my friend, said I, when a man becomes intoxicated,
he begins to have a " tyrannical " temper, does he not ?

' Yes.

' And then again, the madman, when his wits are deranged,
will attempt lordship over gods as well as men, and be
confident (ἐλπίζει) of his power to achieve it.

' Very true, he replied.

' So, said I, to be precise, a " tyrannical " man comes into
being whenever, either by temperament or by habits of life
or by both together, he falls under the dominion of wine or of
love or of insanity.'

That Plato had Alcibiades in his mind is probable from his
language in another dialogue. Alcibiades is living on the
hope (ἐλπίδι) of becoming like Cyrus and Xerxes [1]; and he
has a passion (ἐρᾶν) for becoming the most famous man
among all Greeks and barbarians.[2] Socrates promises not to
give him up unless his worst fear should be realized, namely,
that Alcibiades ' should be corrupted by becoming the *Lover
of the Demos*'.[3] Plato has coined a word—δημεραστής—to
express the relation which Eros, the tyrant passion, has to
the lower desires, and which Alcibiades will have to the
democracy. At the end of the dialogue Socrates proves
that a man ought not to seek a *tyranny* for himself or for
his city.[4]

---

[1] Plat. *Alc.* i. 105 A, cf. E τοσαυτῆς ἐλπίδος γέμειν.
[2] Ibid. 124 E.
[3] Ibid. 132 A.
[4] Ibid. 135 B. Plutarch, keenly alive to the mythical side of Plato's
thought, seized on this connexion of ideas. Recording one of the later
brilliant achievements of Alcibiades, he says, ἤρθη μὲν αὐτὸς τῷ φρονήματι

This association of Eros with 'tyranny' gives a fresh meaning to Thucydides' references to Athens as the tyrant city. Each of the two earlier leaders of the people, Pericles and Cleon, uses the expression;[1] but Pericles would have had the citizens be lovers of *Athens*;[2] and 'tyranny' meant in his original ideal what it had meant to many states of Greece: the supremacy of art and civilization. To Cleon it had meant the iron rule of force over unwilling subjects always plotting rebellion. Alcibiades is the Lover, not of Athens, but of the People;[3] he was suspected of designs for personal despotism, and filled with the tyrant's passion, the lust of conquest and of personal glory.

In the relief,[4] here reproduced, Eros with his great wings stands leaning his hand on the shoulder of Paris, who points upward, whither his dreams are soaring. Over against them sits Helen, scarcely listening to Aphrodite who is beside her, but with eyes fascinated by the love-light from the eyes of Paris; above her is Peitho, with a bird—perhaps the bird of love-magic, the Iynx—in her hand. As Paris swept Helen across the seas, so now the Lover of the People is 'kindling the flame of Desire in Athens, and persuading them to undertake a great expedition to conquer Sicily, suggesting great hopes to the People, and himself coveting yet greater things'.[5]

καὶ τὴν στρατιὰν ἐπῆρεν ὡς ἄμαχον καὶ ἀήττητον οὖσαν ἐκείνου στρατηγοῦντος, τοὺς δὲ φορτικοὺς καὶ πένητας οὕτως ἐδημαγώγησεν ὥστε ἐρᾶν ἔρωτα θαυμαστὸν ὑπ' ἐκείνου τυραννεῖσθαι, *Alc.* xxxiv.

[1] Thuc. ii. 63 (Pericles) ὡς τυραννίδα γὰρ ἤδη ἔχετε αὐτὴν (τὴν ἀρχήν), iii. 37 (Cleon) ὡς τυραννίδα ἔχετε τὴν ἀρχὴν καὶ πρὸς ἐπιβουλεύοντας αὐτοὺς καὶ ἄκοντας ἀρχομένους.

[2] Thuc. ii. 43 (Pericles) ἐραστὰς γιγνομένους αὐτῆς (τῆς πόλεως, not τοῦ δήμου).

[3] Thuc. vi. 89 (Alcibiades) τῷ δήμῳ προσεκείμην μᾶλλον.

[4] This marble relief, now in the Naples Museum, is assigned to the middle of the fourth century at earliest ; ' die hier zum Ausdruck kommende Bedeutung Peithos ist aber sicher viel älter,' Weizsäcker, Roscher, *Lex. Myth.* s. v. *Peitho.* The types of the several figures are probably earlier than this grouping of them.

[5] Plut. *Alc.* xvii ὁ δὲ παντάπασι τὸν ἔρωτα τοῦτον ἀναφλέξας αὐτῶν καὶ πείσας μὴ κατὰ μέρος μηδὲ κατὰ μικρὸν ἀλλὰ μεγάλῳ στόλῳ πλεύσαντας ἐπιχειρεῖν καὶ καταστρέφεσθαι τὴν νῆσον, Ἀλκιβιάδης ἦν, τόν τε δῆμον μεγάλα πείσας ἐλπίζειν, αὐτός τε μειζόνων ὀρεγόμενος. Note how Plutarch preserves all the key-phrases of Thucydides.

In the debate which followed the speech of Nikias[1] 'he who most eagerly urged the expedition was Alcibiades the son of Cleinias. He wished to oppose Nikias, who was always his political antagonist and just now had referred to him disparagingly; but above all he thirsted to command, and hoped[2] that he might be instrumental in seizing Sicily and even Carthage, and at the same time that his success might repair his private fortunes and gain him money as well as fame. For being in conspicuous repute among the citizens, he indulged his desires beyond his means in the upkeep of his horses and other extravagances—a temper which later had much to do in bringing about the utter ruin[3] of Athens. For the people took alarm at the extreme lawlessness of his bodily self-indulgence, and at the far-reaching conceptions which animated his conduct in every detail of any action in which he took part, and thinking he was desirous of becoming tyrant, they set themselves to oppose him. Hence although his management of the war was excellent, individuals took umbrage at his private behaviour, and so they entrusted the war to others and soon shipwrecked the state' (ἔσφηλαν τὴν πόλιν).

Alcibiades begins by asserting his claims to command, and defending his personal magnificence as a public benefit. No other private individual had ever sent seven chariots into the lists at Olympia; and, though a display of this kind may excite murmurs at home, it impresses foreigners with the strength of Athens. Such 'folly' (ἄνοια) is not useless. One who knows his own superiority cannot be expected to treat others as equals. Men of a lofty and disdainful spirit are hated during their lives, but when they are dead their country boasts of them and posterity are eager to claim descent from them.[4] Such are his ambitions; and as for his

---

[1] Thuc. vi. 15.        [2] ἐπιθυμῶν καὶ ἐλπίζων.

[3] καθεῖλεν, a technical word for Ate. Aesch. *Agam.* 404 τὸν δ' ἐπίστροφον τῶν | φῶτ' ἄδικον καθαιρεῖ. Of Elpis Thuc. v. 103 κἂν βλάψῃ, οὐ καθεῖλεν.

[4] Bruns has remarked a reference to the exaggerated cult of Alcibiades after his death—a proof that this speech was written later than that event. Busolt iii. 2674[n]. Aristotle's remarks on heredity furnish a strange comment: 'There is a kind of crop in the families of men (φορά, as Cope

public policy hitherto, who can show a better record? His
youth and 'folly', now held to be so monstrous, won the
Peloponnesians with well-sounding words and his heartiness
gained confidence for his persuasions.[1] Let them not take alarm
now; but while this youth of his, like Nikias' reputation for
success, is still in its flower,[2] take full advantage of both.

Alcibiades proceeds to make light of the power of Sicily
They are a motley rabble, disunited and unable to defend
themselves; the numbers of their heavy infantry have been
greatly exaggerated.[3]    And at home Athens, strong in her
navy, has little to fear.  The Peloponnesians were never more
hopeless than now.  Athens has no excuse for hanging
back from helping her allies in Sicily, on whose assistance
she relied for harassing her own enemies there.  Our empire,
like others, was acquired by readiness to respond to invita-
tions for help.  We cannot play the housewife with an empire
and pick and choose how far it shall extend.  We must keep
our grasp on what we have and contrive occasions against
others.[4]  If we do not rule, others will rule us.[5]

observes, here implies an alternation of φορά and ἀφορία, of good and bad
crops), just as there is in the produce of the soil; for a certain time remarkable men grow up in them, and then (after an interval of unproductive-
ness) they begin again to produce them.  When clever families degenerate,
their characters acquire a tendency to *madness, as for instance the descendants
of Alcibiades* and Dionysius the Elder, whereas those of a steady character
degenerate into sluggishness or dullness, as in the case of those of Conon and
Pericles and Socrates.'  Ar. *Rhet. β.* xv, Cope's version.  Cf. Plato, *Alcib. I.*
118 E, Alcibiades calls Pericles' sons ἠλιθίω, and his own brother Cleinias
μαινόμενον ἄνθρωπον.

[1] ὀργῇ πίστιν παρασχομένη ἔπεισεν.

[2] ἕως ἔτι ἀκμάζω μετ' αὐτῆς (τῆς νεότητος).  Cf. Plut. *Nic.* xiv πρὶν ἐγγηράσα
μὲν τὴν ἀκμὴν τῆς ἐλπίδος.

[3] Thuc. vi. 17. 2 ὄχλοις ξυμμείκτοις πολυ νδροῦσι ... 4 τὸν τοιοῦτον ὅμιλον.
So Mardonius : The Ionians in Europe are 'worthless' (ἀνάξιοι) and their
method of fighting is foolish, Herod. vii. 9.    Artabanus reproves him for
slanderously making light of the Greeks in order to ' exalt ' (ἐπαείρειν) Xerxes'
self-confidence.

[4] Thuc. vi. 18. 3 (Alcibiades) ἀνάγκη ... τοῖς μὲν ἐπιβουλεύειν, τοὺς δὲ μὴ
ἀνιέναι.  iii. 45 (Diodotus) ὁ μὲν ("Ερως) τὴν ἐπιβουλὴν ἐκφροντίζων.  Compare
iv. 60 (Hermocrates) ἐπιβουλευομένην τὴν πᾶσαν Σικελίαν ὑπ' Ἀθηναίων, coming
just after the allusion to Diodotus' speech (iii. 45 fin.) : οὔτε φόβῳ, ἢν οἴηταί
τι πλέον σχήσειν, ἀποτρέπεται (iv. 59).

[5] Thuc. vi. 18. 3 διὰ τὸ ἀρχθῆναι ἂν ὑφ' ἑτέρων αὐτοῖς κίνδυνον εἶναι, εἰ μὴ

A display of activity in attacking Sicily will lay the pride of the Peloponnesians in the dust[1]; and the conquest of the island will lead to the conquest of all Hellas.[2] As masters of the sea we can withdraw safely at any time. Do not be diverted by Nikias' doctrine of indolence or his attempts to set old against young. Our fathers, old and young taking counsel together, brought Athens to her present greatness: you should endeavour to lead her yet further in the same way.[3] Inaction will lead to internal friction and decay; conflict and exercise bring gain of experience and new strength for active defence.

The most remarkable part of this speech is the opening defence of the speaker's lavish magnificence, as being a public benefit; following as it does immediately upon the historian's statement that this very quality was a principal cause of Athens' utter downfall. It seems very unlikely that Alcibiades at such a moment would have actually used language so offensively boastful. Once more Thucydides is straining probability in order to give the impression of a certain state of mind. The case is analogous to the Melian dialogue, where the speeches of the Athenian representative were used to portray the insolent and impious cruelty, hardly distinguishable from madness, which was exhibited by Athens as a whole in the massacre of Melos. Now, this early part of Alcibiades' speech—the rest of it may be very much what was actually said—is similarly designed to illustrate, in a typical way, another condition—that which we distinguished

αὐτοὶ ἄλλων ἄρχοιμεν. Herod. vii. 11, Xerxes says: ποιέειν ἢ παθεῖν προκέεται ἀγών, ἵνα ἢ τάδε πάντα ὑπὸ Ἕλλησι ἢ ἐκεῖνα πάντα ὑπὸ Πέρσῃσι γένηται.

[1] Thuc. vi. 18. 4 ἵνα Πελοποννησίων τε στορέσωμεν τὸ φρόνημα. The humbling of pride is God's business: Ζεύς τοι κολαστὴς τῶν ὑπερκόμπων ἄγαν | φρονημάτων ἔπεστι, Aesch. Persae, 827.

[2] Cf. Xerxes: 'We shall extend the Persian territory till it is conterminous with the ether of Zeus. The sun will shine on no land beyond our borders' &c. Herod. vii. 8.

[3] Xerxes: 'I but follow a custom handed down by our fathers. Our older men tell me our race has never reposed since we conquered the Medes ... I, since I mounted the throne, have not ceased to think how I might rival those who have gone before in this honour, and increase the power of Persia as much as any of them.' Herod. vii. 11.

as the sanguine, hot-spirited kind of 'Insolence' (Hybris). The pride of illustrious birth, the splendour of an Olympian victory such as no private person had ever gained, the superiority which cannot be expected to treat acknowledged inferiors as equals, the successful treachery practised on the Spartans—all these are the subjects of almost fatuous boasting; and, as we have seen, there is hardly a point in the speeches of Mardonius and Xerxes which is not echoed in the words of Alcibiades.

The effect of the speech was that the Athenians 'were much more eager than before for the expedition'.[1] We need not linger over Nikias' second speech, in which, seeing that 'he could not *avert*[2] their purpose by repeating the same arguments', he tried to win over the assembly by insisting on the greatness of the armament required. We will only note the peroration where Nikias' 'formula' is once more repeated:

'Such are my fears. I know that we have much need of good counsel, and yet more of good luck—a hard thing for mortals to ensure. Hence I desire *to trust myself as little as possible to fortune* on the expedition, and to start upon it with the security of reasonable preparations. This I think the surest course for the whole state, and for us who are to be sent it means preservation. If any one thinks otherwise, to him I resign my command.'

The next chapter describes in very remarkable language the fevered excitement of the Athenians. Once more all the leading ideas we have dwelt upon are reiterated.

'Nikias said thus much, thinking that by dwelling on the vastness of the undertaking he would either *avert* the purpose (ἀποτρέψειν) of the Athenians, or, if he were compelled to go on the expedition, he would thus have the best chance of starting safely. But the Athenians were not delivered of their passion for the voyage[3] by the burdensome nature

---

[1] vi. 19. 1 ὥρμηντο στρατεύειν; 20. 1 (Nikias) πάντως ὁρῶ ὑμᾶς ὡρμημένους στρατεύειν.

[2] vi. 19. 2 ἀποτρέπειν again.  [3] vi. 24. 2 τὸ ἐπιθυμοῦν τοῦ πλοῦ.

of the preparation needed; rather they were much more
eagerly bent upon it (ὥρμηντο). So Nikias found his position
reversed;[1] for they thought his advice sound and that now
at any rate there would be complete safety. And *a passion
seized* upon all alike to start upon the voyage;[2]—the elder
men being confident either that they would conquer the
power against which they were sailing or else that no disaster
could befall so large a force; the youth *longing to see the
marvels of that distant land, and in high hopes of a safe
return*.[3] The general mass of the soldiers hoped to gain
money at once and further to acquire an inexhaustible mine
of pay for the future. Thus *owing to their excessive desire
for more*,[4] even if there were any who disapproved, they
kept quiet, fearing to be thought unpatriotic if they voted
on the other side.'

The most striking sentence in this paragraph—' a passion
seized upon all alike for the voyage '—recalls by the very
turn of the phrase the sinister foreboding of Clytemnestra, in
the passage already quoted, where she is speaking of the
return of the conquering army from Troy.

> Yet may some passion seize upon the host,
> Some lust of rapine and forbidden gain;
> I fear it;—half their race is yet to run,
> Ere they win home in safety.[5]

Must not Thucydides have intended this dark allusion which
so terribly fits the sequel?—' Of the many who went few

---

[1] τοὐναντίον περιέστη αὐτῷ. Another curious dramatic detail of resemblance
between Nikias and Artabanus, who, in consequence of the vision, ' whereas
he had formerly been the only person openly to oppose the expedition, now
appeared as openly to urge it.' Herod. vii. 18.

[2] Ἔρως ἐνέπεσε τοῖς πᾶσιν ὁμοίως ἐκπλεῦσαι.

[3] τοῖς δὲ ἐν τῇ ἡλικίᾳ τῆς τε ἀπούσης πόθῳ ὄψεως καὶ θεωρίας, καὶ εὐέλπιδες ὄντες
σωθήσεσθαι.

[4] διὰ τὴν ἄγαν τῶν πλεόνων ἐπιθυμίαν.

[5] Aesch. *Agam.* 353:

> Ἔρως δὲ μή τις πρότερον ἐμπίπτῃ στρατῷ
> πορθεῖν ἃ μὴ χρὴ κέρδεσιν νικωμένους·
> δεῖ γὰρ πρὸς οἴκους νοστίμου σωτηρίας
> κάμψαι διαύλου θάτερον κῶλον πάλιν.

returned home again. Thus ended what happened concerning Sicily.'[1]

Another curious phrase: 'the youth, longing to see the marvels of that distant land' (τῆς ἀπούσης πόθῳ ὄψεως καὶ θεωρίας) not only reminds us of Nikias' reference to 'the fatal passion for what is out of reach'; there is also a hint of the lust of the eye which accompanies the pride of life. Besides urging the motive of vengeance, Mardonius too had dwelt upon the 'exceeding beauty' of Europe with its variety of cultivated trees and the great excellence of its soil, worthy only for the king to possess.[2] *Pothos* is the special name for the desire of what is distant;[3] Love in absence is the brother of Love in presence, Himeros.[4] Both, like Eros, are associated with the eye, which was popularly regarded as the channel through which the image or phantom (εἴδωλον) of the desired object entered to inspire love in the soul.[5]

An allusion to the lust of the eye is suggested by the occurrence of a similar phrase (again in conjunction with high *hopes*) where the magnificent spectacle of the departing fleet is described:[6] 'the armament excited wonder no less by its astonishing daring and *the brilliance of the sight* than by the great disproportion of the force to the power against which it was sent, and because never had a greater voyage been undertaken across the seas from home,[7] and never was enterprise

---

[1] Thuc. vii. fin. ὀλίγοι ἀπὸ πολλῶν ἐπ' οἴκου ἀπενόστησαν. ταῦτα μὲν τὰ περὶ Σικελίαν γενόμενα.

[2] Herod. vii. 5 περικαλλὴς χώρα. Xerxes recurs to this point vii. 8 § 1.

[3] καὶ μὴν πόθος αὖ καλεῖται σημαίνων οὐ τοῦ παρόντος εἶναι, ἀλλὰ τοῦ ἄλλοθί που ὄντος καὶ ἀπόντος, ὅθεν πόθος ἐπωνόμασται, ὃς τότε, ὅταν παρῇ οὗ τις ἐφίετο, ἵμερος ἐκαλεῖτο, Plato, *Cratylus*, 420 A. Pind. *Pyth.* iii. 20 (quoted above, p. 206) ὅστις αἰσχύνων ἐπιχώρια παπταίνει τὰ πόρσω. Compare also the πόθου κέντρον which is implanted in the drone and goads him to frenzy, in the description of the tyrant passion quoted above (p. 207) from Plato, *Rep.* 572.

[4] *Himeros* is used of Mardonius' desire to take Athens; Herod. ix. 3 ἀλλά οἱ δεινός τις ἐνέστακτο ἵμερος τὰς Ἀθήνας δεύτερα ἑλεῖν.

[5] Plato, *Phaedrus*, 250 c. Cf. also Xen. *Symp.* i. 9, and Plato, *Cratylus*, 420 A, Eros derived from ἐσρεῖν, 'flowing in.'

[6] 31. 6 τόλμης τε θάμβει καὶ ὄψεως λαμπρότητι.

[7] Herod. vii. 20 'Of all the expeditions known to us this (of Xerxes) was by far the greatest.'

undertaken with *higher hope* in the future in proportion to present power.'[1]

Thucydides, we are told, did not believe in omens : certainly he treats oracle-mongering with ironic scorn. But whatever the cool opinion of the rationalist may have been, the artist cannot forgo the opportunity offered by the mutilation of the Hermae, occurring as it did on the eve of the fleet's departure. It would have been perfectly consistent with his earlier method to omit all mention of this incident until the moment when it affected the course of ' what actually happened in the war ', by causing the recall of Alcibiades. The Thucydides of the first two Books would have postponed the episode and briefly recurred to it at that point ; but the Thucydides of Book VI is alive to its indispensable value as an element in his effect. The impenetrable mystery which will never be solved, the stir and outbreak of superstitious panic, the atmosphere tainted with sacrilege and poisoned by suspicion —all these are needed to cast a shadow, just here, across the brilliant path of Alcibiades. The art with which this impression is given culminates in the concluding sentence of the paragraph—one of the most characteristic in the whole history. It cannot be rendered in any other language, for besides its bare simplicity, its effect depends partly on the order of words and partly on the use of the definite article with a proper name : καὶ ἔδοξε πλεῖν τὸν ᾿Αλκιβιάδην.

The disregard of omens is another constant motive in the legend of Hybris, and we can predict its appearance at the proper place. Xerxes, at the moment of crossing into Europe, just after he has allowed himself, without reproof, to be addressed as Zeus, makes no account of a prodigy which might easily have been interpreted. He had neglected a similar warning while still at Sardis.[2] Whether Thucydides

---

[1] Cf. also above, 30. 2 μετ᾽ ἐλπίδος τε ἅμα ἰόντες καὶ ὀλυφυρμῶν, and 31. 1 τῇ ὄψει ἀνεθάρσουν.

[2] Herod. vii. 57. So also Mardonius before Plataea obstinately rejects good advice, refuses to take notice of the adverse omens of the victims, and misinterprets an oracle predicting the fate of the Persians, Herod. ix. 39–42.

believed in omens or not, the bulk of the Athenians did; and
their disregard of them is a note of the peculiar state of mind
portrayed in the Melian dialogue. 'The affair of the Hermae
was construed in an exaggerated way, for it was thought to be
an omen for the voyage and to have been part of a conspiracy
for revolution and the overthrow of the democracy.'[1] Charges
of another act of profanation were rife against Alcibiades, but
by the contrivance of his enemies they were left suspended
and not brought to trial. Καὶ ἔδοξε πλεῖν τὸν Ἀλκιβιάδην—that
is the last we hear of him till the fleet has sailed.

'And after this, when midsummer had come, they set
about the dispatching of the fleet to Sicily.'[2] The pages
that follow are a masterpiece of description. In the lumbering
roll of these Thucydidean sentences[3] we hear the clatter
and rumble of preparation, the dockyard hammer, the hoarse
cries of mariners, the grinding rush of the trireme taking
the water from the slips,—all the bustle and excitement of
launching this most splendid and costly of expeditions.[4]
'Each captain strove to the utmost that his own ship might
excel all others in beauty and swiftness'; for the spirit of
rivalry was in the air, 'rivalry with one another in the
performance of their appointed tasks, rivalry with all Greece;
so that it looked more like *a display of unrestrainable power*
than a warlike expedition.'[5]

'When the ships were manned and everything required
for the voyage had been placed on board, silence was proclaimed by the sound of the trumpet, and all with one voice
before setting sail offered up the customary prayers; these
were recited, not in each ship, but by a single herald, the

[1] Thuc. vi. 27. 3.

[2] Thuc. vi. 30. 1.

[3] One of them (31. § 3) contains 121 words.

[4] vi. 31 πολυτελεστάτη καὶ εὐπρεπεστάτη.

[5] vi. 31. 4 ξυνέβη δὲ πρός τε σφᾶς αὐτοὺς ἅμα ἔριν γενέσθαι, ᾧ τις ἕκαστος
προσετάχθη, καὶ ἐς τοὺς ἄλλους Ἕλληνας ἐπίδειξιν μᾶλλον εἰκασθῆναι τῆς δυνάμεως
καὶ ἐξουσίας ἢ ἐπὶ πολεμίους παρασκευήν. This rivalry was characteristic too of
Xerxes' preparations. The Persian officers competed eagerly for the prize which
the king offered for the most gallantly arrayed contingent at the muster,
Herod. vii. 8 δ; 19; 26. The associations of *Exousia* are already familiar to us.

whole fleet accompanying him. On every deck both officers and men, mingling wine in bowls, made libations from vessels of gold and silver. The multitude of citizens and other well-wishers who were looking on from the land joined in the prayer. The crews raised the Paean, and when the libations were completed, put to sea. After sailing out for some distance in single file, the ships raced with one another as far as Aegina.' [1]

Across the waters of Salamis! Even so, with prayer and libation from golden vessels, had the armament drowned in those very waters traversed the Hellespont. 'All that day,' says Herodotus, 'the preparations for the passage continued; and on the morrow they burnt all kinds of spices upon the bridges, and strewed the way with myrtle-boughs, while they waited anxiously for the sun, which they hoped to see as he rose. And now the sun appeared; and Xerxes took a golden goblet and poured from it a libation into the sea, praying the while, with his face turned to the sun, "that no misfortune might befall him such as to hinder his conquest of Europe, until he had penetrated to the utmost boundaries." After he had prayed, he cast the golden cup into the Hellespont, and with it a golden bowl and a Persian sword.' [2]

Xerxes too had set his ships racing in a sailing-match, and 'as he looked and saw the whole Hellespont covered with vessels of his fleet, and all the shore and every plain about Abydos as full as possible of men, Xerxes congratulated himself on his good fortune; but after a little while, he wept'.[3] And now, as the Athenian ships in their turn race over the sea, within sight of the promontory where the Persian monarch watched from his throne the judgement of God fall upon presumptuous ambition, there, on one of the foremost and most luxuriously furnished galleys,[4] an eager and beautiful figure stands, flushed with triumph. The shield at his side is inwrought with ivory and gold, and bears an

[1] Thuc. vi. 32 Jowett.      [2] Herod. vii. 54 Rawlinson.
[3] Herod. vii. 44, 45 Rawlinson.      [4] Plutarch, vit. Alcib. xvi.

emblem which is none of the hereditary blazons of his house;
the self-chosen cognizance of Alcibiades is the figure of Love
himself—of Eros with the thunderbolt in his hand.[1] Over
the rich armada, hastening with full sail to Corcyra and
the West, floats the winged, unconquerable Eros who makes
havoc of wealth, ranging beyond the seas,[2]—Eros who planned
the enterprise and now leads the way. Behind him follows
another unseen, haunting spirit—Nemesis, who 'in later
times was represented with wings like Love, because it was
thought that the goddess hovers chiefly in Love's train'.[3]

We cannot follow in detail the fortunes of the great
expedition; through most of the account the military interest
of the siege predominates. But there is one passage in the
description of the last retreat which concerns our subject
and forges the final link in our chain. In the speech addressed by Nikias to the despairing army one mythical
motive, so far wanting, is supplied—the motive of φθόνος,
the divine Jealousy. It could not be mentioned till this
moment; for Thucydides cannot speak of it in his own
person; he must put it in the mouth of the pious Nikias, as
Herodotus had put it in the mouth of Artabanus.[4]

'Although,' says Nikias, 'there was a time when I might
have been thought equal to the best of you in the happiness
of my private and public life, I am now in as great danger,
and as much at the mercy of fortune, as the meanest. Yet
my days have been passed in the performance of many
a religious duty, and of many a just and blameless action.
Therefore *my hope of the future remains unshaken*[5] and
our calamities do not appal me as they might. Who knows

---

[1] Plutarch, *vit. Alcib.* xvi ἀσπίδος τε διαχρύσου ποίησιν οὐδὲν ἐπίσημον τῶν πατρίων
ἔχουσαν, ἀλλ' Ἔρωτα κεραυνοφόρον. Athen. xii. 534 E καὶ στρατηγῶν δὲ ἔτι καλὸς
εἶναι ἤθελεν· ἀσπίδα γοῦν εἶχεν ἐκ χρυσοῦ καὶ ἐλέφαντος πεποιημένην, ἐφ' ἧς ἦν
ἐπίσημον Ἔρως κεραυνὸν ἠγκυλημένος.

[2] Soph. *Ant.* 781 Ἔρως ἀνίκατε μάχαν, Ἔρως ὃς ἐν κτήμασι πίπτεις...φοιτᾷς δ'
ὑπερπόντιος...ὁ δ' ἔχων μέμηνεν.

[3] Paus. i. 33. 6.

[4] Herod. vii. 10. Thuc. vii. 77.

[5] vii. 77 ἡ μὲν ἐλπὶς ὅμως θρασεῖα τοῦ μέλλοντος.

that they may not be lightened? For our enemies have had
their full share of success, and *if our expedition provoked
the jealousy of any God*,[1] by this time we have been punished
enough. Others ere now have attacked their neighbours;
*they have done as men will do and suffered what men can
bear*.[2] We may therefore begin to hope that the Gods will
be more merciful to us; for we now invite their pity rather
than their jealousy.'[3]

The hope, as we know, was vain—a last delusion of
Elpis.[4] In a few weeks 'the best friend of the Lacedaemonians in the matter of Pylos and Sphacteria'[5] was lying
dead beside their worst enemy in the same affair, Cleon's
colleague, Demosthenes. What need of further comment?
Tychê, Elpis, Apatê, Hybris, Eros, Phthonos, Nemesis, Atê—
all these have crossed the stage and the play is done.

> The flower of Pride hath bloomed, the ripened fruit
> Of Suffering is all garnered up in tears:
> Ye that have seen the reapers' wages told,
> Remember Athens![6]

---

[1] εἴ τῳ θεῶν ἐπίφθονοι ἐστρατεύσαμεν.

[2] ἀνθρώπεια δράσαντες ἀνεκτὰ ἔπαθον. Note the reminiscence of δράσαντι
παθεῖν.

[3] Thuc. vii. 77 Jowett.

[4] So Plutarch (*Nic.* xviii) speaks of Nikias, after Lamachus' death, as
being in high hope (ἐλπίδος μεγάλης), and παρὰ φύσιν ὑπὸ τῆς ἐν τῷ παρόντι ῥώμης
καὶ τύχης ἀνατεθαρρηκώς.

[5] Thuc. vii. 86. Observe how this phrase carries our thoughts back to the
first of the train of mythical causes: Fortune at Pylos.

[6] Aesch. *Persae*, 821:

> Ὕβρις γὰρ ἐξανθοῦσ' ἐκάρπωσεν στάχυν
> Ἄτης, ὅθεν πάγκλαυτον ἐξαμᾷ θέρος·
> τοιαῦθ' ὁρῶντες τῶνδε τἀπιτίμα
> μέμνησθ' Ἀθηνῶν. ...

# CHAPTER XIII

## THE TRAGIC PASSIONS

THE question which we have now to face is more obscure and difficult than any we have yet considered. In the language used by Thucydides when he speaks of the tragic passions, are we to see mere poetical metaphor, out of which all literal meaning has faded; or does some of this meaning still linger behind the words, as an unanalysed fund of mythical conception? When Thucydides borrowed the form of the Aeschylean drama, much, certainly, of the explicit theological theory which had been the soul of that form, was left behind in the transmission. On the other hand, there seems to be a residuum of implicit mythical belief which is inherent in the artistic mould, and so inseparable from it that the adoption of the mould might involve an unconscious or half-conscious acceptance of some of its original content. This content is more primitive than the philosophy of Aeschylus himself, and much older than the drama in which it became incorporated. We now propose to trace back the tragic theory of human nature as far as we can follow it, in the hope that a sketch of its development may help us to answer our question, how much of it survives in Thucydides.

When we look at the passage in Diodotus' speech [1] which contains in summary form the motives of Cleon's drama and of the tragedy of Athens, we observe that the so-called 'personifications' named in it fall into a series or cycle. We begin with the various conditions (ξυντυχίαι) of human life; and in particular the two extreme conditions of grinding Poverty and licentious Wealth—Penia and Ploutos

---

[1] Thuc. iii. 45. See above, p. 122, for text and translation.

(ἐξουσία).[1] These are possessed by irremediable and mastering powers—Daring (τόλμα), sprung from Poverty; and Covetousness (πλεονεξία), Insolence (ὕβρις), and Pride (φρόνημα), sprung from Wealth.

Then come Eros and Elpis, the inward tempters; with Fortune, the temptress of external circumstance, completing the intoxication. These lead finally to Ruin—the wreck and downfall of a human life or of a nation's greatness.

The first terms in the series, Wealth and Poverty, are themselves ξυντυχίαι, the outcome of lucky or unlucky coincidence—of Fortune. Our chain of causes leads us back to a mysterious and unknown agency, which appears again at the crisis, in 'reversal'. The circle of thought revolves round the very simple and universal observation of the mutability of Fortune, chance, or luck. In ages before the laws of causation and of probability were even dimly divined, this mutability must have been the most terrible and bewildering phenomenon in human events—more terrible, because more incalculable, than death itself. Not only in the great catastrophes, in flood and avalanche and earthquake, but again and again in the turns of daily experience, man finds himself the sport of an invisible demon. Now, by some unforeseen stroke, his long-cherished design is foiled; now, with equally unintelligible caprice, goods are heaped on him which he never expected.

A reversal of Fortune, coming *suddenly*, is the primitive root of all tragedy. Professor Bradley [2] quotes the conclusion of the monk's tale of Croesus in the *Canterbury Pilgrims*:—

> Anhanged was Cresus, the proudè kyng;
> His roial tronè mightè hym nat availle.
> Tragédie is noon oother maner thyng,
> Ne kan in syngyng criè ne biwaille
> But for that Fortune alwey wole assaille
> With unwar strook the regnès that been proude ;
> For whan men trusteth hire, thanne wol she faille,
> And coverè hire brightè facè with a clowde.

---

[1] i. 38 ὕβρει δὲ καὶ ἐξουσίᾳ πλούτου : Ar. *Rhet.* β 17 φιλοτιμότεροι καὶ ἀνδρω-δέστεροί εἰσιν τὰ ἤθη οἱ δυνάμενοι τῶν πλουσίων διὰ τὸ ἐφίεσθαι ἔργων ὅσα ἐξουσία αὐτοῖς πράττειν διὰ τὴν δύναμιν.      [2] *Shakespearean Tragedy*, p. 8.

Professor Bradley continues: 'a total reverse of fortune coming unawares upon a man who "stood in high degree" happy and apparently secure—such was the tragic fact to the mediaeval mind. It appealed strongly to common human sympathy and pity; it startled also another feeling, that of fear. It frightened men and awed them. It made them feel that man is blind and helpless, the plaything of an inscrutable power, called by the name of Fortune or some other name— a power which appears to smile on him for a little, and then on a sudden strikes him down in his pride.'

The external agencies to which these reversals are attributed will vary at different stages in the development of thought. In a primitive stage they would be thought of simply as spirits; later, perhaps, as a single spirit, called Fate (Μοῖρα) or Fortune (Τύχη), who will be placated or 'averted' by magical rites and observances. In any case, the overthrow was thought of as coming *from without*—an unexpected stroke out of the surrounding darkness.

To the early Greeks not only the sudden fall from prosperity, but equally the sudden rise from adversity, was a part of the tragic fact.[1] Both the extreme conditions are dangerous the transition from either to the other is a 'reversal'. Ploutos and Penia are also known as Resource and Resourcelessness (Poros and Aporia, or Amechania[2]), and again as Licence

---

[1] In this point the Greek view is darker than the Mediaeval. Thus at the conclusion of the Monk's Tale above quoted, the Knight breaks in :

> Hoo! quod the Knyght, good sire, namoore of this!
> That ye han seyd is right ynough, y-wis,...
> I seye for me it is a greet disese,
> Where as men han been in greet welthe and ese,
> To heeren of hire sodeyn fal, allas!
> And the contrarie is joye and greet solas,
> As whan a man hath ben in poure estaat,
> And clymbeth up, and wexeth fortunat,
> And there abideth in prosperitee ;
> Swich thyng is gladsom, as it thynketh me.

[2] Herod. viii. 111. Themistocles, demanding money of the Andrians, said he had brought 'two mighty gods, Peitho and Anankaia', to enforce his demand. The Andrians replied that they were cursed with 'two unprofitable gods, Penia and Amechania', and could not pay.

and Constraint (Exousia and Ananke,—both of which terms
are used by Diodotus). Eros and Elpis may be associated
with either. In the *Symposium*, Plato for his own purposes
makes Eros the child of both: he was born, in the garden
of Zeus, of Poros and Penia. But in an earlier stage Elpis,
at any rate, was more closely associated with Poverty.

As a personality, she first appears in Hesiod, who mentions
her twice. He warns the labouring man to pass by the
sunny portico where the poor gather for warmth in the
winter season, when the frost has stopped work in the fields.
Otherwise, in the hard winter-time, Amechania and Penia
will swoop down on him. 'An idle man, waiting on empty
Hope, gathers many evils to his heart. Hope is an ill guide
for a needy man,' sitting there and chattering when he has
not enough livelihood.[1] Such are the sinister associations
of Elpis, the temptress, prompting evil thoughts which we,
with our different conception of Hope, associate rather with
the daring of *despair*.

No less significant is Hesiod's other mention of her, which
occurs in the second, and more primitive, of the two versions
which he gives of the Pandora myth. Mankind originally
lived free from evil and pain and the sprites (*Keres*) of
disease. These were all shut up safely in the great jar; but
'a woman' lifted the lid and they all flew abroad, filling
land and sea. 'Only there, in a house not to be broken into,
abode Elpis, inside the mouth of the jar, and flitted not

---

[1] Hesiod, *Erga*, 493 ff. μή σε κακοῦ χειμῶνος Ἀμηχανίη καταμάρψῃ σὺν Πενίῃ . . .
Ἐλπὶς δ' οὐκ ἀγαθὴ κεχρημένον ἄνδρα κομίζει. Proclus (Schol. ad loc.) para-
phrases as follows : 'Those who live in idleness and have empty hopes—
empty because they know of no work they can do to bring them to prosperity, must indeed fall into many evil thoughts, because of having no
resource (ἀπορίαν), to gain a living. Hence some will turn footpads or temple-
robbers,' &c. Thucydides was familiar with this conception; Pericles (ii.
42. 4) speaks of men being corrupted either by the enjoyment of wealth, or
πενίας ἐλπίδι, ὡς κἂν ἔτι διαφυγὼν αὐτὴν πλουτήσειεν. Democr. *frag.* 221 (Diels)
Ἐλπὶς κακοῦ κέρδεος ἀρχὴ ζημίης. *Theognis*, 649 :

Ἆ δειλὴ Πενίη, τί ἐμοῖς ἐπικειμένη ὤμοις
σῶμα καταισχύνεις καὶ νόον ἡμέτερον,
αἰσχρὰ δέ μ' οὐκ ἐθέλοντα βίῃ καὶ πολλὰ διδάσκεις,
ἐσθλὰ μετ' ἀνθρώπων καὶ κάλ' ἐπιστάμενον;

forth; for the woman first shut down on her the lid of the jar.'[1]

It seems probable that several notions are confused in the myth. The uppermost and latest stratum, like the story of the Erichthonius snake, is tinged with satire against feminine curiosity. Woman is the source of evil, as she is in Hesiod's other version of the Pandora myth. But the woman herself is tempted by Elpis, who is one of the baneful sprites inside the jar. Perhaps in the earliest version there was no woman at all, but only Elpis, the temptress, who stays with man in his utter destitution and besets him with dreams of wealth. This idea is crossed by the opposite (and later) notion that hope is the sole comforter of poverty;[2] and finally the introduction of the curious woman who lets out the evil sprites completes the confusion.

However the story is to be disentangled, it is certain that

----

[1] *Erga*, 90-105 μούνη δ' αὐτόθι 'Ελπὶς ἐν ἀρρήκτοισι δόμοισιν ἔνδον ἔμιμνε. The ancient commentators on this passage are instructive. One takes the view that Hesiod's single jar corresponds to the two jars which Homer speaks of, one full of goods, the other of evils. Hope is the one good among so many ills, consoling the unfortunate with expectation of better days. But this interpretation does not sound primitive, and is not grim enough for Hesiod. Aristarchus seems nearer the truth when he distinguishes two Hopes. The Hope of good things, he says, escaped ; the expectation of evils remained. Hesiod, he adds, improperly uses 'Hope' to mean expectation of evil. The thought is here a good deal confused. From the other passage in the *Erga*, it seems likely that Hesiod does not mean expectation of evil, but a false and flattering expectation of goods, which will not be realized. Another critic says : ' The jar (πίθος) is appropriately introduced, because of the allurement (πειθώ) that comes from women; *it is empty of goods and contains only vain hopes.*' This writer shows that he is on the true scent, by associating Elpis with Peitho, though, of course, the word-play (πίθος—πειθώ) is late. He sees, too, that Elpis is not a good, but an evil; and this, we believe, was what the authors of the myth intended.

[2] *Theogn.* 1135 ff. 'Ελπὶς ἐν ἀνθρώποισι μόνη θεὸς ἐσθλὴ ἔνεστι, Pistis, the Charites and Sophrosyne have all deserted mankind, and fled to Olympus. Plut. *vii sap. conv.* 153 D τί κοινότατον ; 'Ελπίς (ἔφη Θαλῆς)· καὶ γὰρ οἷς ἄλλο μηδέν, αὕτη πάρεστι. The two notions of Elpis as *both a comforter and a delusion* are combined by Sophocles in the Antigone chorus (616) : ἁ γὰρ δὴ πολύπλαγκτος 'Ελπὶς πολλοῖς μὲν ὄνασις ἀνδρῶν, πολλοῖς δ' 'Απάτα κουφονόων ἐρώτων, and by Thucydides (v. 103) in the parallel passage from the Melian dialogue (see above, p. 184).

Elpis is a *Ker*; and this gives us one primitive form in which the passions were conceived as external spiritual agencies. Eros retained to the last some resemblance to the *Keres*; the Erotes are always winged sprites.[1] These figures are something very different from what we think of as 'personifications of abstract ideas'. They are not the intolerable, bran-stuffed dummies which stalk absurdly through eighteenth-century verse. They are spirits, unseen, and swift, and terrible in onset. How did they come into being?

The solid fact from which we must start is that many of these 'personifications', as we call them, were objects of established worship, possessing shrines and altars. In Athens alone we know of altars to Aidos, Pheme, Horme, Anteros, Ara, Eirene, Eleos, Eukleia, Lethe, Nike, Peitho, Philia, Tyche, and others.[2] Of those which specially concern us here, Tyche is known to have been worshipped at a great number of places; Penia had an altar at Gades; Elpis was not, so far as we know, the object of any cult; Eros, on the contrary, is the most real and personal of all, and finds his way—much transformed, it is true—into Olympus.

Now it is certainly possible, in an advanced state of civilization, for a cult to be artificially founded in honour of an abstraction. Democratia, to whom the Athenian Generals made offerings in Boedromion, must always have been little more than an epithet of Athena, never an independent person. In such an instance the cult must have been established merely from political motives, and it remains as unreal and artificial as the worship of the Goddess Reason at the time of the French Revolution. But the case is not the same with others of the names above enumerated: some

---

[1] See Miss J. E. Harrison, *Prolegomena to the Study of Greek Religion*, p. 632. Eros, as a developed personality, seems to be a complex product of several different elements. We are here only concerned with one of these—the psychological affection of violent desire, whether sexual or other. Democritus, *frag.* 191 (Diels), calls Jealousy, Envy, and Hatred Κῆρες: ταύτης ἄρ' ἐχόμενος τῆς γνώμης εὐθυμότερόν τε διάξεις καὶ οὐκ ὀλίγας Κῆρας ἐν τῷ βίῳ διώσεαι, Φθόνον καὶ Ζῆλον καὶ Δυσμενίην.

[2] The evidence will be found in Roscher's Lexicon, s. v. *Personificationen*.

of these cults were too ancient to have been anything but genuinely religious. In an early state of society we cannot suppose that personified abstractions, *regarded as such*, could become the objects of a permanent cult. How, then, did these cults arise?

Looking through the list, we find that a fair number of these entities are psychological. Aidos, Anaideia, Eros, Anteros, Eleos, Elpis, Himeros, Horme, Hybris, Phobos, Pothos, are all names of states of mind; and to these we will confine our attention. Their origin must be sought in mental experience; and we may suppose that it occurs in some such way as this. At moments of exceptional excitement, a man feels himself carried away, taken hold of, 'possessed' by an impulse, a gust of emotion, which seems to be not a part of himself, but on the contrary a force against which he is powerless. This is even to a civilized person a somewhat terrifying experience. The inexplicable panic which will suddenly run through an army, the infectious spirit of a crowd, the ecstasy produced by intoxicants, the throes of sexual pleasure, the raving of the seer and of the poet—all these are states of mind in which the self appears to be drowned and swept away. By what? There can be but one answer: some spirit, or daemon, has entered the soul and possesses it. This is the very language used by Diodotus;[1] and, centuries later, Porphyry[2] describes in very similar terms the invasions of maleficent spirits. 'Having in general a violent and insidious character, which moreover is without the tutelage of the higher spiritual power, they for the most part make their assaults, as though from an ambush, with vehemence, so as to overpower their victims, and suddenly, since they try to escape notice. Hence the passions that

---

[1] iii. 45 αἱ δ' ἄλλαι ξυντυχίαι ὀργῇ τῶν ἀνθρώπων ὡς ἑκάστη τις κατέχεται ὑπ' ἀνηκέστου τινὸς κρείσσονος. See above, p. 122.

[2] Porph. *de abst.* ii. 39 βίαιον γὰρ ὅλως καὶ ὕπουλον ἔχοντες ἦθος ἐστερημένον τε τῆς φυλακῆς τῆς ἀπὸ τοῦ κρείττονος δαιμονίου, σφοδρὰς καὶ αἰφνιδίους οἷον [ἐξ] ἐνέδρας ὡς τὸ πολὺ ποιοῦνται τὰς ἐμπτώσεις, πῇ μὲν λανθάνειν πειρώμενοι, πῇ δὲ βιαζόμενοι. ὅθεν ὀξέα μὲν τὰ ἀπ' ἐκείνων πάθη, αἱ δὲ ἀκέσεις (cf. Diodotus' ἀνηκέστον) καὶ κατορθώσεις αἱ ἀπὸ τῶν κρειττόνων δαιμόνων βραδύτεραι δοκοῦσιν.

come from them are swift and keen; and the remedies and restorations due to the higher spirits seem to be too slow.'

When we have traced these agencies back to this stage, it is only one step further to the most primitive theory of causes and motives which we find among existing savages.

'I can see,' says Mr. Sidney Hartland,[1] 'no satisfactory evidence that early man entertained any great faith in the order and uniformity of nature ... If he took aim at his enemy and flung his spear, or whatever primitive weapon served the same purpose; if it hit the man, and he fell; he might witness the result, but the mere mechanical causation, however inevitable in its action, would be the last thing he would think about.' What he does think about, Mr. Hartland, surveying the whole field of savage life as now known to us, and drawing evidence from every part of it, explains in convincing terms. Every known object has to the savage an elementary personality, endowed with qualities which enable it to persist and to influence others; and by virtue of these qualities it possesses, inherent in it and surrounding it, a sort of atmosphere charged with power. The Iroquois in North America call this atmosphere or potentiality, *orenda*. A good hunter is one whose *orenda* is good, and baffles the *orenda* of his quarry. At public games, in contests of skill or endurance between tribes, 'the shamans—men reputed to possess powerful *orenda*—are employed for hire by the opposing parties respectively to exercise their *orenda* to thwart or overcome that of their antagonists.' [2] When a storm is brewing, it (the storm-maker) is said to be preparing its *orenda*. Of one who has died from witchcraft it is said 'an evil *orenda* has struck him'. This idea of *orenda*, says Mr. Hartland, although it may not receive everywhere the same explicit recognition, 'is implied in the customs and beliefs of mankind throughout the world.'

[1] Presidential Address to the Anthropological Section of the British Association, 1906.

[2] Quoted from J. N. B. Hewitt, *American Anthropologist*, N.S. iv. 38.

The savage whose spear has struck down his enemy does not, and cannot, think of the two *events*—the spear-blow and the enemy's death—as *cause and effect*. His view is that 'his own *orenda* felt in his passion, his will, his effort,[1] and displayed in his acts and words, the *orenda* of the spear, either inherent in itself, conceived as a personal being, or conferred by its maker and manifested in the keenness of its point, the precision and the force with which it flies to its work and inflicts the deadly wound—these would be to him the true causes of his enemy's fall. His *orenda* is mightier than his enemy's and overcomes it.'[2]

We have here the notion of cause traced to its root—the psychological experience of effort, the putting forth of will to constrain or master an opposing effort. Now, in states of violent excitement, man feels himself controlled and swept away by something which seems to exercise over his will a compelling force of the same kind as that which he is at other times conscious of putting forth out of himself. He regards this as the *orenda* of a spirit coming from outside.

At first the invading daemons will be associated only with the peculiar experiences which they severally cause. *Phobos* is simply the spirit which falls upon an army and inspires panic ; *Eros* the spirit which possesses the lover, and so on. For a long time they may have had no fuller personality, and not even a continuous existence. They were momentary beings, sweeping into the soul from nowhere and passing out again into nothingness. Their continuous existence would begin when first some rude, unshapen stone was set up and conceived as their dwelling. The invisible agency can be conveyed by incantation into a rock or tree, which thus becomes a fetish. The famous unwrought stone at Thespiae was the habitation, not the image, of Eros—his baetyl, or beth-el. The personalities would gradually fill out, as stories

---

[1] In Homeric language, his ἱερὸν μένος.

[2] When Thales said that 'all things are full of spirits' (δαίμονες), and that 'the magnet has a soul (ψυχή) because it moves iron', he was using a notion very like that of *orenda*. Like a savage, he thought that what moves something else must have a 'soul', a life-force in it.

were told about them. Cult would secure their perma-
nence; myth would invest them with a character and history.
In the transition from aneikonic to eikonic cults, we see
the figure literally emerging out of its pillar habitation and
growing into human shape.[1]

We must think of all this as occurring long before the
earliest literature we know. Homer and Hesiod preserve
much that is primitive, but they preserve it in a late and
artificial dress; far behind them stretches a period of
popular myth-making, and it was in that period that these
'abstractions' reached their fullest reality and life. This
growth of a mythical person is something utterly different from the allegorical personification of an abstract
idea. To grasp an abstraction distinctly and then to assign
it personal attributes is a proceeding which can only occur
in a very advanced state of culture. These figures which
we are now considering are originally not allegorical, but
mythical; not personifications, but persons.

Allegory is a kind of story-telling, and in so far akin to
myth; but, in order of genesis, the fabrication of allegory is
the very reverse of myth-making. Allegory starts with a consciousness of the prosaic truth and then invents an artificial
parable to clothe it withal. Christian sets out with neighbour Hopeful on a pilgrimage from the city of Mansoul to
the New Jerusalem. The company he meets by the way,
Giant Despair and Mr. Worldly Wiseman, are personifications
which can only impose upon a child. Delightful as he is,
we never quite forget that Apollyon is a pantomime bogey
in pasteboard armour. It seems that an abstraction, once
escaped, can never get back into the concrete; abstract and
lifeless it must always remain. Allegory is an artificial
business from the first, and foredoomed to failure. It is not
thus that children—even modern sophisticated children—tell
themselves stories; it was not thus that primitive man told
himself myths. Eros and Elpis, Menis and Eris, Nemesis
and Ananke—these and their like are not allegorical fictions.

---

[1] Note, for instance, that Peitho, in the relief (p. 209), is sitting on the top
of her pillar; Aphrodite, in the vase-painting (p. 195), is emerging from hers.

Man has not made them; it is they who make him, and bitter his fate if he defy them. They have a long course to run before the dissolution sets in, whereby the body falls away from the soul, the presentment from the spirit. They will become personifications only when they die.

How these discarnate passions came to develop into personalities, which could be represented in human shape, we can only guess. It is the work of myth-making imagination, helped probably by the fully developed anthropomorphism of the Olympian religion. Hesiod, by the devices of affiliation and marriage, somehow brings them into his multifarious pantheon; but they look queer and unreal when they get there, because they properly belong to a more primitive, non-anthropomorphic, system of belief. They dwindle into pale shadows beside the radiant and solid inhabitants of Mount Olympus. Some of them, we remark—though our impressions on this point are not very trustworthy—have won and retained a fuller degree of personality than others. Aidos, Peitho, Eros are more real to us than Eleos, Horme, or Philia. It seems certain that to the Greeks also some were fainter, others more vividly conceived. How far any one of them would advance towards complete divinity would depend on all sorts of accidents, and partly on the real frequency and importance of the states of mind which the power in question inspired.

Their later history confirms this impression. Some of them retain their independence, others lose it. It is suggested by Hermann Usener in an illuminating discussion of this subject[1] that the fact that their names have a known meaning weakens them as against the completely developed personal god with a *proper* name, the meaning of which is forgotten. It is easy to see what would happen if this world of daemons were invaded by a hierarchy of gods who had reached full anthropomorphic concreteness. The originally independent, but shadowy, personalities would yield to the stronger and become attached to them as attendants or even as epithets. So we hear of Athena

---

[1] *Götternamen*, p. 369.

Nike, Athena Hygieia, Artemis Eucleia, and so forth. The weakest will in this way almost disappear; their personality is absorbed and they sink into adjectives. Others however maintain their independence. Nike is not lost in Athena; Peitho never becomes Aphrodite. A long-established cult would be an anchor to save these ancient figures from being swept away. If myth has wrought for them a fairly distinct character and history, their personality will resist absorption. Though many of them take lower rank as attendant and ministering spirits, they will long retain a hold of their own in the minds of their simple worshippers. If in one way they are less human than the gods, in another they have remained closer to the elementary feelings of humanity.

Figurative art will also contribute its help. If it is markedly anthropomorphic and has advanced far enough to fix a traditional human type with well-known traits and attributes, its figures will not give way altogether to newly-imported personalities whose traits and attributes are different. In actual fact, Eris, Apatê, Peitho, and some others do remain in Greek vase-painting. They are only subordinated to the Olympians, not effaced by them, and often the divinity and the attendant spirit appear side by side. The existence of a familiar art-type counts for much, especially as polytheism has no objection to indefinite multiplication of divine or daemonic personalities, and all religions have a remarkable power of 'reconciliation'. Christianity finds room for as many saints and martyrs as Greece had daemons and heroes. In the modern world saints are kept alive and independent by local cults. They are also preserved by literature which gives a fixed and enduring form to popular hagiology. Greek poetry did the same service to the primitive daemons, for the clear imagination of poets arrested the flux of popular myths, and prevented the disappearance of figures which might otherwise have melted.

In the *Ker* stage, before they became humanized under the influence of Olympian anthropomorphism, Eros and Elpis were beings of the same order as that out of which the

Erinyes and the Moirai developed.  They were closely akin
to the *angry* ghosts and the *avenging* spirits; and it was
easy for them to be associated with the malevolent daemon
who causes reversals of fortune,[1] since these reversals are often
due to excess of confidence, intoxication, the sudden access of
blind and violent feeling.  Thus the passions take their place
in the cycle of the tragic fact—Elpis beside Penia, Eros beside
Ploutos.  This first stage of the tragic theory is religious, but
not theological; and it is quite non-moral.

With the advent of the Olympian gods we reach a second
stage, which, though still non-moral, is theological.  The
spirits of vengeance are now employed by the gods to punish
man, not for moral offences, but for arrogant presumption.
The notion of the divine Jealousy (Φθόνος) is now prominent.
If man seeks to overstep the limits assigned him and to
become as a god, he excites the resentment (νέμεσις) of higher
powers.  Great prosperity is one of the divine prerogatives,
and the tragic passions of unrestrained desire and ambition
are offences against the gods.  The reversal of fortune,
formerly attributed to an independent daemon, now becomes
an act of divine punishment.[2]  'God is wont to lop and cut

---

[1] As the Erinyes are in Aesch. *Agam.* 468 κελαιναὶ δ' Ἐρινύες χρόνῳ τυχηρὸν
ὄντ' ἄνευ δίκας παλιντυχεῖ τριβᾷ βίου τιθεῖσ' ἀμαυρόν.  Ἐλπίς occurs in the Orphic
Hymn (lix) to the Moirai: αἵτ' ἐπὶ λίμνης | ὀρφναίης ... | ναίουσαι πεπότησθε
βροτῶν ἐπ' ἀπείρονα γαῖαν. | ἔνθεν ἐπὶ βρότεον δόκιμον γένος ἐλπίδι κούφῃ | στείχετε
—a reminiscence of the winged (κούφη) Ker-Elpis.

[2] One of the earliest expressions of this theory is in a recently deciphered
Babylonian book, dated before 2000 B.C., the story of Tabi-utul-Bel, King of
Nippur :

'How can mortals fathom the way of a god ?
He who is still alive in the evening may be dead the next morning ;
In an instant he is cast into grief ; of a sudden he is crushed ;
One moment he sings and plays,
In a twinkling he wails like a mourner.
Like day and night their fate changes ;
If they hunger they are like corpses,
When they are satiated they think themselves equal to their god ;
If things go well they talk of ascending to heaven,
If they are in distress, they speak of going down to Irkalla.'

Morris Jastrow (*A Babylonian Job, Contemp. Review,* Dec. 1906, p. 805),
from whom the above rendering is taken, discusses the document.

down all excess'; [1] it is Zeus who 'abases the high, and exalts the low'. [2] Countless stories of the attempts to scale Olympus, and of men who have aspired to the love of goddesses, belong to this order of thought. These latter sins are the offences of Eros; but Elpis, who dares to count upon the future as assured, is also guilty of impious presumption. 'Some day,' says Pindar, 'I may say for certain what shall be; but now, although I hope, with God is the end.' [3] Such is the cautious language of piety. 'In every matter,' says Solon to Croesus, 'one must look to the end and see how it will turn out; for there are many to whom God gives a glimpse of prosperity and then overturns them root and branch.' [4] It is not safe to call a man happy until he is dead; premature congratulations will bring ill luck on him.

As a third stage in the development of these ideas, we next encounter the Aeschylean notion that *God uses the tragic passions themselves as agents of punishment*, and brings the sinner to ruin by increasing the arrogant delusion. His ministers of Justice are Delusion ('Ἀπάτη), and Blindness ("Ἄτη); [5] the former sometimes takes the shape of Elpis or of Eros. Thus the very causes of offence are enhanced by God to lead the guilty man deeper into the snare which Ruin spreads. This is the theory stated by Sophocles in the chorus we have already quoted. Elpis, the Delusion who wings the dreams of Desire, steals upon the sinner unawares. He is blinded and becomes unable to distinguish

---

[1] Herod. vii. 10 φιλέει γὰρ ὁ θεὸς τὰ ὑπερέχοντα πάντα κολούειν.

[2] Laert. Diog. i. 3. 2 Chilon asked Aesop how Zeus was employed; φάναι δ' αὐτόν· τὰ μὲν ὑψηλὰ ταπεινῶν, τὰ δὲ ταπεινὰ ὑψῶν.

[3] Pind. *Ol.* xiii. 103. Cf. *Theogn.* 659 οὐδ' ὀμόσαι χρὴ τοῦθ', ὅτι μήποτε πρᾶγμα τόδ' ἔσται· | θεοὶ γάρ τοι νεμεσῶσ', οἷσιν ἔπεστι τέλος.

[4] Herod. i. 32 fin.

[5] Aesch. *fragm.* 301 Ἀπάτης δικαίας οὐκ ἀποστατεῖ θεός. One means of delusion, used by the gods, is the riddling oracle, which is of the nature of an *ordeal*. If a man is right-minded, he will interpret it correctly and take warning; but if he is infatuated, it will mislead him. Cf. the terms in which Thucydides (v. 103 *cit. supr.* p. 178) speaks of oracles, divination, καὶ ὅσα τοιαῦτα μετ' ἐλπίδων λυμαίνεται, and Dionysius' paraphrase, ἡ παρὰ τῶν θεῶν ἐλπίς.

right from wrong.[1] Moral offences, as distinct from presumption against the gods, gradually become more prominent. One of the earliest is excess in vengeance,[2]—though this, perhaps, was at first only a theological offence against the divine prerogative of cruelty.

The notion that a passion like Eros can be the instrument of the divine Jealousy finds an interesting expression on a vase[3] of the same class as the Darius *krater* figured on p. 195. In the central field the death of Meleager is represented inside a house. Outside, and on a higher level, sits Aphrodite, with her head inclined in sorrow, watching the scene. In her left hand she holds a bow and arrow; and beside her stands Eros. He is unmistakable, but the name inscribed above him is not his own, but Phthonos (ΦΘΟΝΟΣ). The significance is clear: Aphrodite symbolizes the love of Meleager for Atalanta, of which she is the supernatural cause, the παραιτία; Eros-Phthonos is the enhanced passion which has led Meleager to overstep the bounds assigned to man, and brought on the doom by which the Jealousy of Heaven is appeased.[4]

This moral and theological theory and the drama based on it concentrate attention more on the abasement of pride than on the exaltation of the lowly; and the tragic fact comes to consist chiefly of the former. Hence the original associations of Penia and Elpis have faded for us, while those of Ploutos and Hybris are vivid. Elpis and Eros, too,

---

[1] Soph. *Ant.* 622 τὸ κακὸν δοκεῖν ποτ᾽ ἐσθλὸν | τῷδ᾽ ἔμμεν ὅτῳ φρένας | θεὸς ἄγει πρὸς ἄταν. Lycurgus *in Leocr.* 92 (cit. Jebb *ad loc.*) quotes from ‘ancient poetry’: ὅταν γὰρ ὀργὴ δαιμόνων βλάπτῃ τινά, | τοῦτ᾽ αὐτὸ πρῶτον ἐξαφαιρεῖται φρενῶν | τὸν νοῦν τὸν ἐσθλόν, εἰς δὲ τὴν χείρω τρέπει | γνώμην, ἵν᾽ εἰδῇ μηδὲν ὧν ἁμαρτάνει. Similarly the chorus in the *Antigone* (791) addressing *Eros*: σὺ καὶ δικαίων ἀδίκους φρένας παρασπᾷς ἐπὶ λώβᾳ.

[2] Herod. iv. 205 ὡς ἄρα ἀνθρώποισι αἱ λίην ἰσχυραὶ τιμωρίαι πρὸς θεῶν ἐπίφθονοι γίνονται. The moral, and non-theological, equivalent of this is expounded in Hermocrates’ words (Thuc. iv. 62) quoted above on p. 170.

[3] From Armentum, now at Naples in the Museo Nazionale Coll. Santangelo, No. 11. Interpreted by Kekulé, *Strenna festosa offerta a G. Henzen*, Roma, 1867.

[4] See Koerte, *Ueber Personificationen psychol. Affekte in der späteren Vasenmalerei*, Berlin, 1874.

become almost indistinguishable; both are characteristic of Hybris, and ministerial agents of Nemesis.

We have entered upon this short and imperfect description of primitive psychology with a view to bringing out the pre-Aeschylean beliefs about the tragic passions and their relation to reversals of fortune—their place in the cycle of the tragic fact. Unless our description of the form of Aeschylean tragedy was altogether fanciful, we found in the double structure of his drama certain features which pointed back to the primitive, mythical theory of the passions. Aeschylus conceives them as ministerial agencies, external to man and yet embodied and personified in him. On the ideal plane of the lyric they seemed still to keep something of their old independent existence as elementary, supernatural persons. Hybris was not a mere name for Agamemnon's pride; Eros was something more than the lust of rapine in the conquerors of Troy. The old notion of incarnation or spiritual possession, combined with the subordination of daemons to the gods, provides at this stage of development a working theory to reconcile the supernatural with the natural causation of human action. The characters of the play are not merely the blind puppets of higher powers; they have inward springs of motion, and yet these are agencies sent from God. Thus for a moment is the balance poised between the two sets of powers which shape human destiny.

But only for a moment. The theory involves so delicate an equilibrium between natural and superhuman, so nice a compromise of faith and knowledge, that it cannot be maintained for long. The balance must turn, and there is no doubt which scale will sink. The supernatural must fade and recede. The gods must surrender again to man the life with which, as he slowly learns, himself at his own cost has lavishly endowed them. Human nature re-enters upon its alienated domain, conscious of itself, and of nothing else but a material world which centres round it. Desire and Hope must resign their dream shapes, and all that will be left of them is a hot movement of the blood, the thrill of a quickened nerve. Vengeance and Ruin will be at last transformed into facts of heredity and causal sequences of physical excess and pain. Destiny will give place to Law.

The question which can no longer be postponed is, how far this process, with all the loss and gain it carries with it, had advanced for Thucydides. The common assumption is that the language of Diodotus is only poetical metaphor,— that it means no more than a writer of our own day would mean by it. 'Thucydides,' we are told, 'has made a clean sweep of the legendary and novelistic sympathies, and primitive beliefs, rarely mitigated by the light of criticism, which marked Herodotus.' In a single generation he had leapt across the whole gulf which separates us from Aeschylus and Pindar.

In the course of this study the conviction has been growing upon us that the comparisons commonly made between Thucydides and Herodotus are based on false assumptions and misleading. It is usual to speak of Herodotus as primitive, and religious to the point of superstition; of Thucydides, as advanced and sceptical to the point of irreligiousness. Herodotus is treated as a naive and artless child; Thucydides as a disillusioned satirist and sometimes as a cynic. These representations seem to us to be founded simply on the external fact that Herodotus was by a generation the older of the two, and on the false assumption that, because their books are both called histories, Thucydides must have started where Herodotus left off, and developed the tradition he originated. Our own view is almost exactly the reverse. If either of the two men is to be called religious, it is Thucydides; if either is sceptical, it is Herodotus. Naivety and artlessness are not terms we should choose to apply to either; something closely akin to cynicism and flippancy is common enough in Herodotus; there is not a trace of either in Thucydides.

A single passage at the beginning of Herodotus' history

will illustrate our meaning. In tracing the earlier stages of the quarrel between East and West, Herodotus has occasion to relate the story of Io, the cow-maiden beloved of Zeus and persecuted by Hera.[1] Putting quietly aside the Greek legend,[2] which was primitive, gross, and supernatural, Herodotus gives the story as told by the Persian chroniclers. In this version Io, an Argive princess, was carried off to Egypt by some Phoenicians who were trading along the Aegean coasts. Herodotus also gives a slightly different version, current among the Phoenicians, in which Io became the captain's paramour, and, to escape her parents' anger, sailed to Egypt of her own free will.

' It is curious,' says Rawlinson,[3] ' to observe the treatment which the Greek myths met with at the hands of foreigners. The Oriental mind, quite unable to appreciate poetry of such a character, stripped the legends bare of all that beautified them and then treated them, thus vulgarized, as matters of simple history. Io, the virgin priestess, beloved by Zeus, and hated by jealous Hera, metamorphosed, Argus-watched, and gadfly-driven from land to land, resting at last by holy Nile's sweet-tasting stream, and there becoming mother of a race of hero-kings, is changed to Io, the para-mour, &c. . . . Herodotus, left to himself, has no tendency to treat myths in this coarse, rationalistic way: witness his legends of Croesus, Battus, Labda, &c. His spirit is too reverent, and, if we may so say, too credulous. The super-natural never shocks or startles him.'

The critic's mind is filled with the Io legend as presented in the *Supplices* and the *Prometheus*, and he quarrels with the Phoenicians for not having read and appreciated their Aeschylus. But what was the story of Io, before Aeschylus made it mysterious and beautiful? Apollodorus preserves the edifying tale[4] which ' the Semitic race, unable to enter

---

[1] Herod. i. 1 ff.

[2] i. 2 οὕτω μὲν Ἰοῦν ἐς Αἴγυπτον ἀπικέσθαι λέγουσι Πέρσαι, οὐκ ὡς Ἕλληνες. That is *all* he says about the Greek story.

[3] Translation of Herodotus, note *ad loc.*

[4] Apollod. *Bibl.* 2. 1. 3. Io was priestess of Hera, and Zeus violated her. Caught in the act by Hera, he changed the maiden into a white cow, and

into the spirit of Greek poesy ',[1] vulgarized and stripped bare of its beauty. Herodotus, ' left to himself,' would have been too reverent to be shocked by it; but apparently the Persians and Phoenicians stood over him with a stick and terrorized his ' reverent, and if we may so say, credulous ' spirit. They did their work pretty thoroughly. They corrupted their innocent victim to the extent of making him repeat a comment, which is not quite the sort of thing we expect to hear in the nursery. ' Now the Persians argue that to carry off a woman must of course be considered as the act of a wicked man ; but, when the elopement has taken place, to make great ado about vengeance is the mark of a very foolish man, and to take no notice whatever is the mark of a very wise one. For obviously, if the victim herself had not wished it, there would have been no elopement. Now they themselves (they maintain) had acted like wise men,' &c.[2]

Where else in Greek literature shall we find this flippant, Parisian, man-of-the-worldly tone ? Not in the Athenian authors—Aeschylus, Sophocles, Thucydides, Euripides, Plato —no, nor yet in Aristophanes. It is not Athenian, but Ionian ;[3] we must look for a parallel to the latest and most decadent passages of the Ionian Epos ; just as, to match the ' Milesian ' tale of Gyges, to which Herodotus next turns, we must look to Boccaccio and Brantôme. Herodotus stands, not

swore he would not touch her again. That is why, says Hesiod, the breaking of lovers' vows does not draw down the anger of the gods. Hera begged the cow from Zeus, and set Argus to watch her. He tied her to an olive-tree. Then Zeus sent Hermes to steal the cow, but Hermes was detected by Hierax (the Hawk) and he killed Argus with a stone. Hera sent a gad-fly to drive Io from land to land, till at last she came to Egypt, was changed back into a woman, and bore Epaphos.

[1] Rawlinson, *ibid.*

[2] Herod. i. 4. Plutarch, *malig. Herod.* ii. (856) protests against this utterance as an ' apology on behalf of the ravishers ' and as involving impiety, since, if the women were carried off willingly, the punishment of the gods upon the ravishers was unjust.

[3] The contrast between the Ionian spirit and the Athenian was suggested to me by an unpublished lecture of Mr. Gilbert Murray, which I have been privileged to read, and which suddenly illuminated this part of my subject. Whatever truth there is in the view expressed is due to him, though he is in no way responsible for the expression of it.

at the beginning, but at the end of a tradition. He is not the father of history; he is the last of the Homeridae, turning the refined and polished product of centuries of festal recitation into material for his amusing and instructive tale of the quarrel of East and West. The process is, to our eyes, unscientific; but it was then the most advanced and enlightened treatment of saga. There is not a word in either of the two versions given by Herodotus which might not be literal fact.[1] Such incidents must have occurred as frequently when the Phoenicians bartered beads and gaudy stuffs with the simple natives along the Aegean coasts, as they do now when European traders ply exactly the same business along the shores of Africa. Herodotus is, to our minds, unscientific only in three respects. First, he does not understand that primitive myths are not garbled history, any more than he was aware that garbled history *is* a sort of myth. Second, he imports into the heroic age the international courtesies and decently conducted negotiations by herald and envoy, which prevailed in his own time. Third, he does not care which story—the Persian or the Phoenician—is true. 'About this matter,' he says, 'I am not going to say whether it happened this way or that.' 'I will tell no lies, George, that I promise you,' says the younger Pendennis; 'and do no more than coincide in those which are necessary and pass current, and can't be got in without recalling the whole circulation.'[2]

---

[1] The treatment of this myth illustrates a remark we made above (p. 133), to the effect that rationalization may easily efface the clues by which the elements of fiction and truth can be discriminated. Herodotus leaves only the name of Io and the voyage to Egypt, suppressing the transformation into a cow. Now it is almost certain that the element of historical fact which lies behind the story is a primitive cow-worship at Argos, probably even earlier than the worship of Hera. Io is possibly a primaeval cow-goddess whom Hera replaced. The voyage to Egypt is purely mythical, having been invented when Io was identified with Isis. Thus the most rational part of the story is absolutely unhistorical; while the gross and supernatural features of it, which rationalism refines away, are the clue to historical truth.

Rationalization is the converse of the mythical 'infiguration' of history: it imparts the form of a possible series of events to a supernatural and impossible story.

[2] Thackeray, *Pendennis*, lxviii.

It is against this light and careless Ionian temper that Thucydides protests, as Aeschylus, in his way, had protested before, and Plato, in his, will protest later. To Aeschylus it seemed irreligious; to Thucydides, regardless of truth; to Plato, immoral. Aeschylus had taken Homer and made the religion of Zeus spiritual by incorporating with it a profound interpretation of those gross and primitive myths, like the story of the cow-maiden, which the Ionians had rejected or turned to ridicule in the parodies of mock Epic. Plato finds Homer too thoroughly penetrated with immorality to be rendered serviceable even by drastic expurgation.[1] To Thucydides the Ionian tradition of Epos and story-telling is anathema; his introduction is a judicial and earnest polemic against it and all its works. There was as little of the Ionian in his temperament as there was in his blood. It is almost certain that he was related on his mother's side to the Philaidae, for his tomb was to be seen close to those of Kimon and Miltiades.[2] His father bore a Thracian name, and came probably of that hard-drinking and fighting stock which worshipped Ares and the northern Dionysus; and it is to the religious drama which grew up at Dionysus' festivals in Pelasgian Athens, not to the Epos which had flowered at the Ionian gatherings and now was overblown, that Thucydides turns for his inspiration.

Herodotus picks up a good story where he can. His dramatization of the expedition of Xerxes is tinged with Aeschylean religion, because Aeschylus had created the Persian legend on this type and fixed the lines which any one who wished to glorify Athens and to please an Athenian audience must follow. But in Herodotus the religious notions are ill-digested and lie close to the surface. They are the theme of illustrative and fabulous anecdote, not the deep-set framework of earnest thought. It is not in this manner that Thucydides works when he turns the great moral of Aeschylus' *Persians* against the Athenian Empire.

[1] When Homer is called 'the Bible of the Greeks', these points tend to be overlooked.

[2] The Philaidae were an Aeginetan family. Miltiades, the victor of Marathon, married a Thracian wife.

In doing so, the historian inevitably borrowed much of the structure of Aeschylean tragedy. This unhistoric principle of design came in on the top of his first, chronological plan, and he allowed both to shape his work, leaving long tracts of uncoloured narrative between the scattered episodes of his drama. The tragic theory of human nature involved in the dramatization differs from the Aeschylean in being *non-theological*—at least on the surface and so far beneath it as we are allowed to see; for in place of all-seeing Zeus, Thucydides has Fortune. In thus removing the theological element, he has reverted in a curious way to the *pre*-theological conception of the tragic fact, which existed long before Aeschylus. The language of Diodotus expresses that conception in its completeness and with great precision. We have in fact in that statement an instance of *rationalizing*. The accretion of theological belief is removed; but what is left is a mythical construction which contains and carries with it conceptions still more primitive. Just as Thucydides in rationalizing the story of Pausanias cut away the fabulous anecdotes, and never saw that what remained was not fact, but dramatized legend; so in rationalizing the theology of Aeschylus, he was unaware that what remained was mythical in origin, and not a fresh statement of the facts of life drawn from direct and unbiassed observation. We have traced the theory through three stages: (1) a primitive, pre-Olympian stage, in which it might be called religious, but neither theological nor moral; (2) a theological, but still non-moral stage, in which the Jealousy of the Olympians is a dominant conception; and (3) a stage both theological and moral, in the drama of Aeschylus. Thucydides adds a fourth stage in which this train of thought ceases to involve theology, while it remains moral. But through all its phases it is more or less mythical.

How much warmth and life these primitive ideas still held for him, what degree of reality Fortune, Elpis, and Eros retained—these are questions which cannot be answered with certainty. Our own impression is that the anthropomorphic mode of thought was so habitual and vivid in the Greek mind, that only the most determined rationalists could shake it off. Perhaps even they could not get free of it. Euripides, like Thucydides, is hailed as a modern of the moderns, and (to our thinking) with better reason. The tragedian has none of the historian's detachment; he will risk the success of an artistic effect to gain a point in theological controversy; he is not coolly, but fervently, rationalistic. And yet, when we read the *Hippolytus*, and still more when we see it played, the feeling grows upon us that reason falls back like a broken wave. A brooding power, relentless, inscrutable, waits and watches and smites. There she stands, all through the action, the white, implacable Aphrodite. Is she no more than a marble image, the work of men's hands? Is there no significance in that secret smile, no force behind the beautiful mask, no will looking out of the fixed, watching eyes? And yet, how can there be? Is she not one of the outcast, dethroned Olympians, a figment of bygone superstition, despised and rejected of an enlightened age? No, she is more than this, and much more. But what can she be?—a personification of the 'life-force'? A thousand times, no! It must be that poetry has forced on reason some strange compromise. We cannot detect the formula of that agreement; but we know that somehow a compact has been made. Had the poet, in one of the long days of musing in his seaward cave on Salamis, seen a last vision of the goddess, rising in wrathful foam?

In the *Hippolytus* we are approaching the modern conception of the tragic fact, in which the interest lies in the inward conflict of purely natural motives; but we have not yet quite reached it; and if the supernatural quality of the elementary human passions is still felt by Euripides, it is no great paradox to find traces of it in the historian, who looked to drama of a much more primitive type.

# CHAPTER XIV

## THE CAUSE OF THE WAR

THE play, we said, is done;—that is the feeling which every reader has, when he closes the seventh Book; and we fancy it was the writer's feeling too. He had traced the 'causes' of the Sicilian expedition from Fortune at Pylos to Nemesis at the quarries of Syracuse. From this point onwards he has little interest in his task; the eighth Book is a mere continuation on the old chronological plan, unfinished, dull, and spiritless. The historian patiently continued his record; but he seems to grope his way like a man without a clue. The last seven years of the war he left altogether unrecorded, preferring to spend his time in retouching, amplifying, and shaping the earlier narrative, where he could see clearly. His chain of 'causes' runs through Books IV to VII. At the earlier end it pointed back to foreshadowing events as far as the beginning of Book III (the Mytilenean debate), but no further. To link the Sicilian enterprise to the origin of the war, he would have had to get completely out of himself, become 'a modern of the moderns', and study the economic situation—an entity he never dreamed of. Looking back to this point, where his clue seemed to fail him, he must have puzzled and cast about for some light. The historically insoluble riddle of Pericles' attack upon Megara—how he must have turned this over, as again and again he took up his first Book, to revise it once more.

Now, to almost all his contemporaries that riddle presented no difficulty whatever; for there can have been very few who did not belong to one or other of two classes. There was the thoughtless mass of ordinary folk who were quite content with the notion that Pericles had some personal rancour against the Megarians. These had not known Pericles; their minds were not on a scale to measure his. Their foolish opinions are not so much as stated, for a tacit disproof was enough for them. But there was also a large body of reflective, serious people, who were satisfied with a very different explanation. About their opinion these facts are certain: namely, that Thucydides, at some time in his life, thought it worth mentioning, if only indirectly and by implication; that he mentioned it with no expression of belief or disbelief on his own part; and that he described at some length what he thought to be the facts on which it was based. This explanation was that there was a curse—a taint of guilt and of madness—in the house to which Pericles, on his mother's side, belonged.

We hasten to say that Thucydides' detailed narration of the incidents of the Kylonian conspiracy, to which this taint was traced back, is *sufficiently* accounted for by a desire to correct the version given by Herodotus.[1] Herodotus says the Alcmaeonids were 'considered responsible'; the 'accusation was laid upon them',[2] and tells the story very briefly. Thucydides tells it with much precision and detail, and especially insists that the nine archons (not, as Herodotus says, the 'presidents of the Naucraries') were absolutely responsible.[3] The effect is to fix the guilt of the sacrilege on the Alcmaeonid archon, Megacles; and doubtless Thucydides believed that so it was. Both historians have in view

---

[1] It has been observed that Herodotus, here as in other places where the Alcmaeonids are concerned, gives the version current in that family. Thucydides (who, by the way, was connected with the rival house of the Philaidae—the family of Miltiades and Kimon), here as elsewhere, gives a version which is, at least, without any bias in favour of the Alcmaeonids. Another instance is the expulsion of the tyrants: Thucydides (vi. 54 ff.) barely mentions the Alcmaeonids; Herodotus gives them as much credit as possible. See Herod. vi. 123.

[2] Herod. v. 70 εἶχον αἰτίην τοῦ φόνου ... 71 φονεῦσαι δὲ αὐτοὺς αἰτίη ἔχει Ἀλκμεωνίδας.

[3] Herod. v. 71 τούτους ἀνιστᾶσι μὲν οἱ πρυτάνιες τῶν ναυκράρων, οἵ περ ἔνεμον τότε τὰς Ἀθήνας. Thuc. i. 126 οἱ Ἀθηναῖοι ... ἀπῆλθον ... ἐπιτρέψαντες τοῖς ἐννέα ἄρχουσι τήν τε φυλακὴν καὶ τὸ πᾶν αὐτοκράτορσι διαθεῖναι ᾗ ἂν ἄριστα διαγιγνώσκωσιν· τότε δὲ τὰ πολλὰ τῶν πολιτικῶν οἱ ἐννέα ἄρχοντες ἔπρασσον.

a current controversy on the subject roused by the Lacedaemonians' demand that the Athenians should expel 'the
Accursed'—a 'pretext' for the war which provides Thucydides with an occasion for telling the story and correcting
Herodotus. The occasion is sufficient; the desire to correct
accounts for the precision and detail.

The story is told with great reserve.[1] 'The followers of
Kylon were besieged and were in distress for lack of food
and water. So, although Kylon and his brother escaped,
the rest, since they were in straits and some were dying
of hunger, took sanctuary as suppliants at the altar which
is on the Acropolis. And those Athenians who were charged
to keep watch, when they saw them dying in the holy place,
caused them to rise, promising they would do them no harm,
and they led them away and slew them. And some who,
as they passed by, took sanctuary *actually at the altars of
the Venerable Goddesses*,[2] they dispatched. And from this
they were called accursed and banned of the goddess, they
and the race that came from them. Now the Athenians
drove out these accursed, and Cleomenes, also, the Lacedaemonian, drove them out later when the Athenians were in
civil strife; and when they drove out the living they also
took up the bones of the dead and cast them out. They
were, however, restored later, and their race is to this day
in the city.

'This then was the Curse which the Lacedaemonians bade
them drive out; pretending that they were first of all
avenging the gods, but knowing that Pericles, the son of
Xanthippos, was connected with it on his mother's side,[3]

---

[1] Die Erzählung des Thukydides macht den Eindruck einer im ganzen
objektiven, wenngleich mit Bezug auf die Beteiligung der Alkmeoniden,
deren Name gar nicht genannt wird, äusserst zurückhaltenden Darstellung.
Busolt, *Gr. Gesch.* ii. 204⁵.

[2] i. 126. 11 καθεζομένους δέ τινας καὶ ἐπὶ τῶν Σεμνῶν Θεῶν τοῖς βωμοῖς ἐν τῇ
παρόδῳ ἀπεχρήσαντο. The καί is ambiguous: it may mean 'also' or 'even',
'actually.'

[3] Observe that the curse follows the *female* line. Aeschylus had not
eradicated that belief. Alcibiades also was an Alcmaeonid, certainly through
his mother, probably also through his father.

and thinking that if he were exiled their affairs at Athens would go more smoothly. However, they did not so much expect that this would happen to him as that they would bring him into ill-odour with the city, and make them think that the war would be partly because of his misfortune (ξυμφοράν). For being most powerful in his day and leading the state, he was in all things opposing the Lacedaemonians and not suffering the Athenians to give way, but was urging them into the war.' [1]

This narrative is very serious and solemn. Thucydides, moreover, has neither directly nor by implication given any opinion about the beliefs connected with it. He implies, indeed, that to avenge the gods was not, as the Lacedaemonians pretended, the 'first', the primary motive of their demand. The phrase which describes their primary object— διαβολὴν οἴσειν αὐτῷ—is ambiguous; for a διαβολή is any charge brought with malicious intention to discredit a man—whether the charge be true or false. The most pious believer in the curse of the Alcmaeonidae could have used the expression; on any view the revival of the curse to gain an end in diplomacy was 'malicious'. That the Lacedaemonians believed in the curse, Thucydides implies when he says that the religious motive was not, as they pretended, the primary one. In the next chapter he records that the Spartans did believe in their own curse—the ἄγος of the Brazen House—and thought it caused the earthquake which preceded the Helot revolt.

Thucydides' reserve is impenetrable; we can only fall back on our general impression of the tone and manner of his narrative. We are stating what is a mere matter of personal opinion when we say that this story does not strike us as the work of a man who was clearly convinced that the curse or 'taint' of the Alcmaeonidae could not conceivably have had any causal connexion with Pericles' action in 'urging the Athenians into the war', because there was no such thing as

---

[1] ἐς τὸν πόλεμον ὥρμα τοὺς Ἀθηναίους, the one explicit statement made by Thucydides on his own account about Pericles' action in forcing on the war. We have seen how elsewhere he minimizes it.

an hereditary taint of guilt, obscurely working in the blood, a seed of madness which might be a wise and innocent man's 'misfortune'. We feel that a writer who had altogether rejected that conception would have given some indication that he thought the whole controversy about the curse a piece of silly superstition; and that he would not have told the story of Kylon in so solemn a tone, or have added a still longer and equally serious history of the curse of Taenarus. That Thucydides believed in the religious and dogmatic theory of hereditary guilt, we do not for one moment suppose. He did not, we may be quite sure, think of an ἄγος as Aeschylus thought of it,—as a spirit, an evil genius (δαίμων), which could be incarnate in a series of descendants. But there was nothing irrational or superstitious in believing that when a man commits what is to him an awful religious crime, remorse and terror may madden his brain; and that this taint of madness may be transmitted to his posterity. The first of these propositions no one would deny; the second is, we believe, not yet finally disproved.

It seems, then, just possible that Thucydides thought there might be some touch of madness in Pericles which explained his violence against Megara—the otherwise inexplicable problem. But why against Megara? and why connect the madness with the curse of the Alcmaeonidae? Is it altogether fanciful to point out that the Kylonian conspiracy was an incident in the feud between *Megara* and Athens? 'Kylon was an Athenian in olden time who won a victory at Olympia and was well-born and powerful; and he had married a daughter of Theagenes, a Megarian, who in those days was tyrant of Megara.'[1] Theagenes, we are further told,[2] supplied him with forces for his attempt on the Acropolis of Athens. So most, at any rate, of the suppliants who were sacrilegiously slain by the Alcmaeonid archon, were Megarians. And now Megacles' descendant is 'urging' the Athenians into a war sooner than revoke a violent decree against the descendants of his victims. A strange coincidence, if it is nothing more!

[1] i. 126.   [2] Ibid.

However this may be, the point is, perhaps, clear, that Thucydides' attention was occupied with topics like these, and so diverted from thof e factors in the economic situation which might have enabled him to read the origin of the war in the light of the Sicilian expedition. All contemporary thought was similarly directed to mythical causes. The Lacedaemonians, for instance, explained the war on the same lines. Their first open quarrel with Athens, says Thucydides,[1] dated from the Helot revolt at Ithome, when they had dismissed Kimon's contingent slightingly. The Helot revolt was occasioned by an earthquake.[2] The earthquake was, as the Lacedaemonians thought, caused by Poseidon, whose sanctuary they had violated by killing suppliants.[3] Their chain of 'causes' led them back to an ἄγος—the curse of Taenarus— of just the same kind as the ἄγος of the Alcmaeonidae. Such were the 'causes' men looked for in Thucydides' day. Can we wonder that the origin of the Peloponnesian war is somewhat obscure ?

Thucydides was one of those prophets and kings of thought who have desired to see the day of all-conquering Knowledge, and have not seen it. The deepest instinct of the human mind is to shape the chaotic world and the illimitable stream of events into some intelligible form which it can hold before itself and take in at one survey. From this instinct all mythology takes its rise, and all the religious and philosophical systems which grow out of mythology without a break. The man whose reason has thrown over myth and abjured religion, and who yet is born too soon to find any resting-place for his thought provided by science and philosophy, may set himself to live on isolated facts without a theory ; but the time will come when his resistance will break down. All the artistic and imaginative elements in his nature will pull against his reason, and, if once he begins to produce, their triumph is assured. In spite of all his good resolutions, the work will grow under his hands into some satisfying shape, informed by reflection and governed by art.

[1] i. 102.    [2] i. 101.    [3] i. 128.

When Thucydides records his own military failure and the exile by which the Athenians punished it, he neither extenuates the blunder nor complains of the penalty. Perhaps he knew that during those twenty years of banishment in his remote Thracian home, he had gathered the maturer fruits of solitude and silence. It must have been bitter at first to quit the scene of a drama so intense and passionate, to step down from the stage and find a place among the spectators; but as the long agony wore on, as crime led to crime and madness to ruin, it was only from a distance that the artist who was no longer an actor could discern the large outlines shaping all that misery and suffering into the thing of beauty and awe which we call Tragedy.

# INDEX

AEGINA and Egypt, 38.

AESCHYLUS, *Agamemnon*, 144; *Agam. 293–328*, 149; *330* ff., 156; *353* ff., 214; *717* ff., 193; *801–965*, 160; *1371–1576*, 161; *Persians*, 134; Art-form of his drama, 139 ff.; psychology, 154 ff., 234, 236; free-will, 154.

ALCIBIADES, Melian massacre, 186; idealized, 188; deludes Spartan envoys, 191; Sicilian expedition, 205 ff.

ALCMAEONID curse, 245 ff.

ALIENS, influx of, 19.

ALLEGORY, 230.

ANAXAGORAS, 73, 107.

APATE, on Darius vase, 196; in Aeschylus, 234.

ARISTOPHANES, *Acharnians*, 83, 26; *Frogs, 1425*, 193; *Knights*, *125* ff., 22; *1303*, 45.

CARTHAGE, 44.

CAUSE, and pretext, 53; Polybius' distinction, 57; meaning of αἰτία, 57 ff.; only psychological causes in ancient historians, 64; causes of human events, 68.

CLEON, leader of Piraeus, 22; Thucydides' treatment of, 80; 'malignity' against, 96, 110; Pylos negotiations, 110–114, 119; Mytilenean debate, 114; Sphacteria, 116; Amphipolis, 118; his career dramatized, 125; as Elpis, 171.

CLYTEMNESTRA, as Peitho, 160.

COMMERCIAL PARTY, 18; policy, 31.

CORCYRA, alliance, 40, 43–44, 51.

CORINTH, position on Isthmus, 34.

COUNTRY against town at Athens, 16.

DAEMONS, and passions, 157; and gods, 231.

DARIUS vase, 195.

DIODOTUS, Mytilenean speech, 121, 221, 242.

DIONYSIUS, on Melian Dialogue, 174 ff.

DRAMA, influence on Thucydides, 137 ff.

ECONOMICS, 71.

EGESTA, 199.

EGYPTIAN expedition, 37.

ELPIS, in Diodotus' speech, 122; Cleon, 171; Melian Dialogue, 178, 184; conception of, 167; in Hesiod, 224; as Ker, 225, 232.

EROS, in Diodotus' speech, 122; in *Agamemnon*, 156, 214; Alcibiades, 206 ff.; and tyranny, 207; Phthonos, 235.

EURIPIDES, *Hippolytus*, 243.

EVERYMAN, 141.

FORTUNE, as agency, 97 ff.; and foresight, 104 ff.; in Diodotus' speech, 122; and 'reversal', 222.

GOMPERZ, 68.

HARMODIUS and Aristogeiton, 132.

HERODOTUS, *i. 1*, 60, 237; criticized by Thucydides, 74; dramatization of Persian War, 134; compared with Thucydides, 237.

HISTORIANS, ancient and modern, 65 ff., 127.

INFIGURATION, mythical, 131.

Io myth, 238.